UNSETTLED FAMILIES

Stanford Studies in Human Rights
Mark Goodale, editor

Unsettled Families

Refugees, Humanitarianism, and the Politics of Kinship

Sophia Balakian

Stanford University Press
Stanford, California

Stanford University Press
Stanford, California

Printed in the United States of America on acid-free, archival-quality paper

Library of Congress Cataloging-in-Publication Data available on request.

Library of Congress Control Number: 2024027048

ISBN (cloth) 9781503639652
ISBN (paper) 9781503641198
ISBN (ebook) 9781503641204

Cover design: Michele Wetherbee
Cover painting: © Uman, *Untitled*, 2019, Black gesso on primed canvas, 48 x 48".
Courtesy of the artist and Nicola Vassell Gallery.

For all my kin

By valorizing refugees as innocent, vulnerable, naïve, and lacking responsibility for their circumstances, the category enables the criminalization of all those who want to change their circumstances, who see better lives and refuse to accept inequality or its accompanying forms of violence.

Miriam Ticktin, "On Refugees and Innocence," *Public Seminar*, 2020

I see that in identity papers there is space allotted to biological parents and to guardians but none to somebody like Misra.

Nuruddin Farah, *Maps*, 1986

Contents

Foreword

IN HER BEAUTIFULLY CRAFTED and moving ethnographic account of refugee resettlement and global humanitarian governance, Sophia Balakian opens our eyes to the bureaucratically and politically obscured worlds of people who are both enmeshed and on the move. Her study documents the human consequences and lived experiences of what Saskia Sassen has described as "savage sorting": the ways in which political, legal, and economic categories are created by dominant states and the institutions that do their bidding in order manage, regulate, and (attempt to) circumscribe the "brutality and complexity" of the global political economic order. Yet what *Unsettled Families* demonstrates so convincingly, so unforgettably, is the fact that savage sorting *through* international refugee law and policy is no match for the infinite resilience of the millions of people who find themselves caught up in the multiscalar, multinational project of categorization, institutional adjudication, and exclusion.

Although Balakian's research took her along many of the pathways of global migration and resettlement from East Africa to Columbus, Ohio, her work is anchored in the granular trajectories and recovered memories of people living in what she calls the "commercial, tech, development, and humanitarian hub of Nairobi, Kenya." While moving seamlessly between intimate portraits of her many key interlocuters and penetrating analyses of the institutions that seek to regulate movement in an "age of global security," Balakian introduces us to a courageous group of Somali refugees, including Mohamed, Ahmed, Issa, and Samira. She allows us the privilege of following their lives and viewing the experience of migration and survival through their eyes. In this sense,

Balakian's book is also a powerful reaffirmation of the value and urgency of a methodology grounded in engagement, empathy, and solidarity.

Among all of the many ways in which the global governance of forced migration is suffused with contradiction, violence, and dehumanization, Balakian's critical narrative narrows the focus on one in particular: the use of the category of "the family" as an instrument for both bureaucratic moral judgment and a kind of regulatory lawfare. Moreover, the insistence upon specific models of "the family" across the entire assemblage of refugee resettlement underscores the ways in which seemingly technocratic determinations of things like relatedness, culpability, and vulnerability encode ongoing legacies of imperial control and ethnocentrism.

As she argues, when people are forced to navigate the perils of resettlement bureaucracy, they do so in relation to a bitter paradox. If a particular conception of the family has become one of the most important sociolegal objects of humanitarian investment, it also, at the same time, has become a crucial "locus of suspicion and investigation for those in charge of selecting the beneficiaries of refugee aid and resettlement," as Balakian explains. As the research in her book conveys so strikingly, people in the midst of extraordinary processes of dislocation and displacement must nevertheless quickly learn the multiple and often mutually incompatible grammars of national and international refugee governance.

And yet, through it all, as Balakian's tenacious cast of interlocuters reveals to us with such undeniable moral force, the imposed categories of refugee resettlement, including "the family," do not come close to defining the boundaries of either the necessary or the possible. Although she treads lightly around the more radical implications of her account, of the ways in which people "positioned as refugees" in fact learn to bend to this positioning while at the same time subverting it with their lived interstitiality, the implications are always there, refusing to be ignored.

As she puts it with both subtlety and depth of vision, people on the move have "always been part of the human story." This is not the prevailing and widely mediatized story of "disconnected individuals" in crisis, without real agency, consigned to fates beyond their control. On the contrary, migration, movement, uprooting, even in the face of different kinds of duress, tell the story of purposeful, even heroic, action, of the "desire to protect and care not only for oneself but also for others . . . in a world of increasing global interconnection and inequality." Although migration—forced and otherwise—now partly takes place within the shell of the international resettlement system, which is more universal, which is more enduring: the human compulsion to be on the move, to create meaning and value beyond the gaze of empire or the bureaucratic systems that seek to govern this compulsion, to exclude and banish these meanings?

Mark Goodale
Series Editor
STANFORD STUDIES IN HUMAN RIGHTS

Acknowledgments

THE RESEARCH FOR THIS book was generously funded by the Social Science Research Council, the Wenner-Gren Foundation for Anthropological Research, a Mellon/ACLS Dissertation Completion Fellowship, the Nelle M. Signore Graduate Scholarship in International Relations, and the Graduate College of the University of Illinois at Urbana-Champaign. Professor Simiyu Wandibba and the University of Nairobi's Department of Anthropology, Gender, and African Studies supported me in procuring government research permission in Kenya. I'm grateful to friends in Nairobi, especially Mercy Kimathi and family and Angie Kagume and Sid Anand.

The Harvard Academy for International and Area Studies, where I was an Academy Scholar in 2019–20, and 2022–23, provided tremendous support for writing this book. I thank Bruce Jackan, Kathleen Hoover, Melani Cammett, Timothy Colton, Jocelyn Viterna, and the other senior scholars there. A book workshop sponsored by the Academy informed important aspects of the book and gave me a road map. I thank George Meiu, Catherine Besteman, Samar Al-Bulushi, Gilberto Rosas, and Susan Thomson for their invaluable feedback on the manuscript. Claire Rostov, graduate student at the Harvard Divinity School, transcribed several crucial interviews with staff in refugee resettlement organizations. I'm also grateful for the friendship, advice, and intellectual energy of fellow Academy Scholars. All were wonderful colleagues, and I especially thank Suzie Ferguson, Chris Gratien, Rabiat Akande, Zachary Howlett, Brinton Ahlin, Yang-Yang Zhou, Taylor Moore, Nishita Trisal, Ping-hsiu Lin, Matt Shutzer, Egor Lazarev, Ruslan Yusupov, who informed this project with questions and conversations. They were brilliant guides to and comrades in navigating early-career life. In 2019–20, conversations with Molly Schen helped me claim what I cared most about in this project. Carolyn Mugar generously allowed me stay at her apartment in Cambridge when I was based at Harvard in 2022–23, and I am so grateful for that consistent place to land near the river.

I am immensely grateful to colleagues who commented on individual chapters of this book. I received valuable perspectives on a chapter from members of the Political Anthropology/Political Ecology Working Group at Harvard in 2020. Rawan Arar, Andrew Bush, Nishita Trisal, Ellen Moodie, and Lisa Gilman gave invaluable feedback on various chapters. At George Mason, colleagues in the School of Integrative Studies have been supportive, and I especially thank Andrew Wingfield, Cher Chen, Levi Van Sant, Graziella McCarron, and Kelly Dunne for support and solidarity. In Anthropology, I thank Rashmi Sadana, who gave generous and incisive feedback on my book proposal. I also thank SIS staff, Stephanie Zeher and James Zhao, for their essential support. At Penn State, I thank Bill Dewey, who offered me my first academic position, and friends and colleagues from the African Studies and African American Studies programs.

At the University of Illinois, where this project began, I am especially grateful for the mentorship and teaching of Alma Gottlieb, Ellen Moodie, Virginia Dominguez, and James Brennan. They have each shaped this book and supported my career in fundamental ways. I think especially of Alma's kinship course and her comments on many, many drafts of funding proposals; Ellen's course on insecurity, her pointed feedback, and conversations over meals; a readings course with Virginia on humanitarianism and human rights, and many projects in which she has included me; and Jim's seminar on East African history, which gave me a whole new perspective. The teachings of Nancy Abelmann, Gilberto Rosas, and Alejandro Lugo are also alive in these pages. I am grateful to fellow grad students from Illinois, especially Tim Landry for his comments on drafts, advice, and humor. I began my academic journey in anthropology at Cornell University as an undergraduate and was inspired by courses taught by Andrew Willford and Viranjini Munasinghe and by studying abroad with Kath March and David Holmberg. Michael Peletz (who also gave generous feedback on the proposal for this book) and Elayne Zorn were early guides to the field.

I am deeply grateful to Stanford University Press, especially Dylan Kyunglim White, who has been a professional and humane shepherd of this book and its author, and Austin Araujo, for his kind and proactive communications. Thanks to series editor Mark Goodale, who found value in this project. I am grateful to the anonymous reviewers who gave essential feedback on the manuscript that helped shape the book and chart my way to its completion.

This book was made possible by women who took care of my children while I worked: first and foremost, my mother, who watched my daughter nearly full-time during my first semester teaching at George Mason when other childcare options shut down during the early pandemic and who has spent nearly every Sunday afternoon with my daughter for the past two and a half years. I am also deeply grateful to Tanya, Thelma, Jennifer, Belikiz, Jesse, Dorothea, Yime, Erin, Liza, Brooke, Lilly, Rina, Tonya, Toni, Karen, Shira, and many George Mason students who have worked as classroom assistants at the George Mason University Child Development Center. In fall 2020, my dad also took my daughter every Sunday; pancakes were served. Thanks also to my in-laws, Carol and Irl Don, who have never hesitated to travel to see their grandchildren, including when I was away at conferences.

Most of this book was written at a desk that my parents bought me when I was around twelve or so. It's large and solid wood—hard to come by now in an age of wood veneer and particleboard. Its legs have been unscrewed so it could be packed in trunks, and later loaded into U-Haul trucks. It has been a friend over decades, where I can spread out printed drafts and stack books and rest coffee cups. My parents gave me many things that have allowed me to write this book. I am grateful for their endless support. My mother, Helen Kebabian, read the entire manuscript and gave copy-edits; my father, Peter Balakian, was always available for conversations about the process. My brother, James, has always been a source of moral support and understanding. My many aunts and uncles have always been supports—have loved and fed me—especially Aunt Jan, fellow traveler on the road of the teaching and writing life. I thank my lifelong friends from Hamilton Central School—my roots. I thank my friends from Cornell—my source of advice on all matters working-parent.

My spouse, Michael Don, has supported me in innumerable ways through the unsteady challenges of graduate school and early-career academic life. His interest in anthropological knowledge; his life as a writer; and our conversations about teaching, literature, and storytelling have helped make work and life good. His doing the lion's share of laundry, dishes, grocery shopping, bills, and car maintenance for years has allowed us to live in some semblance of order while I had more time to write. Though he rarely appears in this book, he accompanied me to Kenya in 2012 and from 2013 to 2015, during which time he taught writing and literature at St. Paul's University in Limuru. He has been an ever-present sounding board from start to finish. Samara, born in 2018, and Leo, born in 2021, emerged into the world and grew alongside this book. Thank you, Samara and Leo, for being who you are.

This book is made of stories about people living as refugees in Kenya, and people who came to the US through the Refugee Admissions Program. To them I owe the greatest thanks. There are several people who worked with me as research assistants in Nairobi without whom I would not have written this book. Many of them are described in these pages using pseudonyms. I wish I could acknowledge them by name. In keeping with standard ethical protocols of the field and their own positions amidst changing security contexts, I won't. I also thank people working at UNHCR and NGOs in Nairobi and the US who opened their doors to me and spent time talking with me about their work. In Columbus, I am deeply grateful to staff members at the organization I have called Ohio Refugee Assistance and their clients, many of whom are also described here using pseudonyms. Many, many people shared stories with me that informed this book. Trying to do right by those stories has been a humbling journey. Thank you.

Acronyms

AMISOM—African Union Mission in Somalia
AOR—Affidavit of Relationship
DHS—Department of Homeland Security
DRC—Democratic Republic of the Congo
FBI—Federal Bureau of Investigation
INS—Immigration and Naturalization Service
IOM—International Organization for Migration
JVA—Joint Voluntary Agency
M23—Movement du 23 Mars
NGO—Non-governmental organization
ORA—Ohio Refugee Assistance (a pseudonym)
RCK—Refugee Consortium of Kenya
RPF—Rwandan Patriotic Front
RSC—Resettlement Support Center
SAO—Security Advisory Opinion
UICs—Union of Islamic Courts
UN—United Nations
UNHCR—United Nations High Commissioner for Refugees
USCIS—United States Citizenship and Immigration Services
USRAP—United States Refugee Admissions Program
VOLAG—Voluntary Agency

UNSETTLED FAMILIES

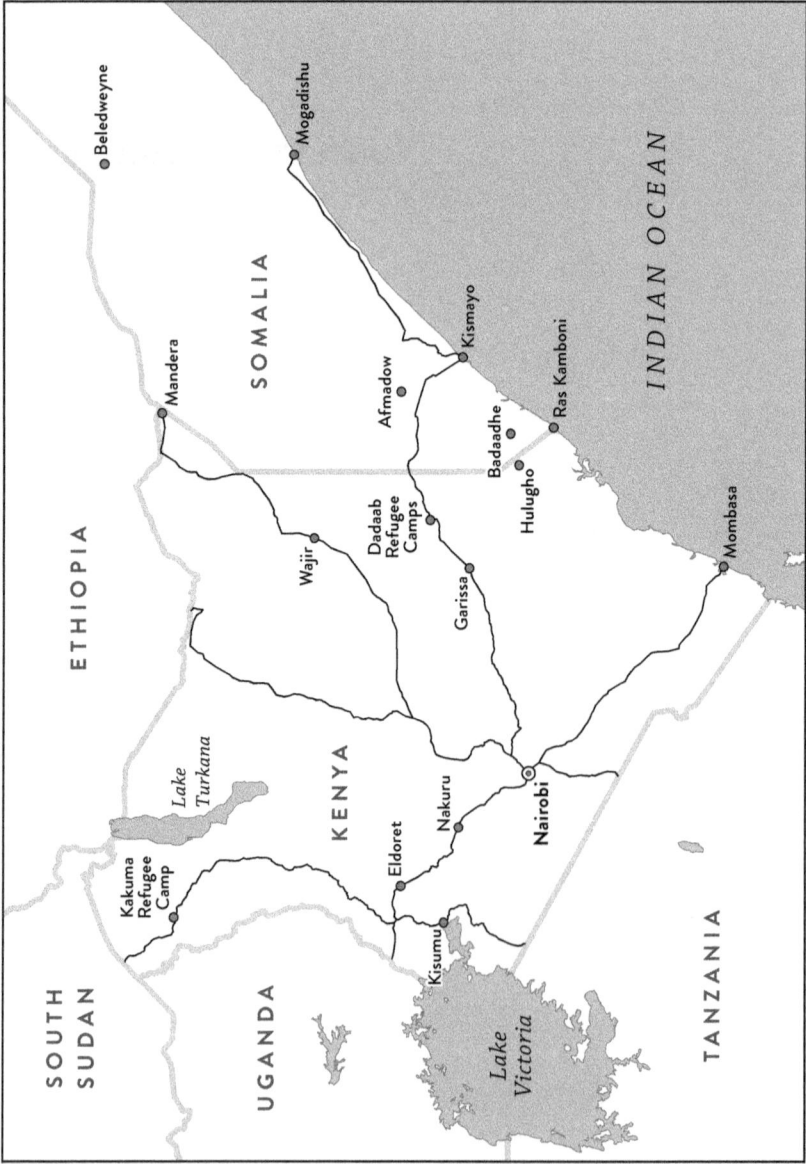

KENYA, SOUTHERN SOMALIA, AND BORDERING COUNTRIES

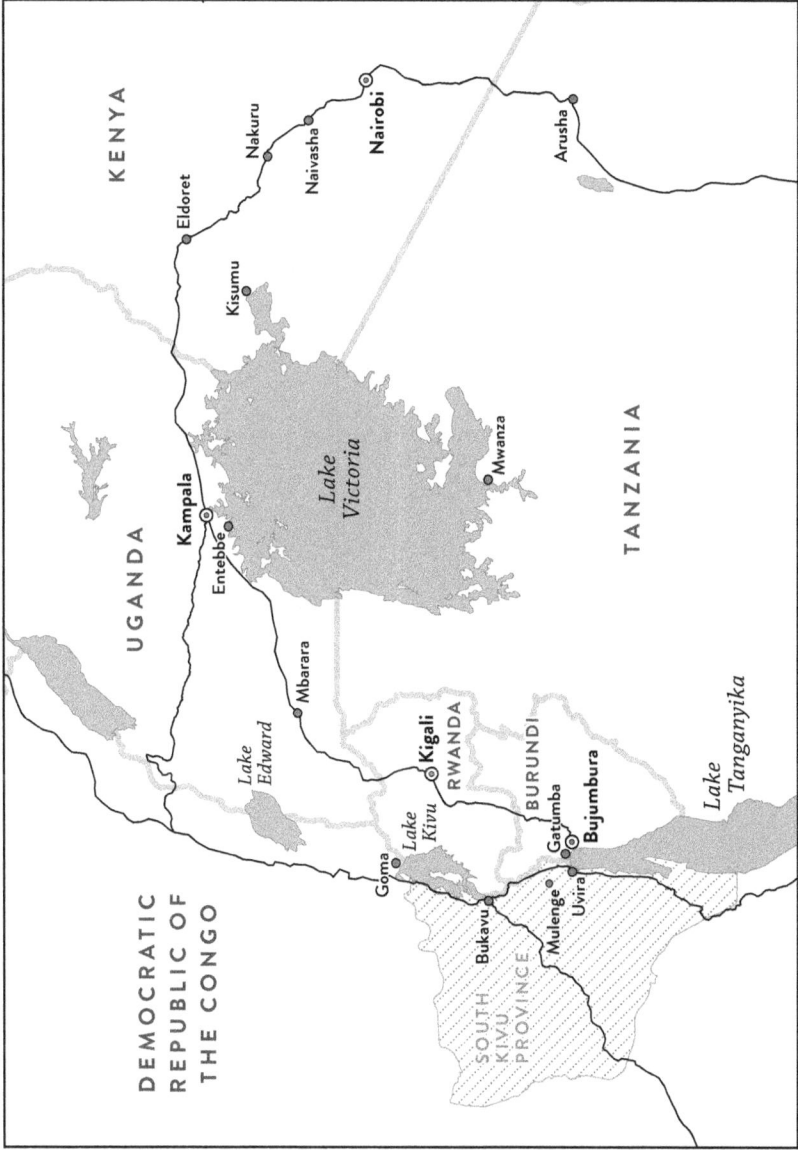

EASTERN CONGO AND NEIGHBORING COUNTRIES IN THE GREAT LAKES REGION

Introduction

HABIBA DRUMMED HER FINGERS on the table, staring out at the bright lot where her minivan was parked.[1] She didn't often talk about her two sets of parents, though the always present facts of her family occasionally rose into conscious thought. At age four, she had been sent several hours from her family's home in northern Somalia to live with her maternal grandmother, who was otherwise alone. Soon after, in 1988, with President Barre's military regime violently retaliating against a northern rebellion, they fled together south to Mogadishu. Her parents had had to stay in the north with their other children. With the US quitting their long financial support of the dictator, Barre's regime crumbled, and a genocidal war broke out in 1991 in the capital. Habiba's grandmother could not keep moving, so she sent Habiba with her maternal uncle and his family, who were fleeing Mogadishu for Kenya. By the time the family was identified for resettlement to the United States years later, Habiba's memories of her birth parents had grown hazier. Though she still thought of them as *hooyaday iyo aabbahay* (my mom and dad), she had, over years, come to call her uncle and his wife Mom and Dad, as well.

Turning from the parking lot back to the table where condensation pooled around an iced coffee, she offered, "My parents raised me as their own, really and truly," noting that at the time of their resettlement case in the 1990s, no one asked questions about the genealogical basis of their relationships. There had been no need to say anything about being different from her siblings— her genealogical cousins. The requirements of care and piecing together social worlds amidst death, separation, and grief meant that Habiba, like many, had two sets of parents and siblings. This was how kinship worked. Amidst both long-standing kinship norms and the turmoil of a war, "family" and everyday practices of care emerge in many forms. Some of them prove distinctly troubling to the humanitarian systems meant to aid, reunify, and resettle refugee families.

In 2008, a decade after Habiba arrived in the United States, Greg Brown was working for the Nairobi-based Resettlement Support Center (RSC), an entity contracted by the US State Department to screen people referred by the UN High Commissioner for Refugees (UNHCR). Greg had worked for the RSC for several years—traveling to refugee camps and cities across the continent to interview people, determining whether or not they could move to a final stage of vetting by US Citizenship and Immigration Services officials, under the Department of Homeland Security. Early that year, Greg received a call asking him to draw up a proposal for a DNA-testing pilot program. A new State Department official based at the US embassy in Nairobi had heard rumors that the US Refugee Family Reunification Program—of which 95 percent was filled by applicants from Africa—was "thoroughly corrupt," as Greg put it, recalling the official's comments about five years later. "And this is a few years post 9/11. 'What happens to my career if I'm the guy who sent a terrorist to the States?' [the official said]. And he would have been responsible," Greg recounted.

Greg and his team drew up a plan to conduct DNA tests for every family slated to be interviewed at their offices in Nairobi that week. The pilot program was then repeated in Ethiopia, Uganda, and several countries in West Africa. Ultimately, three thousand people were tested, mostly from Somalia, Ethiopia, and Liberia. According to the State Department, which released a statement titled "Fraud in the Refugee Family Reunification (P3) Program," over 80 percent of cases included at least one "fraudulent relationship" (Bureau of Population, Refugees, and Migration 2009). The reported results sent shockwaves through governmental and non-governmental agencies involved in US refugee admissions. In the following months, the reunification program was suspended. For people in the US who had been waiting for family members or who had planned to start the reunification process, the suspension was devastating. It wasn't until four years later that the program reopened, this time with DNA testing as a mandatory component.

Because families are often separated in the course of fleeing civil and international wars, many people who arrive in places like the United States through resettlement programs hope to apply for family members who remain living as refugees elsewhere. Meanwhile, households and networks of social care, like Habiba's, can be radically reconfigured while fleeing violence and seeking asylum across international borders. Prior to 2012, many people simply listed a niece or nephew as their child on the required paperwork. In the years following the reunification program's initial suspension and in the wake of its reopening in 2012, families and communities were reconfigured by DNA testing and reconfigured themselves to fit new regulations (Besteman 2016, 89–96; Lowe 2019, 195). People who fell outside the parameters of the biogenetic nuclear family, like Habiba, were often separated indefinitely. Sometimes these people, children and adults alike, became invisible to bureaucratic authorities, because people living as refugees and attempting to migrate would configure their cases to meet bureaucratic requirements. Other times, UNHCR tried to keep a family together by creating a separate "linked" case for a niece or cousin who was a member of the household. Sometimes bureaucratic workarounds were successful, and other times not.

In Ohio, for example, a woman named Hibo applied to reunite with her teenage son, 15, and daughter, 16, who were living in Kenya's Dadaab camps. At the time, Hibo's niece was the primary caregiver for her teenage daughter, who had cerebral palsy. Despite her caregiving role, the niece could not be included on the family reunification case because she was not a member of Hibo's nuclear family—not a biogenetic child or a spouse. Because of her necessary role caring for Hibo's daughter, however, Hibo's niece was granted her own resettlement case. The niece's case went forward, and she arrived in the United States, hoping that the children would soon follow. But they did not follow, owing to a long-stalled security check. Now, Hibo's daughter had lost her primary caregiver; her round-the-clock care fell to her teenage brother; and Hibo still had no idea when or if she would ever see her children.

The 2008 DNA pilot program, the suspension of the US Refugee Family Reunification Program, and its reopening in 2012 were largely invisible events in the United States. There was no media coverage and little writing about the policy change or its effects on families and communities throughout Africa and the United States.[2] Yet these events are emblematic of how displacement and mobility are managed. They tell us about the intersections of humanitarianism and securitization in aid to and governance of people living as refugees in global South locations, and in Africa specifically. These events also reflect the ways in which "the family" as a category simultaneously exists as an object of humanitarian care and as a locus of suspicion and investigation for those in charge of selecting the beneficiaries of refugee aid and resettlement.

Refugee resettlement—programs that bring UNHCR-documented refugees from a country of first asylum to a country that will grant a path to citizenship—is available to fewer than 1 percent of people living as recognized refugees worldwide. How does the current global system of refugee governance, which enables a tiny minority to legally migrate to global North countries, produce the figure of the "fraudulent refugee" and "fraudulent families" that the DNA tests purportedly revealed? How do these figures emerge at the intersection of heightened border control and a humanitarian focus on sorting the "the most vulnerable" from those deemed less or not deserving? How is the family—as a category, a unit, and a symbol—central to those processes? And how do people live with and respond to the logics and categories of humanitarian regimes? These are questions that this book raises as it untangles the patchwork of bureaucratic systems that constitute refugee resettlement from global South to global North today and as it follows people who have been displaced across borders.

Undocumented migration and asylum-seeking processes in global North locations have captured public and scholarly attention (De León 2015; Cabot 2013, 2014; Ticktin 2011). An ethnography of refugee resettlement, told mostly from the vantage point of an African city but also tracing processes and people to North America, offers a distinct but complementary story about migration today. Although refugee resettlement is framed as a humanitarian concept and refugee camps are deemed temporary sites of humanitarian relief, they are part of larger regimes that contain people outside citizenship—sometimes for years, often for generations. Contemporary governance of refugees is part of the same "overarching structure of mobility controls" that characterize what Besteman (2020) calls "militarized global apartheid" (19)—controls that fortify borders to global North states just enough to capture and exploit the labor of people who survive treacherous journeys. Studying refugee resettlement from a postcolonial African city demonstrates the ways in which logics of care are implicated in the same regimes that they also desire to overcome (Oliver 2017). The family, I show, is central to these overlapping imperatives of care and control.

Family ties have always motivated migration and have often structured migration policies. Today, two-thirds of authorized immigration to the United States occurs under the rubric of family reunification, far more than through work visas or political asylum (Coe 2014, 87)—a legacy of the priorities created under the Immigration Act of 1965 (Daniels 2004, 136). Forces of violent conflict, climate change and environmental catastrophe, economic crisis, and the call of opportunities elsewhere have driven countless people to leave home behind and have separated and reconfigured families across borders (Coe 2014; De León 2015; Feldman-Savelsberg 2016; Hannaford 2017; Ong 1999). Policies define "family" and invest the term with specific sociocultural meanings that become differently visible when seen from the vantage point of people trying to migrate (Coe 2014; Piot with Batema 2019). Like kinship reckoned through myriad spiritual (Thomas 2021), technological and biomedical (Carsten 2004; Hargreaves 2006; Thompson 2001; Rapp, Heath, and Taussig 2001), bureaucratic (Piot with Batema 2019), and non-Western, queer, and other non-biological idioms (Alber 2003; Kim 2010; Weston 1991), this book foregrounds kinship beyond the genealogical or nuclear family ideal. It demonstrates the effects of the ways that humanitarian and immigration bureaucracies define the family. How do these definitions come to life in borderland spaces of embassies, UN offices, refugee camps, and urban neighborhoods? As this book reveals, people living as refugees uphold duties to kin and community in ways that are animated by their own moral logics—logics that often run along a different track than those undergirding humanitarian principles and policy definitions.

Centering Resettlement

The beginning of a coordinated, international effort to manage internationally displaced populations began in the aftermath of World War I, under the League of Nations' Office of the High Commissioner for Refugees—a precursor to UNHCR. The organization was created to manage refugees from the dissolving Russian and Ottoman Empires. Following World War II, the Allied powers organized a series of temporary agencies to manage Europe's tens of millions who had been displaced from their home countries. A permanent organization was formed with the creation of UNHCR in 1950. Its mandate was codified in the 1951 Convention Relating to the Status of Refugees, which framed "the unity of the family, the natural and fundamental group unit of society," as an essential right and critical object of protection.[3] While at first temporally and geographically limited, UNHCR's mandate was extended under the 1967 Protocol Relating to the Status of Refugees. The Protocol brought emerging refugee situations produced by Cold War conflicts in Asia, Africa, and beyond under UNHCR's mandate, though displaced people from African countries did not become part of US and other government resettlement programs until decades later (Sandvik 2018). As a "Western-dominated and donor-dependent organization," UNHCR was driven by Western governments' Cold War interests (Loescher, Betts, and Milner 2008, 25–26), and in this sense, US and global refugee resettlement initiatives were always tied to national security interests, decades before 9/11 and other turn-of-the-century forces reshaped them.

UNHCR defines its work around three "durable solutions": local integration, voluntary repatriation to the country of origin, and resettlement to a third country. Many of the conflicts that have led people to leave their home countries and seek asylum in Kenya have persisted for decades now—in Somalia and Congo, for example, since the early- and mid-1990s, respectively—making repatriation impossible for most. Kenya, like most African countries, does not offer legally recognized refugees a path to citizenship. Instead, people live as precarious residents with refugee documents that must be regularly renewed, making local integration severely circumscribed.[4] Resettlement operates as a potent tool for UNHCR and a longed-for opportunity for many, but it is scarce, elusive, and largely beyond the control of those who seek it.

As of 2023, people counted as "refugees" numbered 36.4 million—including those under the mandate of UNHCR, and nearly 6 million Palestinians under the mandate of the UN Relief and Works Agency (UNRWA) (UNHCR 2023). The notion of refugee-ness as a temporary condition—one that will be resolved once people return home or obtain legal citizenship elsewhere—is not borne out by the data. Since the start of the twenty-first century, political conflicts giving rise to mass displacements have cycled through media across the world: Afghanistan, Iraq, Syria, Ukraine, Gaza. As Saida Hodžić writes, "World attention spikes like blood sugar. Disasters and deaths are made visible and then disappear from the public eye," while "for many refugees, the real and unexpected struggles begin after arrival in host countries" (2017, 157). Contemporary modes of managing displacement at both national and global levels mean that people are often stranded in the legal limbo of asylee and refugee status for the rest of their lives. Seventy-eight percent of the world's refugees have lived without citizenship rights for at least five years, and many for as long as forty (UNHCR 2022). People continue living in camps and other so-called temporary conditions long after their situations are perceived as newsworthy events.

African countries typically register as only a blip on the radar of world news in most places outside the continent, even in moments of major political significance. The close to five million refugees and twelve million internally displaced people from East and Central Africa and the Horn of Africa are marginal in public discussion of immigration and refugees in places like the United States (UNHCR 2022). Attention tends to focus on conflicts deemed significant to US foreign policy and economic interests, as well as those that are harder to turn a blind eye to because they pertain to US land borders, which garner earnest concern, or are employed in fear-mongering political rhetoric. The Kenyan context speaks to global South situations broadly, but also offers its own distinct story. It draws little attention on a global stage, but provides critical insights into the intersections of global humanitarian efforts, global North immigration policies, the Global War on Terror, race and white supremacy, and struggles "in the name of the family" (Stacey 1996) that play out transnationally.

Studying refugee resettlement requires attention to multiple scales, communities, places, institutions, and histories (see Arar and FitzGerald 2023). This book is centered in the commercial, tech, development, and humanitarian hub of Nairobi, Kenya. It also follows my interlocutors' memories of Somalia, eastern Democratic Republic of the Congo (DRC), Rwanda, and other places of asylum where they lived, such as Kenya's refugee camps. Toward the book's end, it shifts locations to view resettlement from the space of a US Voluntary Agency that supports people resettling in Columbus, Ohio, and from the perspectives of people resettling there. The ethnography brings readers to two sides of the Atlantic and two sides of a postcolonial city—a city established by British settlers at the close of the nineteenth century, constructed by and for migrants of many kinds. While necessarily partial and incomplete in its attempt to grasp resettlement as a transnational process, the book attends to the patchwork of organizations that manage it. It offers the stories and perspectives of people who live amidst that patchwork—who critique it, make claims on it, and maneuver through and around it. It charts the ways in which people attempting to access refugee resettlement understand and respond to its categories, technologies, and modes of operating, particularly as they pertain to their families and the social networks in which they are embedded.

But who gets access to resettlement, and how does it work? UNHCR outlines seven priority categories: legal and/or physical protection needs, survivors of violence and/or torture, medical needs, women and girls at risk, family reunification, and children and adolescents at risk. The last category, "lack of foreseeable alternative durable solutions," could theoretically apply to most refugees living in Kenya (and many other places), but it is, like others, used sparingly (UNHCR 2011, 287). UNHCR selects people who fit into these categories but also into host-government priorities and regulations. While US government agencies and partnering NGOs often refer to the resettlement "pipeline"—the interlocking of multiple institutions through which people move—the experience of the resettlement process is rarely smooth. Much of this book highlights the ways in which people seeking resettlement become stuck in the interstices of different bureaucratic regimes.

The story of a woman I'll call Esperance, on the other hand, elucidates the broad strokes of how refugee resettlement from Kenya operates in theory—a partial story from a perspective that privileges the interlinking institutions involved. Esperance and her family—a composite based on many people I interviewed—serve as a model to explain the resettlement system before I describe it in more granular ways.[5] Esperance is a minority Banyamulenge[6] woman from the South Kivu province of the Democratic Republic of the Congo—a targeted ethnic minority. After her husband was killed by government-supported *mai-mai* militia and she was assaulted, Esperance escaped her village with her four children. They fled first to the city of Uvira, then traveled to Uganda, and later to Nairobi. Having heard about massacres in refugee camps in bordering countries like Burundi and Rwanda and that Kenya's capital city offered greater security, she used the little money she had to cross borders through unofficial routes made accessible by smugglers and other local people.

When Esperance and her children arrived in Nairobi, she sought out the Banyamulenge community, eventually finding a cousin of her late husband at a Banyamulenge church. Her husband's cousin took her and her children to the Kenyan Department of Refugee Affairs office to register as asylum seekers. There, Esperance's biographical data and photo were taken, and she was given a "waiting" paper to show she had applied for her ID card. She was told that she should return after three months to retrieve her document. Meanwhile, her husband's cousin brought her and her children to UNHCR. There, she was given an asylum seeker's pass, which authorized her stay in Nairobi while awaiting a Refugee Status Determination interview, scheduled for six months later. At the interview, through an interpreter, she described the attack on her village, her husband's death, her assault, and the journey she undertook with her children to arrive in Nairobi. She described her medical complications that resulted from being attacked and her challenges in finding a way to pay rent and buy basic necessities.

As the sole provider for her family, she followed a few other women in her community—mostly widows—who did laundry by hand at homes in a nearby neighborhood. It was a physically demanding job made more difficult because of chronic pain resulting from her attack. She was pressured to have sex for money by a man in whose home she had been working, a terrifying prospect as she faced eviction. People at church helped pool some money for her, but resources were scarce as many community members faced similar problems. The situation caused symptoms of post-traumatic stress that made it increasingly difficult to work and care for her children. One day, while returning from washing clothes, a group of young men from a different Congolese community cornered her and threatened to rob her, stating that they would "finish" her family like the *mai mai* had killed her husband. She was terrified, and although she allowed her children to go to school, she lived in constant fear and rarely ventured outside.

When the day of her UNHCR status determination interview finally arrived, the interviewer found Esperance's story credible: her testimony was consistent with the timeline of documented events in her home area, and her children's testimonies corroborated hers. UNHCR granted her and her children asylum, along with a refugee identity document. Because of the continued threats she faced, along with her medical complications, the Refugee Status Determination Unit referred Esperance to the Protection Unit, giving her an appointment for several weeks later. Advised by both the Refugee Status Determination Unit and members of her community, Esperance brought a police report that her husband's relatives helped her file regarding the harassment she experienced. The interviewer from the Protection Unit deemed Esperance to be particularly vulnerable on account of her minority ethnicity, her experience of gender-based violence and ongoing physical and mental health problems, the documentation of the threat she received, and her status as a single mother. Because the US government had recently agreed to resettle fifty thousand Congolese refugees over five years, she not only fit UNHCR criteria but also a host-government priority.[7]

Esperance and her children were given another appointment to meet with the Resettlement Unit in three months. In her first interview, the UNHCR staff member created a precise record of her family. That record could be used if Esperance made any family-related claims in the future. Esperance knew that the information she provided about her past had to be consistent with the facts she had reported previously. Unexplained inconsistencies, such as different dates or names or unexplained variations in her narrative, could cast doubt on her story and cause her case to be closed. Several months later, Esperance was given an appointment for a final UNHCR interview. Months later, she was notified that their case had been referred to the United States. Now, she and her children waited to hear from the US Resettlement Support Center (RSC).

Finally, Esperance was notified of the interview date. When the day arrived, she and her children traveled to an unfamiliar building, not far from the UNHCR offices. After the interview at RSC, Esperance was notified that she would move on to the final stage of vetting with US Citizenship and Immigration Services (USCIS), an agency under the Department of Homeland Security. While she waited, the US government carried out background checks. She received notice of her USCIS interview but would have to wait nearly a year before USCIS officials would come to Nairobi. Her UNHCR and Kenyan government identity documents had expired since she first arrived, so while she was waiting for USCIS, she returned to the Kenyan Department of Refugee Affairs and to UNHCR to renew her IDs, required for her next interview. Finally, Esperance and her children were interviewed by a USCIS officer, and a few months later they received a letter about the positive determination of their case. The interviewer found that she met the definition of a refugee and did not match any categories of inadmissibility to the United States. Her narrative matched that from her earlier interviews, and the officer deemed her credible. She accepted a loan from the US government for the cost of her family's airline tickets, which she would repay after beginning to work in the US. The International Organization for Migration (IOM) in Nairobi notified her of upcoming medical screenings. Since neither she nor her children had communicable diseases that would delay their travel, their case moved forward again.

At a week-long orientation at the IOM Transit Center, Esperance learned about US climate, laws, and cultural practices. The instructor explained what to expect on her upcoming journey, what her new home would look like, and what she could expect in the first months after arrival. On the day of their flight, Esperance and her children returned to the Transit Center, where they underwent a final medical screening. An IOM staff member handed Esperance a plastic bag with all the documents they would need to depart Kenya, transit through Istanbul, and enter the United States, eventually arriving in Houston. From the time that she arrived in Kenya, over four years had passed.

Since her children were young when they arrived, none had aged out of their dependency status, which would have caused them to be separated from her case—a challenge faced by those with children who reach age twenty-one. At each juncture of the process, Esperance and her children moved forward—a best-case scenario.

This narrative of resettlement foregrounds organizational procedures, priorities vis-à-vis Esperance as a credible victim, and a timeframe bookended by an arrival and a departure. But what happens during the weeks, months, and years of waiting? How does everyday life unfold? How do people make a life and create new social worlds in new places? What does this process look like for people who turn out to be more troublesome to UNHCR or host governments—less ideal objects of humanitarian care? As critical scholars of humanitarianism have shown, real people rarely—if ever—fulfill the criteria of the idealized object of humanitarian assistance: perfectly innocent, totally helpless, endlessly grateful (Besteman 2016; Feldman and Ticktin 2010; Malkki 1996; Ticktin 2011). Not only do individuals turn out to be troublesome, but so do families. As a single mother with biogenetic children under twenty-one, the composition of Esperance's family made it ideal: the absence of a husband made her especially vulnerable, and because she gave birth to all her young children, there were no relations that had to be investigated or family members who had to be excluded.

Ultimately, resettlement is also embedded in shifting local, regional, and global political conditions that make maneuvering through the process unpredictable. Esperance's story is a broad overview of how resettlement ideally works, foregrounding the organizations involved, with a person moving step by step from one institution to the next. In contrast, the following section zooms in on a real moment in time that had major consequences for both people living as refugees and organizations working with refugees in Kenya during the period on which this book centers. It highlights how resettlement unfolds (or doesn't) amidst the forces of local and international politics.

Seeking Resettlement, Nairobi, 2014

What does resettlement look like when, instead of mapping the process from a bureaucratically defined start (recognition by UNHCR) to finish (a plane landing in an American city), we attend to the places where people remain refugees for years, even generations? At the end of March 2014, I was visiting a Congolese family in Kayole, a neighborhood in Nairobi's Eastlands. Though the family was celebrating the birth of a new baby, with visitors stopping by, the main words on everyone's lips were "Shauri Moyo." The Kenyan Department of Refugee Affairs in the Shauri Moyo neighborhood, where one applied for a government refugee document, was closing. This had happened before, causing major disruptions to accessing identification—important for daily life in Nairobi and for accessing humanitarian aid and necessary for the resettlement process. The "alien cards," as they were colloquially called, were required to prove that a person had been lawfully residing in Kenya in order to receive an exit permit to leave the country. This time, things seemed even more uncertain, and the government even more primed to make life difficult for urban residents documented as refugees.

On September 21 of the previous year, just six months prior, and one month and a day after I had arrived in Nairobi for a nineteen-month research stay, Kenya endured its most deadly attack since the 1998 al-Qaeda bombing of the US embassy. The 2013 attack by the Somali militant group al-Shabaab on the upscale Westgate shopping mall left sixty-seven Kenyans and foreigners dead and ignited a renewed public focus on security by the government. The US-backed Ethiopian invasion of Somalia in 2006, spurred by groundless claims about the rise of the Union of Islamic Courts (UICs)—a legitimate and widely supported governing institution inside the country—had further destabilized Somalia in the preceding years. Foreign attempts to quash the UICs ultimately gave rise to the faction known as al-Shabaab (Ibrahim 2018). Citing the instability of its border region with its eastern neighbor, Kenya invaded Somalia in 2011 and joined the African Union Mission in Somalia (AMISOM) in 2012 (Al-Bulushi 2019). The invasion was followed by attacks by al-Shabaab across the border, the Westgate attack being the most dramatic up to that point due to the loss of life and the visibility and symbolic resonance of the location: a hub of upscale international commerce, patronized by Kenyan and international elites. Throughout the country, President Uhuru Kenyatta, who had lost his nephew in the attack, entered Kenyan homes through their televisions to describe the implementation of advanced security technologies from CCTV cameras to facial recognition technology. But a different version of security was also at work.

The day after visiting the new baby in Kayole, I went to meet Mohamed, friend and Somali language partner, at a restaurant in Eastleigh, the bustling commercial and residential neighborhood best known for its Somali community. When I arrived, Mohamed, a young man in his early twenties, slim and fresh faced, was sitting at a table with an older man who managed the restaurant. The man asked to see my newspaper, which featured an article about the arrest of five hundred mostly Somali people the previous night, not far from where we sat. On March 26, as people gathered around a new baby discussed the closure of the office in Shauri Moyo, Joseph Ole Lenku, cabinet secretary for the Ministry of Interior and Coordination of National Government, had issued a directive stating the following:

1. All refugees residing outside the designated refugee camps of Kakuma and Dadaab are hereby directed to return to their respective camps with immediate effect. There are no other designated refugee camps outside these areas. Any refugee found flouting this directive will be dealt with in accordance with the law. Consequently, all refugee registration centres in urban areas . . . are hereby closed.

2. All Kenyans are requested to report to the Police any refugee and/or illegal immigrants found outside the designated refugee camps.

3. Furthermore, an additional 500 police officers will be deployed with immediate effect in Nairobi, Mombasa and their environs to enhance security and surveillance. Other Security organs will support the exercise. (Ole Lenku 2014)

On March 31, the future of the directive still nebulous, Mohamed and I had spent the afternoon with a broker who helped people in Eastleigh with resettlement and other immigration processes. Leaving his office in a narrow alley, we walked along busy First Avenue, passing tables of brightly colored leggings, piles of ballet flats, tables of neatly folded scarves, stacks of blue jeans. Given the new developments, Mohamed said, he no longer had a valid ID. He kept his UNHCR mandate at home now, since "they don't respect it," as he put it. He carried his creased and folded waiting slip for his government alien card (he had lost his original card when his wallet was stolen and had had to reapply), along with his expired student ID from Eastleigh High School. But these were useless if stopped by police, and he needed the ID from Shauri Moyo to see his family sponsorship case to its completion. Without the government ID card, he would be stuck, even if the Canadian government finally issued him a visa.

We talked in low voices as we wound our way back to Ushirika, stopping as we often did at an abandoned truck that had come to mark the juncture between Mohamed's part of Eastleigh and the rest of my way home to Pangani across Juja Road. Vans labeled "Private" bumped past us, carrying children in blue and white school uniforms. "This will be our checkpoint," Mohamed said, as he always did. As I made the rest of my way home, the sound of reggae mingled with the call to prayer. Dark clouds made a blanket over Pangani and wind whipped up a cloud of dust. An airplane coming from nearby Moi Air Base droned low overhead. Near a butcher shop with a goat and a camel painted on the front, an old woman stretched out on the sidewalk looking strangely comfortable, as if she were lounging on a picnic blanket or beach towel. At home, I ate dinner in front of the TV. Kanye West was proposing to Kim Kardashian in a baseball stadium to a hundred-piece orchestra. At 8:15, I received a text from Mohamed: "An explosion just happened @12street no one is out of his house people are really scared." *The Standard*, a national newspaper, was already reporting that the double blasts had occurred at 7:30 and that five people were dead.

In the following days, I stayed in Pangani and other neighborhoods farther from Eastleigh. Mohamed and others described nighttime raids by the police, who would park their big lorries—large enough to fit dozens of people in back—in front of the neighborhood's cinderblock apartment buildings, arresting anyone who had neither a Kenyan national ID nor enough money or luck to negotiate their freedom. At Pangani Police Station, the nearest precinct, shoes were piled high as police crammed barefoot people into cells. Mohamed, feeling emboldened by his chameleonic ability to talk like a local, had gone to the police station to help a relative get a background report needed for the final stage of her resettlement to Sweden. "It was like an auction!" he reported, with people lined up with their money to try to bid for their relatives' release. From Pangani Police Station, people were distributed across the city's other jails and prisons, then to a mass detention center set up at Kasarani Stadium, a national sports arena. From there, people were trucked to the Dadaab refugee camps on the Somali-Kenya border.

The relocation directive had been put into motion with a crackdown on refugee neighborhoods dubbed Operation Usalama (Security) Watch. On April 5, six thousand police had been deployed to Eastleigh, according to Minister Ole Lenku. When I read this in my notes years later, I could not believe that so many officers could have been sent to occupy an area of perhaps two square kilometers—around twenty blocks deep and eight across—but published sources corroborate that at least the minister reported this to be so (Minority Rights Group International 2015).

A couple days later, Mohamed reported that a young man had been shot. "Police called him and he ran. They shot him. Through the neck."

"Did you know him?" I asked.

"No. He was a youth. *Just* like me," Mohamed replied. "The police were gathered around him. Dead." Mohamed described the scene in the market the next day, as community leaders with a microphone addressed crowds. "They were telling people, 'If the police call you, just come.' If they call me, I'll just do like this"—he reached his arms over his head, eyes exaggeratedly wide.

During events like Operation Usalama Watch, what happens to resettlement—a lifeline intended for the most vulnerable? A young man named Saiid was one of many whose cases were disrupted by the operation. Saiid and his brother were at home in Eastleigh the night before their interview at the Canadian embassy when police banged on their door. With only their refugee IDs—IDs that overnight had become evidence of unlawful residence in the city—they were taken to the local police station, then moved to Kasarani Stadium, later to the Industrial Area Prison, and from there they were trucked to the Dadaab camps. Both at Pangani police station and later at a UNHCR office at the camp, Saiid showed his letter from the Canadian embassy, hoping that it would somehow help him get home, but neither the police nor UNHCR were impressed. When his brother received a call informing him that his interview had been scheduled, their cousin in Ontario considered hiring a smuggler to get them back to the capital but ultimately couldn't afford it. Finally, the government Department of Refugee Affairs office at the camp issued them a fourteen-day movement pass. The young men traveled by bus on the long road that stretches from the Northeast and finally becomes an eight-lane highway entering Nairobi, stopped at several police and military checkpoints along the way. They arrived the night before Saiid's brother's interview. In the morning, Saiid's brother showed up at the guarded embassy gates on Limuru Road, only to be told, due to some bureaucratic blunder, "Sorry, your name isn't on the list today." Amidst the operation, countless plans to leave Kenya and to reunify with family elsewhere were unsettled (Balakian 2020).

In resettlement, the system's different requirements, priorities, and technologies, not to mention bureaucratic errors, create gridlocks and impasses that people navigating the process must find ways to overcome. The IOM medical clearance, for example, was infamous for expiring before other clearances were completed. Some people had to undergo the medical screening as many as seven times before all the different checks were valid and aligned. During their years of waiting and hoping to move through the stages of the resettlement process, conflicting bureaucratic systems create obstacles. Every person has stories about how the requirements of one institution conflicted with the demands of another, about how their inability to access a needed document prevented their case from moving forward, about how changing government regulations had stopped their case in its tracks, about how their family situation clashed with rules of case composition, or about how the separation of family members onto different cases caused endless worry, especially when some members departed while others remained.

The bureaucratic complexity of the patchwork of institutions involved in refugee resettlement became especially visible during Operation Usalama Watch. The anti-refugee, anti-Somali crackdown mirrored old patterns of Kenya's hostility toward ethnic Somalis rooted in colonial divisions and Kenya-Somalia border conflicts dating from the era of independence in the 1960s (Lochery 2012; Mburu 2005; Sheik 2007; Thompson 1995; Turton 1972; Weitzberg 2017; Whittaker 2008). It also ran alongside changing forms of policing, surveillance, and violence against Muslims in Kenya in a Global War on Terror more generally (Al-Bulushi 2021). In the aftermath of the directive, not only had the government registration office at Shauri Moyo closed, but so had UNHCR registration. After staff members from an international NGO were arrested for aiding refugees in the city, refugee-serving organizations in Nairobi largely went underground. NGOs removed their signage and halted or altered their services so as not to imperil their staff or draw attention to people continuing to live in the capital against the directive's orders. Due to heightened fear about repeat attacks like Westgate, the US government also suspended travel to Kenya for USCIS officials, so no resettlement cases in the US system could move to the final stage of interviews. Even the very few selected for resettlement were stuck. Ironically, at a time when life for people documented as refugees in Kenya was more insecure than ever, it was also more difficult to leave the country via the resettlement process (Balakian 2020).

For Saiid and his brother and many like them, the question of how resettlement works would be answered differently from how it is diagramed or explained in handbooks or visual aids created by government agencies or UNHCR. And it would be different from the experience of Esperance—an idealized version that leaves out the many events, personal and political, that animate how resettlement works in people's lives. The question of how resettlement works would also be answered differently by the many people whom UNHCR deems not exceptional, not vulnerable enough to be considered.

Researching Resettlement from Kenya

This research on resettlement has several origin points, including my own family's history among the refugees aided by the League of Nations—the beginning of a modern refugee figure and international bodies of refugee management (Arar and FitzGerald 2023, 46). My Armenian family's stories from the twilight of the Ottoman Empire, which involve families dispersed, separated, and remade in new places, have long informed my interest in the issues central to this book. I first came to Kenya in the summer of 2011 with plans to research resettlement and family reunification programs as a Swahili language student in Mombasa on a Foreign Language and Area Studies fellowship funded by the US Department of Education. A graduate student developing a dissertation research project, I began cold calling and emailing organizations like the UN High Commissioner for Refugees (UNHCR) and the US Resettlement Support Center (RSC) to ask for meetings for when I would arrive in Nairobi later that summer. Like much long-term ethnographic research, a slow snowballing of contacts over the course of years led to significant relationships that shaped my understanding of refugee resettlement and family reunification, both from the standpoint of the organizations involved and the people trying to access resettlement as a migration route.

One of the people I first met at UNHCR was a staff member from the US who introduced me to Amina, a UNHCR interpreter who became my first Somali language tutor in the summer of 2012. When I returned in 2013 for long-term fieldwork, Amina had left for the United States through the US resettlement program, but she introduced me by email to Mohamed, who became a close friend and guide. His life, social networks, and insights inform this book in central ways. An internship at a US-based NGO, likewise, connected me to people at the NGO's Kenya office. Greg Brown, who directed that office, also became an important interlocutor whose knowledge of the field informed my understanding of refugee resettlement, the logics and systems that animate it, and the people who work in it.

Gaining access to organizations like UNHCR and the RSC, both of which were relatively closed to researchers, had distinct challenges, though US citizenship facilitated access to the RSC, an entity managed by the US State Department (in comparison, see Jansen 2008, 578). Interviewing former RSC staff provided one route to understanding that organization and its history, as most current staff members were not able to speak with me, and those who did talked only in their official capacity as representatives of the organization. On the other hand, Greg and others guided me to people at UNHCR who would have both the authority and the interest to talk with me about resettlement. My US passport and access to US-based dissertation research funding enabled the multi-sited research that produced this book. My freedom of movement on account of my citizenship status and nationality, as tied to race and class, is of both practical and theoretical significance to this book and its creation.

Working with people living as refugees, who were often desperate to garner a resettlement case or move to the next stage of the process, had specific challenges. As a white American who looked and sounded like many of the people who worked in the gatekeeping offices they frequented, I needed to clearly distinguish myself and my research *about* resettlement from people who worked for organizations that granted access *to* resettlement. Despite the way I identified myself, there were likely still people I met who believed I had some connection to resettlement organizations or the US government. This is one reason that I mostly write about people with whom I developed sustained relationships and who came to know me and understand my identity as a student and researcher. At the same time, as anthropologist Shannon Speed writes, people who are the subjects of research, particularly pertaining to issues of justice and rights, "are likely to expect and demand" commitment to their needs and causes (2006, 72). In this case, that often meant finding ways to be useful to people in their individual quests for resettlement or refugee status. This involved acting as a source of information about ever-changing policies, accompanying people to offices, reading and interpreting documents, and asking questions of people in power. These activities allowed me to participate in the life of Somali and Congolese communities, where many people already operated as unofficial brokers of information to assist others in the resettlement process. Those activities fundamentally shaped this research. Had I been officially based inside an organization, rather than spending most of my time in neighborhoods and moving between communities and the institutions that manage and aid them, the story of refugee resettlement that I would have to tell would be a different one. When I returned to the US to begin conducting research in Columbus, Ohio, I was based at a local resettlement agency—one of the hundreds of organizations across the country that receive funding from the US government to assist people arriving through the US Refugee Admissions Program. Viewing resettlement from that vantage point involved different methods, and enabled new insights about resettlement, which I detail in chapter 5.

As a city, Nairobi has always housed migrant communities: European settlers and British colonial administrators, Somali livestock traders, laborers from South Asia, and workers and seekers from rural communities within and beyond Kenya's colonial and post-independence borders (Carrier 2016; Mutongi 2017; White 1990). Beginning in the late 1980s and in greater numbers through the 1990s, people seeking asylum from many of Kenya's neighboring countries joined that list. Those who came in the late '80s and early '90s—initially from Uganda, then from Somalia and Ethiopia (Horst 2006b, 19), and later from Sudan and other neighboring countries—were fleeing and continue to flee conflicts rooted in the legacies of colonial borders; violence, plunder, and racializing regimes of colonial administration; complex political transitions to independent nationhood; and neocolonial programs and interventions across the region (Besteman 1999, 2016, 2020; Hunt 2008; Mamdani 2001; Mburu 2005; Weitzberg 2017). During the 1990s, in the wake of hundreds of thousands fleeing Somalia and Sudan, the government turned to UNHCR to take over managing refugee camps, which the organization reduced from several small enclaves to two large areas (Horst 2006b, 19). By the 2010s, Kenya was home to over half a million people documented as refugees by UNHCR, many of whom live in Kenya's two major UN-run camp complexes, while tens of thousands reside in the capital city or move between camps and Nairobi (Pavanello, Elhawary, and Pantuliano 2010).

This book focuses on people from two primary countries of origin: Somalia and the Democratic Republic of the Congo. Those from Somalia came from different class and regional backgrounds, including some minority communities. Those from Congo primarily came from the Banyamulenge community—one of multiple ethnic groups in the eastern part of the country. Although the people I write about come from these two communities, this book is not most centrally about those ethnic groups, nor is it a comparative study of them in a traditional sense. Anthropologists studying categories such as "illegality" and "deportability" caution against reifying subjectivities such as "deportee" or "undocumented migrant" (Cabot 2014; Coutin 2000; De Genova 2002; Peutz 2006). Likewise, this book is also not a study of "refugees"—a term that can act as a helpful shorthand but can also undermine the project of investigating the category and unsettling widespread assumptions about it. It can also erase the significant differences between official legal statuses like asylum seeker, refugee, and permanent resident.[8] This book is, in one sense, an "ethnography of a legal process rather than of a particular group of people" (Coutin, cited in Peutz 2006, 219; see also Cabot 2014, 2)—the process of refugee resettlement and how it both facilitates and impedes mobility and both resettles and unsettles families. In it, I mostly refer to "people documented as refugees" and "people living as refugees" to describe people with refugee status (sometimes including people waiting for their status to be determined or those who have been denied but count themselves as refugees). I do so because refugee status has significant legal and bureaucratic meaning in the Kenyan context.

Among eight major nationalities that comprise Nairobi's refugee population, Somalis (who accounted for nearly half the people documented as refugees in the city), and Congolese (who accounted for 10 percent) (Pavanello, Elhawary, and Pantuliano 2010, 13) were well-integrated into US and other national resettlement programs. While other national communities were represented in smaller numbers, in 2015 Congolese and Somalis accounted for the second and fourth most resettled populations worldwide, respectively (UNHCR 2015). The US, which has historically admitted more people through refugee resettlement than any other global North country, admitted close to seventy thousand people in fiscal year 2015, of which Somalis represented 12.7 percent and Congolese 11.3 percent (Zong and Batalova 2015).

People from Somalia and Congo faced many of the same challenges living in Kenya and navigating the bureaucracy of resettlement and aid offered by UNHCR and NGOs and the shifting attitudes of the Kenyan government. On the other hand, Somalis often had long-standing networks to draw on in Nairobi and greater access to remittances because of a larger diaspora in global North countries. Banyamulenge, on the other hand, were newer to Nairobi as a community and, in general, had fewer resources being sent from abroad. At the same time, Somalis faced discrimination in Kenya based on their religion (Islam) and ethnicity and more intensive forms of security screening in resettlement processes. In both communities it was normal for extended kin to rely on one another and sometimes raise each other's children. These practices, along with children fostered by families outside their original kin networks, were amplified by needs that arose in the context of each country's political conflicts.

While narratives included in this book gesture toward these similarities and differences, I recount stories not primarily to explicate those comparisons but to elucidate the core themes of the book: discourses of fraud in refugee resettlement (chapter 1), critiques of the resettlement system by those trying to access it (chapter 2), the role of kinship in forging migration opportunities (chapter 3), the effects of DNA testing on families (chapter 4), and the role of national security regimes after people arrive in the US and are waiting to re-unite with family members left behind (chapter 5). Narratives from Congolese interlocutors primarily feature in the first two chapters, while the last three chapters foreground stories from Somali interlocutors. This is in part driven by the topics at hand: Somalis were among the first communities to experience DNA testing. They face distinct forms of securitization in the resettlement process and surveillance in both Kenya and United States as members of a racialized Muslim community. At other moments, on the other hand, ethnicity was less consequential than the shared fact of living as refugees in Nairobi.

Securing Resettlement

On Waiyaki Way, a major road that stretches north and west from Nairobi's Central Business District, sat the Kenya office of the UNHCR. This was 2015. The office had been there since the early 2010s after moving from a nearby location, and it has since moved again. On the building's right was a gated and guarded entrance for staff and visitors, behind which sat a parking lot, a security pavilion, and the building's staff entrance. In front, shaded by a canopy of large trees, one bursting with bright yellow flowers, was a guarded entrance for people seeking UNHCR's services: a farmer whose fields were now planted by someone else, a business owner whose merchandise had been looted long ago, a teacher whose students had scattered, a herder whose cattle were stolen or dead, a minister and an imam, a DJ, a musician, a politician, students, seamstresses, government workers, mothers, fathers, grandparents. Each person had left a life behind in a city like Kismayo, Goma, Juba, Kigali, or Jijiga or a farm near southern Somalia's rivers, a town in the green hills around Lake Kivu and Lake Tanganyika, a city on the Indian Ocean, or one of thousands of villages across a wide region of varied histories.

Some of those assembled at UNHCR's gates had just arrived in Kenya's capital—a city known as "the green city in the sun" in tourism literature and "Silicon Savannah" in tech and entrepreneurial circles. Others had lived in Nairobi's poor peripheries and bustling multiethnic neighborhoods across town and had been returning to this office for years, a decade, more. Most had traveled from neighborhoods in distant parts of the city, usually requiring at least two *matatus* (minibuses) to reach the office—first traveling into the city's center, then west toward Nairobi's affluent neighborhoods where UNHCR and NGOs have made their homes. Some had appointments, while others had gambled precious money for matatu fare, hoping to get the attention of some-one who might change their situation. Many held refugee documents; the majority of people who seek asylum in Kenya are ultimately granted legal refuge. Some awaited a decision on their case, while others had been denied refugee status but continued to return anyway.

After security guards patted them down and they handed over their cell phones, they waited in a large room with long benches. On the walls here, as in other refugee-serving organizations throughout the city, hung posters with the blue UNHCR logo at the bottom: two hands forming a roof over a person (a person without arms or hands, as a Congolese pastor once pointed out to me in his critique of representation). The posters depict, in cartoon form, refugees tempted by dishonest or opportunistic brokers claiming to offer access to resettlement or to hasten a resettlement case. In one, the protagonist presents truthful information despite a broker tempting him to do otherwise. He has a good outcome: a UN official notifies him that his family has been accepted for resettlement. Other posters have characters who take the advice of an unscrupulous broker. The last frame of one such cartoon depicts the character demoralized, head hanging low in front of angry police officers. The broker has been arrested and the protagonist has been summoned for questioning. Written in large white letters at the bottom of each poster is "Ukweli hauna mwanandani," a Swahili proverb meaning "The truth has no grave" or "The truth has nowhere to hide."

Truth exists in relation to another key concept in refugee work: fraud. The fears of fraud that led to DNA testing in US refugee family reunification were not unique. These kinds of anxieties have a long-standing basis among organizations providing aid to refugees, as well as aid more broadly. In 2016 UNHCR released a fictional anti-fraud film with the Swahili proverb as its title: *The Truth Has Nowhere to Hide*. In the film, a Congolese woman persuades her husband to pay a broker to secure a resettlement case. When this tactic fails and their money is lost, she tries another approach. In an interview, she tearfully reports that during their flight from Congo, her husband was shot and is now unable to provide for their family because of the resulting physical disability. When this lie is exposed at their next UNHCR interview, their case is closed. At the film's end, the husband is furious with his wife, who weeps in despair as they leave the UNHCR offices. A voice-over admonishes, "Be truthful and honest when you tell UNHCR what you went through in your country of origin and the country of asylum. If you are found to be committing fraud, your resettlement case will be suspended" (UNHCR 2016).

Fraud is a central category in policymaking, official discourse, and everyday talk in the world of refugee aid. In the *UNHCR Resettlement Handbook*, a 428-page guide for UNHCR staff, resettlement countries, and NGOs, the word *fraud* appears 262 times (UNHCR 2011). *Resettlement fraud* is defined as "the intentional misrepresentation or concealment of facts or evidence material to the resettlement process with the intent of obtaining a resettlement or other benefit for the refugee concerned or for another individual who otherwise would not be entitled to be resettled or to obtain such a benefit" (UNHCR 2011, 128).

The handbook catalogues three major types of resettlement fraud: internal (perpetrated by someone inside UNHCR); external (perpetrated by someone outside of UNHCR—namely, refugees themselves); and "mixed or complex fraud" (perpetrated by the collusion of people inside and outside UNHCR). For external fraud, UNHCR lists five subtypes: identity fraud, family composition fraud, document fraud, material misrepresentation fraud (including omission and commission), and bribery (UNHCR 2011, 129–30). This taxonomy of fraud highlights its importance to the way UNHCR and partnering non-governmental agencies conceptualize and organize their work (see also Sandvik 2011; Thomson 2012). For governments such as that of the US, fraud prevention also looms large in refugee resettlement work. The US State Department articulates resettlement as reflecting the country's "highest values and aspirations to compassion, generosity and leadership" (US Department of State n.d.[a]). At the same time, the practical features of US resettlement are largely oriented around screening interviews and background checks in which refugees are conceptualized as embodying risk.

What kinds of work does the concept of fraud perform in this context? *Fraud*—often defined as "criminal deception" (Oxford English Dictionary)—works to reinforce that resettlement is an official, rule-governed process. As a category, fraud helps produce official responses to behaviors and activities that confound agencies' abilities to carry out their goals of identifying the most vulnerable refugees. Discourses of fraud and anti-fraud practices—like DNA testing—also frame people living as refugees as always potentially both victim and criminal (Knudsen 1995). The figure of the fraudulent refugee, produced and reproduced in UN and government discourse, draws attention to the intersecting initiatives of securitizing national borders on one hand and protecting refugees on the other. Security procedures and technologies also protect humanitarian logics of sorting people deemed deserving of protection or migration opportunities from people viewed as unexceptional or tainted by characteristics or behaviors that disqualify them. Indeed, some applying for refugee status have participated in war crimes. The vast majority have not— far more have been victims of war crimes.

Mistrust of people who have been forcibly displaced has been documented over time. Of her work with humanitarian administrators in the 1980s, Liisa Malkki wrote, "the ideal construct, the 'real refugee,' was imagined as a particular kind of person: a victim whose judgment and reason had been compromised by his or her experiences." Thus, wounds were "more reliable sources of knowledge than the words of the people on whose bodies those wounds are found." Some aid workers characterized Burundian refugees in Tanzania in Malkki's study as "dishonest, prone to exaggeration, even crafty and untrustworthy" (1996, 384). Asylum seekers in France (Fassin and d'Halluin 2005), aid recipients in Haiti (James 2010), Palestinians in the aftermath of 1948 (Feldman 2007), displaced people, and other (usually racialized) recipients of international humanitarian aid routinely exist in a hierarchy of power and authority that structures mutual mistrust (Voutira and Harrell-Bond 1995; see also Daniel and Knudsen 1995). Those who manage access to aid and resettlement programs enact mistrust in ways that have far-reaching consequences for people living as refugees and seeking humanitarian aid, even as many humanitarian and legal professionals may also advocate for refugees and are well aware of the complexities of the systems in which they work (Cabot 2019).

Recently, the figure of the fraudulent refugee has garnered more widespread anxiety: the displacement of five million people from Syria and the 2015 attacks in Paris that stoked fears about refugees as terrorists; the large numbers of asylum seekers from African and Middle Eastern countries arriving at European borders; and a simultaneous rise in people from countries in Central America crossing the US-Mexico border in the late 2010s. Xenophobic rhetoric has equated refugees and asylum seekers with terrorists and criminals, a vast distortion of the majority of real people attempting to migrate (see, for example, *Guardian* 2015). In his 2016 presidential campaign, Donald Trump attacked the US Refugee Admissions Program, repeating the phrase, "We don't know who these people are," promoting the false idea that people entering the US through refugee resettlement were not vetted prior to arrival (Amos 2016). The rhetoric incited xenophobic ire and became policy in the 2017 executive order barring refugees and immigrants from several Muslim-majority countries, including Somalia. The claim that "we don't know who these people are" reflects that the figure of a fraudulent refugee is not just a category in a UNHCR handbook. Amidst the rise of right-wing populism in the twenty-first century, the figure of the "fraudulent refugee" has taken on a bigger life in US and globalizing public discourse, illuminating the twin imperatives of securing borders against undesirable, racialized Others on one hand and saving a small number of refugees deemed worthy on the other.

Today, humanitarian aid and securitization operate in tandem, with national security projects launched under the banner of human rights and humanitarianism (Abu Lughod 2002) and humanitarian programs like refugee resettlement inextricably connected to national security apparatuses. The first decades of the twenty-first century have seen a world transformed by heightened, violent regimes of border control and security—"the now normalized practices of abandoning people in refugee camps, incarcerating people in secretive detention centers, and interrupting migrant routes in order to push people into life-threatening environments" (Besteman 2019, S33). Oliver (2017) describes the ways in which the "rescue" of migrants blurs together with their incarceration in camps and detention centers, declaring such forms of aid "carceral humanitarianism." Here, I use the term *securitized humanitarianism* to refer to the ways in which refugee resettlement processes are embedded in national security agencies and guided by their logics.[9] A current global order, as Besteman argues, rests on the ability of powerful states "to control mobility and to unilaterally assess the risk of racialized mobile subjects while imposing carceral regimes as the antidote to risk" (2020, 122).

Like Jemima Pierre's (2020) framing of "the racial vernaculars of development," humanitarian work in Africa is premised on racializing hierarchies between Africa and the West. White foreigners are free to live and work in African countries and granted authority to adjudicate which people receive aid there, including resettlement. People living as refugees from African countries, on the other hand, are discursively and practically constructed as ineligible to have an equal seat at that table. Discourses about fraud cast people living as refugees as incapable of making unbiased and appropriate choices about who to help and how (see Sackett 2023). This book centers the effects of such discourses and practices on communities building lives in new places where they are often imagined as dangerous or as charity cases, rather than as people asking for rights that many in different circumstances and in different parts of the world simply take for granted (Weitzberg 2017, 180).

The Figure of the Fraudulent Family

As Habiba's story in the opening of this Introduction reveals, in the course of leaving places made unlivable by violence and staying in places of asylum, families are reconfigured to meet the most basic human needs for care and belonging. But what makes a "family," as anthropologists have long demonstrated, is an unsettled question—a topic of debate in myriad social and political contexts.

Permanently fostering children from within and beyond kin is common across multiple African (and other) societies (Alber 2003; Etienne 1979; Notermans 2004; Talle 2004). Sharing child-rearing responsibilities widely is also typical (Feldman-Savelsberg 2016; Gottlieb 2009; Ivey 2000). Policies of global North governments that take for granted the cohabiting nuclear family often clash with more expansive kinship practices among their own minority communities (Abdi 2015; Besteman 2016; Clark-Kazak 2011; Feldman-Savelsberg 2016). Scholars of Black communities in the US, for example, have noted that child-rearing has often been communally shared and that children's primary guardians may change over time to best meet the needs of both children and their caregivers (Davis-Sowers 2006, 2012; Stack 1974). Such practices conflict with social and legal standards set by white, middle-class US norms (Briggs 2020; Stack 1974), where non-nuclear, nonheterosexual families can be cast as deviant or pathological (Cohen 2004). As Carol Stack wrote in her ethnography of a Black community in the Midwestern US, "Most of the adults . . . had been fostered at one time or another by kinsmen. Some of their own children are currently residing in the homes of kinsmen, or have been kept by kinsmen in the past. These alternatives . . . are possibilities that every mother understands." Yet, "folk sanctions concerning the transfer of rights in children are often in conflict with the publicly sanctioned laws of the state" (1974, 62).

As with forms of policing families inside the United States, including the removal of children from Black and Native American families and separating children from their parents at the US-Mexico border (Briggs 2020), the non-nuclear, non-biogenetic family among people displaced from African countries becomes a racialized and stigmatized social formation. As reflected by child fosterage among aunts, uncles, grandparents, and even friends or neighbors, kin relations are flexible and transform to serve various needs, particularly in times of insecurity (Ellison 2009; Gale 2007; Giblin with Giblin 2005). Yet the necessary expansiveness of kinship—particularly in the context of migration—poses a special problem for UNHCR and governments in global North locations.

For organizations like UNHCR and for government programs like US Refugee Admissions, the family is an object of special care and concern, toward which the "moral sentiments" of humanitarian work are directed (Fassin 2012, 1).[10] UNHCR calls family unity "a fundamental principle of refugee protection" (2011, 176). The organization of refugee resettlement through family units and the humanitarian sentiments directed toward family unity undergird the scrutiny placed on proving so-called genuine family relations. The *UNHCR Resettlement Handbook*, for example, states:

> The definition of a family is culturally specific, and care must be taken to accurately record real relationships, as misrepresentation may not have a fraudulent intent. However, family composition fraud may involve marriages of convenience; fictitious relationships, such as when distant relatives are claimed as sons or daughters; adding fictitious family members; substituting children, which may occur for money or under duress; or "losing" or hiding a family member to get an improved chance at resettlement (such as when a woman hopes to qualify for the Women and Girls at Risk category by claiming that her husband is dead or has disappeared). (2011, 130)

UNHCR describes a wide range of practices under the category "family composition fraud." But this label misnames vastly more complex social realities and motivations than the notion of "fraud" can capture. Haunting the figure of the fraudulent family is the idea that kinship is based in biology or marriage. Behind the "fraudulent family" are also ideas about "real" families that take for granted forms of stability that are often absent from the worlds of people remaking networks of care in countries of asylum. UNHCR and host governments weigh competing interests: a desire to keep "real" families together while also guarding against "misrepresentations" with "fraudulent intent"—in other words, using the guise of family to access humanitarian charity.

In 2013, I interviewed a veteran of refugee resettlement work then based in the US office of an NGO. Prior to working in the NGO world, Beth had worked for the State Department–contracted Resettlement Support Centers abroad. She was a devoted advocate and spent her career thinking carefully about policies and potential for transforming refugee situations. When I mentioned how family is defined in US resettlement policy, she offered that there was, in fact, flexibility in the system, so long as refugees honestly represented their family relations: "I actually think the State Department is fair on this issue—tries to be fair on this issue. They are not in the business of trying to separate real families that *really* are dependent on each other and that *really* are families—had a history of living together, ideally fled together, have lived together in the country of asylum. That, like . . . *families*, you know?" She laughed, seemingly aware of the ways in which her answer might have confirmed the concerns that informed my question. "I know that's a loaded term," she continued, "but, you know—that have the emotional and economic dependency. They're not trying to separate people like that, whether they're biological or not biological. But what they need is people to be honest about the real relationships."

Beth's statement evoked Kath Weston's "know-one-when-you-see-one" family, which Weston argues students of kinship must actively resist (2001, 149). A real family, Beth maintained, is made up of people who lived together prior to fleeing their country, presently live together in the asylum country, and exhibit economic and emotional dependency—all qualities that must be assessed in interviews, usually conducted through interpreters in bureaucratic offices far from the home of the people in question. Beth went on to express that DNA testing—used for reunifying families in which one or more members had already come to the US—had been necessary to curb widespread fraud. Such fraud hurt the most vulnerable, she argued, and led to social problems once people who lacked genuine familial relationships arrived in the US, sometimes leaving children in precarious and dangerous positions. Yet the Somali and Congolese communities that fill the cinderblock apartments in Nairobi neighborhoods like Eastleigh, Kayole, and Kasarani and fill the pages of this book often live in and rely on families and social networks that extend beyond what policies mark as legitimate.

From the pragmatic point of view of many people who conducted resettlement interviews, DNA testing unburdened them of trying to assess family relations in more subjective ways (see Scherz 2011). Indeed, bureaucratic categories and definitions can never capture the complexity of real life. But categories and definitions, as well as the logics that undergird them, have effects in the world. The logic that deems nonnuclear family relations suspicious, less valuable, or unusual has widespread consequences for people trying to access resettlement in the aftermath of war and displacement.

Jacqueline, for example, was a young unmarried woman who had fled her home in eastern Congo in 2009. When she first arrived in Nairobi, she lived with a Kenyan pastor. When his home filled up with others, she moved into an apartment with three young men from her community, a situation that created more insecurity than the safety she was seeking. At church, she met Claire, a young mother with four children (three that she gave birth to and one the bio-genetic daughter of her brother), with whom she bonded, and who invited her to move in with her family. After a couple of years, the family was identified for resettlement based on Claire and her husband Innocent's imprisonment and torture in Congo. Claire and Innocent requested that Jacqueline be included on their case, fearing that she would be vulnerable to the same kinds of economic, physical, and psychological insecurity she had previously faced if they left her behind. But because Jacqueline was not an orphaned minor, nor had they lived together prior to their flight from Congo, UNHCR did not consider Jacqueline part of their family unit.

Jacqueline was not given her own resettlement case either. It was rare for single people to be considered for resettlement. As Greg Brown, who had worked at the Resettlement Support Center and now directed an NGO office, explained, it was more laborious to resettle single people, each of whom constituted a separate case requiring separate interviews and paperwork, than to resettle a large family. One large family allowed an organization to efficiently resettle six or eight people at once, as opposed to six or eight individual cases, which required far more work to hit an organization's target numbers. Furthermore, families were valued in "both cultures," as Greg put it (by which he seemed to mean Euro-American and African), making it a greater humanitarian imperative to resettle families than single people. Jacqueline and many people like her could not be included on the cases of the families and networks of social care that had become their primary sources of emotional, social, and economic stability in Nairobi, nor were they likely to be resettled on their own. Claire and Innocent were up-front about their relationship to Jacqueline, and therefore UNHCR did not claim "fraudulent intent," which could have ruined their case. But Jacqueline was still ineligible—theirs did not comprise a "real" family, and Jacqueline, a single person, was a low priority on her own.

Despite calls to abandon it as an ethnocentric category in the 1960s and '70s (Schneider 1972, [1968]1980, 1984), Kath Weston argued for taking up the study of kinship as an answer to demands "to attend to bitterly fought social struggles that . . . stake their claims in the name of the family" (2001, 150). These are struggles surrounding queer kinship, reproductive rights, transnational adoption, genealogical identities, and others arising in relation to changing laws, social formations, technologies, and scientific knowledge (Bamford and Leach 2009; Franklin and McKinnon 2001). The use of genetic science and specific definitions of family in the context of refugee resettlement bring questions about the contested meanings of the family into a new arena.

The concept of family composition fraud—made dramatically apparent by the 2008 DNA pilot program and the implementation of DNA testing by the US government in 2012 (and other governments around the same time)—reflects competing claims in refugee resettlement and the management of mobility on a global level: protecting refugees on one hand and protecting national borders and humanitarian ideals on the other. At the same time, the figure of the fraudulent family exemplifies a broader trend encompassing many ways in which the family constitutes a site of anxious contestation in the contemporary world (Giddens 2000). Bringing questions about kinship into current discussions on humanitarianism, this book locates "the family" as a crucial category in producing, policing, and contesting borders and boundaries of nation-states and in the production of a securitized humanitarianism in the twenty-first century. Tracing how policies like DNA testing are understood and contested in displaced communities subject to them demonstrates the ways in which "the family" exists as a site of struggle and contestation on global borderlands.

Combatting fraud in a humanitarian program may appear to be a self-evident good. As people working in refugee resettlement often argue, fraud hurts refugees. People with less pressing claims who mislead interviewers about their past or present take limited spots from those with greater needs. But this book suggests that "fraud" as a category is not as self-evident as it may at first appear. Nor is "the family." Viewing these concepts from different vantage points, the categories begin to blur out of focus, sometimes to evaporate altogether; what seems to be contained within them scatters outside their bounds.

Listening to the ways that people living as refugees experience and conceptualize categories like fraud, credibility, DNA, and others, another story also emerges. In one sense, the global resettlement system helps to create the conditions for the very practices it names "fraud." In another, the stories in the following pages show how impossible it is to delineate the exceptionally vulnerable refugee from the imagined fraud, the worthy person from the supposedly ordinary person who must live as a refugee forever, and the genuine family from the purportedly fake or illegitimate one. People living as refugees and asylum seekers who animate this ethnography resist such distinctions by living by and articulating different kinds of imperatives—ones that embrace rights to mobility and the obligation to assist kin.

ONE

The Figure of the Fraudulent Refugee

PEOPLE DOCUMENTED AS REFUGEES and asylum seekers in Nairobi often talked about UNHCR's door: *albaabka* in Somali, *mlango* in Swahili. These words came up repeatedly: "We couldn't even get through the door" or "She went through the door by force." "The door" was a potent symbol of UNHCR as a fortress—difficult or impossible to enter. "The door" pointed to the inaccessibility of the physical building and the challenges of accessing its resources. Instead of traveling across the city and showing up at UNHCR's infamous door, UNHCR's clients, as the organization called them, could text the office a brief message. They did not receive a reply by phone, however, but might see their ID number printed on the paper lists that were distributed weekly to various places throughout the city, summoning a select group to the office that week.[1]

This method of responding contributed to the sense that the text messages disappeared into the ether, as it was difficult for many to check the printed lists week after week, and many people continued to send messages but never saw their ID number listed. While people often spoke about the text message system—how many messages they had sent or how often—most seemed uncertain about what became of the messages, how people were chosen to come to the office, and what would happen if they were. Two young Banyamulenge women, Christine and Solange, told me that they sometimes sent a message twice a day. After receiving no reply, they began going to UNHCR without an appointment, but they were never let through the door, which was fortified by two security guards. People often complained that nothing came of the text messages at all, but they sent messages anyway, some weekly or even daily. This was one of the only available avenues to initiate contact with the organization that held the key to resettlement. For some, it became a necessary ritual that provided a sense that one could *do something*, could actively work toward changing their life instead of just waiting, which was what many felt that their relationship with aid organizations and the resettlement system consisted of (Oka 2014; Thomson 2012).

In September 2014, Louisa, a UNHCR official who had recently arrived in Nairobi after years of working for the organization in other regions, responded to an email I had sent on the recommendation of a friend. She invited me to observe a process at the office called "resettlement counseling." I had been to the office before, accompanying friends or acquaintances, lining up and following them through the front doors. Upon Louisa's invitation, however, I entered through a different entrance—one for staff and their visitors. While people seeking UNHCR's services alighted from matatus across the street, the staff entrance was behind large gates that led to a parking lot on the other side of the building. At a security pavilion outside, two Kenyan guards greeted me. One searched my bag while the other waved a handheld metal detector around my frame. Inside, a woman seated at a desk took my passport in exchange for a visitor's badge, inviting me to sit and wait for Louisa.

Some minutes later, Louisa, a petite, middle-aged woman, appeared on the stairs. She greeted me: "So you live in Eastleigh? That must be great for your research." I wasn't sure how she knew where I lived (I lived in Pangani, next to Eastleigh), but news about people in a broader network of foreign aid workers, interns, reporters, and researchers seemed to circulate quickly. The legacies of colonial-era racial segregation often mean that the people who work in refugee aid infrequently venture to the places where refugees live. Many neighborhoods, like Eastleigh, are "no-go" zones either officially, as for US embassy staff, or in practice, as for many NGO workers. The "architectures of exclusion" of Nairobi (Smith 2019) are part and parcel of how humanitarian aid is spatialized: those who provide aid live and work far from where their clients reside. Most offices are similarly located in places that are easily accessible to foreign "expat" workers (typically white, but not exclusively) and difficult to reach for people trying to use their services.

As Louisa walked me upstairs, I inquired about the day's activity. "Is this only for people who have a resettlement case?" I asked, mistaking the meaning of "resettlement counseling."

"It used to be like that," she replied. "But now we allow people to send an SMS just to meet with us. We don't refer a lot of people from the counseling for resettlement because it would send the wrong message."

It suddenly dawned on me that I was going to see what was on the other side of all those text messages.

Resettlement counseling, it turned out, was mostly a way to tell people directly that they were *not* candidates for resettlement. Louisa communicated that it would be misleading to suggest that resettlement counseling was an avenue toward resettlement itself. Occasionally, someone would present a situation that required further investigation, but that was rare. Indeed, the "wrong message" Louisa referred to was, in one sense, that refugees themselves— usually equipped only with their own narratives and memories—could compel a more powerful person to act on their behalf. The system was not designed for that in any case.

Resettlement is for the exceptional few—fewer than 1 percent, globally. This 1 percent is typically identified by UNHCR during their Refugee Status Determination interviews when they first enter a country of first asylum like Kenya or through other UNHCR units or NGOs that deal with cases of un- usual protection or security needs. In 2015, UNHCR's "assessment of needs" for resettlement came to nearly one million globally, but most were cut, with UNHCR submitting only around 125,000 people based on the small number of places made available by host countries (Suhrke and Garnier 2018, 244–45).

Upstairs, Louisa introduced me to Grace, an experienced Kenyan staff member. She sat behind one of several desks guarded by a tall, transparent barrier. A computer was angled to her right, which she used to look up re- cords. A Somali interpreter—a young man named Abdiweli—sat by her side. People who had found their ID numbers posted the previous week filled the noisy room, lining up behind one of several desks according to their primary language. Most of the staff were either Kenyan or from Europe or North America, and spoke to their clients through interpreters. From 8:30 in the morning until 1:30 in the afternoon, Grace and Abdiweli saw people for about ten minutes at a time without a break, telling most that they were not eligible for resettlement.

Among the group was Luul, who, unlike most, had a pending resettlement case. She sat down at the desk and greeted us through the transparent parti- tion, over the din of other conversations. She slid her UNHCR identity papers across the desk through the opening in the plexiglass barrier. She told Grace that she had last heard from RefAid, the NGO overseeing her case, in February; it was now September. "That's not so long," Grace said as she pulled up the woman's file on her computer. Grace told Luul that staff from RefAid would be coming to UNHCR that day and that she would remind them about her case. Luul then slid a stapled packet of yellow papers, folded in half, across the desk. Grace unfolded it and glanced at it briefly. "There's someone in Eastleigh who writes these letters," she said. "These are form letters. They're all the same. We don't want these. That's why we need to hear from the applicant—we don't want made-up letters." In Grace's view, Luul's paper had been manufactured by someone else and was therefore not a credible source.

What does the routinization of mistrust of people forcibly displaced from their home countries, now often articulated through the concept of fraud, tell us about global refugee governance? The fraudulent refugee is a racialized figure embedded in global North-South hierarchies. Perceived as "working the system," people slotted in this category are deemed potentially dangerous and unworthy of help. How is the figure of a fraudulent refugee produced at the intersection of humanitarian and security priorities and through everyday discourses and practices of refugee resettlement work? In this chapter, I turn to these discourses and practices and will also return to resettlement counseling. But before doing so, I begin by centering the meanings of transnational migration and mobility to the people seeking it. I then tell the story of an unsettled family, separated by contemporary border regimes that make onward migration and citizenship so difficult to access. This story helps bring the meanings of mobility to life. Finally, I turn to the ways in which people living outside citizenship rights are cast as suspects vis-à-vis the aid and migration programs on which many pin their hopes.

Meanings of Mobility

The first time I met Mohamed, who would become my Somali language tutor and friend, we chatted at a restaurant in Eastleigh, where he lived in a room that he shared with two relatives. Our mutual friend, Amina, connected us when I contacted her about finding someone to help me with Somali language study. A few days after corresponding on text, Mohamed met me at the number 6 matatu stage near Garissa Lodge—once accommodations for people arriving from Somalia's civil war, now one of Eastleigh's densely packed shopping centers (Carrier 2016, 61–62). He suggested we go to the nearby restaurant, located in a new hotel catering to Somalis visiting Eastleigh from abroad. It served camel milk tea, goat with rice, and passion fruit juice, but also cheeseburgers and cappuccinos. Entering the restaurant from the street, you climb stairs past shops selling jewelry and perfume. Passing through the men's dining section, where gentlemen in suits or long, white *khameez* are chatting, you enter the room for women and families or the odd, mixed-gender patrons like Mohamed and me.

Soon, over tea, Mohamed was telling me about his own circumstances—a recent high school graduate in his early twenties, who had left his parents in Somalia at the age of ten, he was now awaiting a process of his own. He and two relatives were being sponsored by an uncle in Canada, and he had goals of higher degrees and a career in healthcare. He listened intently to my explanation of my interests and aims. "If you just pass around here," he said, motioning to the tables of women eating lunch, the men with their cups of tea in the room beyond us, and outside, a neighborhood dense with stories of aspirations to be elsewhere, "everyone is talking about two things: politics at home, and resettlement."

The term *resettlement* and its Somali translations, *buufis* and *dib u dejin*, as well as the English words *case* and *process* are typically used in the Somali community in Nairobi to connote not only the official refugee resettlement process coordinated by UNHCR and participating governments (as in the US Refugee Admissions Program) but sometimes also family sponsorship through other immigration programs and visa types, like Mohamed's case. Crossing borders without prior authorization in order to lawfully seek asylum in global North countries, often called *tahriibiye*, referring to the use of a smuggler, might also be wrapped in the language of resettlement and *buufis*. Such crossings to Europe and North America to seek asylum involve long, dangerous, and costly routes, such as traveling to Libya and then crossing the Mediterranean or flying to Latin America using someone else's passport, followed by journeys through the continent and across the US-Mexico border, the latter being less common due to its cost, length, danger, and complexity (Abdi 2015, 50–52).

Like government resettlement programs, family sponsorship visas and asylum seeking are also options that pan out for a small minority of people living as refugees in African countries. Those who choose to leave East Africa by *tahriibiye* have often exhausted less life-threatening options. In sum, government resettlement programs, mainly initiated by UNHCR, are part of a larger constellation of modes of migrating, but the term *resettlement* is used both for the official process and as a broader catch-all. I use *resettlement* to refer to the official process and distinguish where a person's case involves a different avenue, while also noting that the term was used in more flexible ways by people who shared their stories with me. While I initially set out to study resettlement—the process that begins with UNHCR or select NGOs referring people to government resettlement programs—I soon found that I could not draw a boundary around those cases and ignore others that proceeded through family sponsorship visas or traveling without prior authorization and seeking asylum on reaching a global North location. An individual might be attempting to migrate in more than one way. In any given family, different people had migrated or planned to migrate through different channels. Dreams to resettle were not bound to any one route or bureaucratic process.

If resettlement and these other modes of migration reach such a small number of people each year, why do people living as refugees hold such great hope for them and invest so much time and energy in leaving places like Kenya? Dreams of resettlement have pervaded life in Africa's refugee camps and cities in the first quarter of the twenty-first century (Abdi 2015; Horst 2006a, 2006b; Thomson 2012, 2018). Somali desires for resettlement are also rooted in a long-standing value placed on travel and livelihoods linked to mobility, including a nomadic past and pastoral economies (Abdi 2015; Horst 2006a, 2006b; see also Weitzberg 2017). Based on her research in the Dadaab refugee camps in the late 1990s and early 2000s, Cindy Horst writes about the emergence of the term *buufis* to refer to the "hope, longing, desire or dream to go for resettlement," as well as "resettlement itself" and "the madness that at times occurs when the dream to go overseas is shattered" (2006b, 163). Horst was surprised to learn that her Somali interlocutors in the Netherlands were unfamiliar with this meaning. The word originally signified "air, *hawo*, which also stands for a longing or desire for something specific, an ambition or even daydream" (Horst 2006b, 162). As the resettlement process began in Kenya's refugee camps, the term transformed to specifically refer to dreams of going abroad and the resettlement process itself (162–63). The same meanings were attached to the term *buufis* in Nairobi when I conducted research years after Horst's study.

Post-1991 refugee resettlement for Somalis has been incorporated into a much longer history of travel and mobility, which Horst calls a "nomadic heritage": "looking for greener pastures; . . . a strong social network that entails the obligation to assist each other in surviving; and risk-reduction through strategically dispersing investments in family members" (2006b, 2). This nomadic heritage has been drawn upon as a resource and transformed in the context of Somalia's civil war to make "transnational nomads," to use Horst's term. In the 1970s and '80s, Somalis used the word *jannalle* (those who had reached "earthly Jannah," or paradise) to refer to people who migrated to the Gulf States for work in the oil and construction industries (Abdi 2015, 87–88). North America and Europe, Cawo Abdi writes, have become the "earthly Jannah for Somali refugees" today (106). Civil war–era migration and refugee resettlement programs more specifically are incorporated into long-standing modes of understanding the world and one's place in it, where mobility and migration have long been central (see also Weitzberg 2017). Although this has been written about more extensively in the Somali context, before the civil wars in Congo, Banyamulenge Congolese (who figure centrally in this book) also had long histories of mobility and movement, including their migrations to South Kivu as early as the seventeenth century (Prunier 2009, 51), but also through their pastoralist tradition.

The preoccupation that many living as refugees and asylum seekers have with resettlement and going abroad is also rooted in multiple conditions of their lives in Kenya. These conditions were not uniform across nationality, ethnicity, age, class, gender, sexuality, family composition, and other forms of identity and experience. However, some common aspects of life that compelled people to seek resettlement include lacking citizenship or a path to citizenship and its attendant rights and opportunities in Kenya; widespread discrimination in Kenyan society and harassment by police, especially of Somalis; poverty and lack of physical security; persecution by compatriots on the basis of identity for ethnic, religious, gender, and sexual minority groups; and the inescapable awareness of the differences between those who had left Kenya and those who remained (Abdi 2015; Horst 2006a, 2006b; Lochery 2012; Pavanello, Elhawary, and Pantuliano 2010).

What I aim to point out in brief is that a desire to access resettlement programs is tied to conditions of insecurity, poverty, immobility, and incarceration in camps, as well as to what Keren Weitzberg describes as a political imagination linked to "older forms of cosmopolitanism, diaspora, and nomadic life" in Somali history (2017, 3), and what Achille Mbembe describes as an African "archive" of networks and crossroads, borders defined by porousness and permeability, and "a whole repertoire of alternative forms of membership" between citizen and foreigner in African contexts more broadly (2018). Resettlement has meanings for Somali and Congolese (and other) communities living in Kenya that are different from the meanings given to refugee resettlement by the states and organizations that control it.

Access to technology and social media means that curated photos of friends' and relatives' lives in places like Minneapolis, Houston, Stockholm, or London posted on Facebook or Instagram or sent via WhatsApp create the sense that one can see over to the other side of the fence. While some understand how difficult life is in places like the United States for their kin, seeing past the images created on social media or by Hollywood can be nearly impossible. Even for those who understand intellectually the difficulties faced by their kin and compatriots who resettled in the United States, there are always stories of good jobs, degrees, houses, and cars and always dreams of achieving the same. These migration dreams are part of a particular economy of resettlement that is tied to displacement and aid in an African context, but they are also part of much broader trends related to how many in the global South imagine life elsewhere (Ferguson 2006; Piot 2010). On a more local level, these dreams and ways of pursuing them fit into the logics of Nairobi's "hustle economy," in which "feelings of precarity and futility can be enmeshed with the fierce desire to create an alternative future" and the sense that "anything and nothing are equally likely to happen," as Constance Smith writes of Kenyans in their capital city (2019, 6). In one sense, resettlement is just one avenue or opportunity in a wider schema of resources—scarce but present—of possible alternative futures.

An Unsettled Family

In the years following my first meeting with Mohamed, I talked to many people—in formal interviews, casual conversations, and fragments in waiting rooms at UNHCR or the offices of other organizations—about their resettlement hopes, plans, and challenges. I learned that kinship both structures and motivates resettlement. Kin provide "information, link the migrant to the organizational infrastructure that enables migration and often provide the financial resources necessary for movement" (Horst 2006b, 198). Migration is never a story of a solitary individual but rather involves complex networks of social attachment, affect, care, and obligation. Kinship networks enable migration through resources of many kinds, but kinship also structures the feelings—love, longing, envy, desire, duty—that motivate many to seek reset-tlement and join family and community members spread around the world.

Take the story of Hamdi. Hamdi was a Somali mother of three young chil-dren, whose husband had gone to the United States by *tahriibiye*. "We had very little money—we had no support. [My husband] used to work in a shop in Eastleigh. His sisters in the US contributed money. But we couldn't get a process. We needed an emergency process, so we went from here."

The young couple didn't have enough money to leave together, and they realized that traveling as a family, with two young children and Hamdi preg-nant with their third, was too dangerous. Using a Kenyan passport, Hamdi's husband went to the Middle East. From there, he traveled to Cuba and then Mexico and finally crossed the US-Mexico border. There, he was detained for six months before being granted asylum. Mohamed used to be Hamdi's neigh-bor and he told me, "I remember when she was very happy. She would be in the kitchen very early in the morning while everyone is sleeping. I would ask her, 'Were you here all night talking to him?'" Those mornings had been over for quite some time when I met Hamdi.

Prior to Hamdi's husband leaving Kenya, they had agreed that if he made it to the United States, he would prepare for them, and then bring her and their three young children via family sponsorship—a much safer and more straightforward route than seeking asylum as he had. If he died, she would take care of their children. They would each make a sacrifice: his was embark-ing on a dangerous journey; hers was managing three young children alone. If he was successful, their reward would be reunification. That was the plan they had made together, six years before I met her.

After he made it to the US and began working, Hamdi's husband sent money back to support his family. "Her house is beautiful," Mohamed told me before Hamdi and I met. Her house was proof of her husband's devotion. Hamdi was always nicely dressed. The children were coiffed and well-dressed, too. But after a couple of years, things changed. Hamdi expected her husband to start the process of bringing her and their children as soon as possible. But he hesitated. First, he expressed that he didn't want their children raised in the United States. Let them wait, he said, until they had grown up a bit. His brother, also in the US, had gotten into trouble—had started drinking, and was now in jail. He didn't want their children to end up the same way. Hamdi was close to her husband's sisters who lived nearby in Eastleigh. Two of them lived with her for a while after her husband had left. Another sister in the US pressed him to bring his family, but to no avail. Other family members secretly sided with Hamdi but didn't interfere. On the other hand, his *habaryar*, his mother's sister, also in the US, warned him that bringing a wife and young children would be a terrible burden. He couldn't support them alone. Instead, she told him, he should marry someone already in the United States, who was established, working, and didn't need to be helped from square one. Once, the *habaryar* had called Hamdi's sister-in-law (her husband's sister) while Hamdi was in the room. His sister had put her on speaker phone and Hamdi heard everything. The family was divided.

Hamdi's husband became more and more distant. She began to suspect he had a new wife. One day, she received a text message from a woman demanding, "Why are you always calling my husband?" She called the number back, but no one picked up. She called her husband, who admitted that yes, he had married another woman—polygyny being a lawful and accepted practice in the community. Hamdi fell into a deep depression. For four months, she didn't pick up her phone. Finally, his relatives and hers sat down to discuss the situation. Hamdi realized that without his financial support, she couldn't manage life with three children. She had a small business with her sister and was applying for a grant from an aid agency, but this didn't come close to covering her rent and other expenses. With the old plan dead, Hamdi dreamed up new ones.

"The main thing is to get resettlement independent of him," she told Mohamed and me in her home one day.

"What is plan B, if you can't get resettlement without him?" Mohamed asked her. Mohamed always talked about "plan B."

"I'll wait. I'll just live here and raise my kids. I will see if he comes back. I'm convincing him to come back. If he comes back, I will leave the kids with him and go. I want to tell some relatives of mine to send me money and go by Mediterranean Sea to Europe. I want him to feel the pain I felt raising the kids as a single person."

"Is that because you're jealous of the other wife?" Mohamed asked.

"I have a lot of problems," she replied, her three children playing in the next room. "I've been raising three kids on my own for six years. I have been patient—hoping that your husband will be very successful and you'll see him one day. And that patience does not seem like it's going to bear anything."

The day after Mohamed and I visited Hamdi, we met for tea. Mohamed, who had suffered his own losses and who had known Hamdi when she was a hopeful young wife, in love and waiting for a devoted husband, was disturbed by Hamdi's story and her state of mind. He tapped his fingers on the table, his brow furrowed. "We didn't even ask her, she just vomited it all up. If you see someone who talks and talks about a certain issue when you sit with them, that thing is a nail in their body causing endless pain," he said.

Hamdi's story was especially painful because of the betrayal it involved, but in many ways it is common. Countless families like hers are separated in the course of making difficult decisions about how to support families and carve a path for a future beyond camps and cities where their rights are severely circumscribed by refugee status. Resettlement program criteria and the expense of asylum journeys and family reunification programs mean that some family members go abroad while others stay behind (see also Horst 2006b, 196). Resettlement and going abroad by any avenue, as I explore further throughout this book, are typically carried out with an expectation that one person's opportunity will benefit many. The fruits of one's labors working in a place like the US or Canada will be shared to support not only a nuclear family left behind but usually a wider web of kin. In the meantime, people go about their lives with the ache of separation that often lasts years, with little more than faith and resolve that they will someday be reunited with their families. Desire for resettlement must be understood in the context of that wider web of affect and obligation.

For Hamdi, her husband's migration was planned to support and ultimately bring her and the children to the US. When his plans changed, Hamdi's dreams of resettlement changed, too. Far from letting them go, she created new resettlement plans. They were hatched in the everyday deprivations and insecurities of refugee status, as well as in the winding labyrinths of love, betrayal, longing, obligation, and the desire and "madness" known as *buufis*. But those dreams and plans were not just alive in her mind. They were enacted in the day-to-day work of seeking information, visiting bureaucratic offices, making phone calls, filling forms, and obtaining documents, as well as in the hours, days, years of waiting that those activities entailed.

The many people like Hamdi rarely see resettlement as a privilege for a few, as it is deemed by the organizations that control and manage it. Rather, they view resettlement as a resource that they have a right to access like any other. It exists in a cultural schema that is quite different from the one in which it is located for people who work in humanitarian aid or government immigration bureaucracies. People like Hamdi know that "if you have an American passport you can basically go wherever you want. The world belongs to you" (Mbembe 2018). With that knowledge of vast inequality of mobility, many living as refugees reject the notion that mobility is a privilege for them rather than a right.

"A Privilege, Not a Right"

Back at UNHCR resettlement counseling, Grace noticed a woman out of the corner of her eye. "That woman comes here all the time," she said in a low voice. "She strips!" she exclaimed, without explaining more. When the woman finally reached the front of Grace's line, I could see her more clearly. I guessed she was about seventy, but she might have been younger. She was thin and wore a black *cabaaya*, the long, loose-fitting garment often worn by Somali women, with pink flowers embroidered on the sleeves. She explained that she sent a text message every Friday but never heard back. "I want resettlement," she said. "I've been detained two times. I used to sustain myself selling coffee, but I can't anymore."

Operation Usalama Watch, launched several months after the Somali militant group al-Shabaab's attack on the Westgate shopping mall, sought to remove refugees from urban areas. If the stated objective of deporting refugees to Kenya's peripheral, UN-run camps had limited success, it achieved other objectives. As described in the Introduction, it became a cover for extortion by police and paramilitary. It also succeeded in making life more difficult and terrifying for people marked as "refugee" either by their documents or their appearance as foreign. Selling goods like coffee, housewares, or clothes in marketplaces, on which many livelihoods rested, became difficult or impossible. Many of the people to whom Grace spoke that morning complained of the same inability to work and survive and of police harassment and violence. To this, Grace replied, in keeping with Kenyan government policy, "Go to the camps."

The woman now standing before us, whose name I never heard, told Grace that she had been in Kenya since 1992—"since the time of Barre," she added, referring to the Somali president whose ousting ignited the country's decades-long civil war. She began taking off her hijab, revealing a headscarf wrapped tightly around her head. "Oh wait, now she's going to start taking her clothes off," Grace whispered to me. But the woman went no further, and I never had a chance to clarify what Grace meant exactly. All that was revealed was her hairline, dyed red with henna, and her ears, both pierced with many silver hoops.

"Do you have any other problems?" Grace asked her.

"I don't have documents. I can't get a job."

"These are general problems," Grace replied. "Everyone has these problems."

The woman went on, looking increasingly distressed. She tried a different approach, explaining that her neighbor informed authorities that there was a refugee in the building. At two in the morning she was in the bathroom when she heard banging on the door. She locked the door but they broke the windows.

"Who broke the windows?" Grace asked.

After some back and forth, Abdiweli, the interpreter, explained that it was the police. They arrested her, but another neighbor paid 5,000 Kenyan shillings (about US$50), for her release. This was a scenario that played out hundreds of times each day during Operation Usalama Watch of 2014: police banged on the door at night, asked for identification, and the occupant showed the ID they had—government and UN refugee documents. The very documents the government and UN had issued them to legalize their residence in Kenya were now criminalizing—identifying them as refugees residing in the city against the new relocation directive (Balakian 2016). The police threatened arrest, and the occupant or a neighbor negotiated their release by paying. Without a bribe, they would be arrested and either have to arrange for payment by a relative once they were facing an overcrowded jail cell or eventually be trucked to Dadaab.

"Any other problems?" Grace asked.

"I've been here for twenty-three years," the woman said. "Since the time of Barre," she repeated. "Don't I have a right? I'm not eligible for resettlement?"

"Resettlement is not a right," Grace replied. "It's a privilege." She paused. "It's for very few people, in very serious situations."

The woman began to explain that she had been in Utange and Kakuma refugee camps, trying to express the longevity of her time as a refugee and the hardships she had endured.

"We have strict criteria," Grace cut her off. "If we submitted your case, the country would wonder why we had submitted it. They'd ask, 'What else happened to this person?'"

Grace echoed the fact of UNHCR's "extreme dependence" on participating states. The organization is funded by a few major governments, and the majority of resettlement slots are made available by only a few countries. In 2013,

85 percent of all resettlement slots came from the US, Australia, and Canada alone, and the US historically has accounted for more resettlement slots than all other countries combined (Suhrke and Garnier 2018, 247). Because of most global North nations' reluctance to take large numbers of refugees, "resettlement is maintained as a small 'niche' program, designed for refugees in situations of grave risk" (249) and who suit host countries' geopolitical interests. At the same time, UNHCR relies on the Kenyan government to authorize its operations within its borders. The government directive to forcibly relocate refugees from urban areas further constrained UNHCR's capacity to work in the capital, leading the organization to temporarily shut down the refugee-status-determination process and halt issuing documents there. It also led to Grace's slogan, "Go to the camps."

At the start of the twenty-first century in France, asylum judges "gradually internalized the rate [of acceptance] they were encouraged to aim for," 10 percent—a transformation from accepting "nine times more in the 1970s" (Fassin 2012, 120). Judges adjudicating asylum cases accepted an increasingly limited set of eligibility criteria and a narrow set of evidentiary rules and norms in order to meet new immigration regulations—relying on medical experts to verify claims of torture, rather than accepting asylum seekers' own narratives. Didier Fassin writes that the "tension between a high number of applications for asylum and a low rate of granting refugee status, which was obviously problematic for a nation that continued to present itself as the 'cradle of human rights,' had been resolved ideologically by increasingly discrediting the word of asylum seekers so as to justify the progressive reduction in the rate of acceptance of their request" (2012, 109).

The pattern Fassin identified can be observed in different sites of asylum and in refugee resettlement. UNHCR and NGO standards for resettlement criteria are shaped, by necessity, to meet the numbers made available by governments that participate in third-country resettlement. UNHCR and other organizations can resolve the problem of scarcity of available resettlement spots by defining resettlement as a privilege for a select minority. This leads people like Grace to reply to grievances with the statement that "these are general problems." That a problem is experienced by many and is unexceptional makes it disqualifying despite the severity of its effect on people's lives. The paucity of legally authorized avenues toward onward migration to a place that offers a path to citizenship creates a climate of mistrust (Voutira and Harrell-Bond 1995) and pressure for institutions that manage resettlement to doubt or downplay people's claims.

Papers and Words: The Double Bind of Oral Testimony

When Grace rejected the papers that Luul slid under the glass barrier as a fabrication—something written by a shady broker in Eastleigh (a place that, for many, automatically colored their view of anything associated with it), she expressed a commonly held view that documents presented by people living as refugees were suspect. Oral testimony, by contrast, was perceived as being less mediated and more authentic, and although people could fabricate or embellish their stories, it was easier to perceive truth from falsehood when the story emanated from a physical person. The interviewer could read body language and facial expressions and ask questions to verify the consistency and credibility of the story. "That's why we need to *hear* from the applicant," as Grace had put it.

In the first half of the 2010s, there were about half a million people documented as refugees living in Kenya. There is no trial or legal counsel for either asylum access or refugee resettlement. In interviews with UNHCR and NGO staff, oral testimony is the center of asylum and resettlement determinations. Yet, as Greg Brown, the director of an NGO, once put it, "In an environment with no documentation, or at least documentation you can trust, oral testimony is everything. But oral testimony . . . is not reliable." How does a system work that relies on a form of evidence that is deemed unreliable?

While we were meeting in his office, Greg slipped behind his desk and opened up a website on his desktop computer. He chatted as he typed, then waited for a page to load: "Okay. So, the basis of pretty much all refugee work is oral testimony. As I used to say in my trainings, 'Man with a gun comes to the front door, you don't stop to pick up your passport and national ID papers when you run out the back door.' We also found . . . if I was to say, 'You need to get me fake documentation . . .'" He paused just a beat, recognizing his Freudian slip. "Pardon me. 'You need to get me *documentation* proving whatever,' you would get it for me. I'll give you a couple examples. When Mogadishu fell, some clever person went into the foreign ministry and grabbed a couple of boxes of blank passports, carried them down to Eastleigh, and so when you bought a fake Somali passport in the nineties, it wasn't a fake passport! It was the real thing! [But] the information in there was fake, so that's why nobody accepts old Somali passports anymore."

Greg's webpage loaded, and he quickly printed a diploma accrediting me as Dr. Sophia, PhD in Reiki Healing.

"So, this is why," Greg stated, handing me my diploma, "documentation doesn't work. So, without documentation to prove identity, what have you got?" He continued,

> Well, oral testimony, which has got a long-standing legal basis as long as you're able to talk. Um . . . you need to be consistent. If today you say you're Dr. Sophia, tomorrow you say you're Dr. Sophia, [but] on another day, six weeks later, you say you're Dr. Susan. Well, wait, hang on . . . certain basic facts about your identity should be consistent and repeated. If you have—and this gets into a tricky area—if you've gone through major life events, there's a broad expectation that you'll remember the details. Consistently. Now, leave aside what trauma does to memory . . . but, um, how do you now figure out, is this a real family? Can they actually say the names of each other? If you and your husband were put in different rooms and we interviewed you separately, would you know basic facts about each other?

On another occasion, a US government official explained how the State Department–contracted RSC staff and USCIS officials assessed cases, exclaiming, "I could get a document that says I'm in a polygamous marriage with you and Madonna tomorrow!" Like Greg, he provided a colorful example of why documents were not trusted. (I suddenly had a fake PhD and was in a sham polygamous marriage, but that requires unpacking of a different type.) In these pedagogical demonstrations for me, the young researcher, both brought up the necessary reliance on oral testimony: "The basis of pretty much all refugee work is oral testimony," as Greg put it.

Anything written by people seeking resources and many documents produced in their countries of origins were by nature suspect and often deemed fraudulent, or "fake," as Greg put it, like the old Somali passports. The political breakdown of the states from which refugees had fled meant that documents produced by their governments were often no longer considered legitimate, and the ability to forge documents was too widespread for anything to be trusted. How could there be a Somali government document, so the logic went, if there was no functioning Somali government? Documents crafted or commissioned by clients—for example, a written version of their narrative, such as Luul's—were similarly seen as suspicious, untrustworthy, or fraudulent. Corruption has become a potent racialized stereotype of Africans, and, as Jemima Pierre notes in her work on white supremacy and development in Africa, this stereotype "works not only to deny the universality of corruption but also to limit corruption to the Global South, and especially Africa, while excluding the West, foreign private corporate interests, donor governments and financial institutions, and international NGOs from its scope" (2020, 90). This is an issue treated more centrally in the following chapter.

And yet, spoken narratives were also considered flawed. That more powerful gatekeepers mistrust the narratives of people seeking humanitarian aid, charity, asylum, resettlement, or government welfare is well documented in anthropological literature (Cabot 2014; Fassin and d'Halluin 2005; James 2010; Malkki 1996; Sandvik 2011; Petryna 2013). Indeed, mistrust has been categorized as a fundamental element of humanitarianism itself (Daniel and Knudsen 1995; Voutira and Harrell-Bond 1995). People who conducted resettlement interviews in Kenya insisted that truth was essential to their process. One UNHCR staff member noted that she prefaced her interviews by saying, "You have to tell me the truth, or I can't help you." At the same time, these interviewers acknowledged that determining some imagined, objective truth was always out of reach. Yet, the ideal of a True Story—unmediated by people's knowledge of how the system worked, what kinds of narratives were effective, and also memory, time, and trauma—provided people working in the refugee field with an ideal that gave their work meaning: that they could accurately assess people's experiences in order to choose the correct recipients of scarce, coveted resettlement opportunities. The flip side of the True Story was the ever-present possibility of false stories, or fraud. But the fact that people living as refugees utilized their knowledge of which stories elicit sympathy is intrinsic to the system itself: they did not see constructing their narratives in ways that would be heard and understood as legitimate as "committing fraud" but rather "part of a flawed, intrinsically human system" and as "a symptom of the injustices of the system" itself (Thomson 2018, 217; see also Garnier, Sandvik, and Jubilut 2018; Sandvik 2011).

Camp Stories

It was Greg who first introduced me to the term *camp story*, which he defined succinctly in his informal way: "Once a story is told that works, everyone uses it." Greg had worked in the refugee field for close to two decades when I met him in 2013. Earlier that year, I had spent several months volunteering in the US for the organization for which he served as the country director in Kenya. When I arrived in Nairobi that August, I stayed for a few weeks with a friend from the US who serendipitously lived in an apartment across from his office, as I searched for a more permanent home. This was not totally coincidental since American foreigners with elite educations often lived in the same neighborhoods where global North–headquartered NGOs established their bases. A fellow volunteer from the US had arrived in Nairobi around the same time to continue working for the organization and helped introduce me to the Nairobi staff, including Greg, who was a gregarious talker and storyteller.

Greg arrived in Kenya in the mid-1990s, shortly after completing a master's degree, to visit relatives who had been living in Kenya for many years. He was disillusioned with the field to which he had devoted his master's study: "Problem was that in the process of getting that master's, I realized that a lot of what I believe[d] was wrong. . . . When a lot of the facts that you thought were facts turn out to be wrong, the decisions you make based on that are all messed up," he reflected. He started to look for a job. Being already connected to a network of North American foreigners living in Kenya—and being perceived as a valuable asset on account of whiteness, nationality, and education—finding a job in Nairobi did not pose a major challenge. At a happy hour, Greg was advised to "go talk to the blonde lady; carry a gin and tonic with you." Soon after, he was employed by the nascent US Joint Voluntary Agency (JVA) for the African region, later renamed the US Resettlement Support Center (RSC) Africa.

The US Resettlement Support Centers, set up in locations worldwide, are run by NGOs contracted by the US State Department to screen people referred by UNHCR and NGOs like the one Greg went on to head. The RSCs serve as regional hubs from which the US manages refugee resettlement across the globe. As of early 2024, there were eight RSCs facilitating the US Refugee Admissions Program based in Kenya, El Salvador, Poland (after temporarily moving from Ukraine), Austria, Turkey, Jordan, Malaysia, and Thailand. RSC Africa, contracted out to the nonprofit Church World Service, works in forty-nine countries on the continent, with field staff based in its Nairobi headquarters. The staff conduct circuit rides—periodic trips to screen people for resettlement in camps and cities across the continent; successful interviewees then meet officers from USCIS, under Homeland Security.

Prior to the establishment of the RSCs, there was little communication or coordination between people screening refugees abroad and the "voluntary agencies" (VOLAGs) in the US that received new arrivals. Staff at the small VOLAGs in US cities could be called at any hour of the day or night by airport security to alert them that a group of people had arrived with their telltale white and blue International Organization for Migration bags. The complex global process required greater coordination so that local organizations could not only prepare for airport pickups but also secure appropriate housing, interpreters, and other services in advance. To fill these needs, the US government created the Joint Voluntary Agencies (JVAs), renamed Resettlement Support Centers (RSCs), I was told, to communicate that they were not in fact "joint" or equal partners with the domestic agencies in the US, but rather more powerful entities controlled by the State Department.

RSC Africa opened in 1991, shortly after refugees from African countries became "formally incorporated into extraregional resettlement schemes" and into the quotas of the three major resettlement countries: the US, Canada, and Australia (Sandvik 2018, 47). Africans had been excluded from resettlement until the 1980s, and even then they were admitted in very small numbers throughout that decade (Sandvik 2018, 59). As Sandvik writes of their long exclusion, "African refugees were considered too numerous, dispersed, premodern, and poor to make individual assessments to establish the elements of the refugee definition possible or necessary (Holbron 1975, 836). This, of course, was a political choice unrelated to the actual needs or traditions on the ground" (2018, 56). Although the US had admitted more than 2 million people as refugees between the end of World War II and 1980, refugee admissions had been oriented around Cold War interests, prioritizing people fleeing Communist regimes and initially focusing on Europe. Under the Refugee Relief Act of 1953, for example, most visas went to Germans and Italians (Daniels 2004, 125).

The Immigration Act of 1965 abolished the US's race-based quota system that allocated most immigrant visas to people from Northern and Western Europe—85 percent in 1952, for example (US Department of State n.d.[b]).[2] Following an uncoordinated set of programs bringing 400,000 people from Southeast Asian countries in the 1970s (Daniels 2004, 203), the Refugee Act of 1980 granted decision-making power about refugee admissions to Congress and formalized coordination between UNHCR and US government agencies (Besteman 2016, 68). The 1965 and 1980 legislation helped pave the way for greater immigration from African countries starting in the late twentieth century, including through refugee resettlement. Congress's new role in refugee admissions allowed the Congressional Black Caucus to promote resettling refugees from African and other Black countries, such as Haiti (Besteman 2016, 69). US military intervention in Somalia in the 1990s also precipitated larger allocations for people from Somalia and other African countries in the United States Refugee Admissions Program (Daniels 2004, 212).

Greg Brown joined the JVA in Nairobi in 1996 amidst these changes, which, along with changes in UNHCR's institutional orientation toward human rights, made African countries more central to its operations (Sandvik 2018). After fifteen years working for JVA (later RSC Africa) and seeing the organization change after 9/11 to a more security-oriented institution with the advent of the Department of Homeland Security,[3] Greg left to head the Kenya office of the NGO RefAid.[4] From this vantage point, he spoke with authority and a sense of intimacy with the field's history, as well as some nostalgia. He seemed to enjoy remembering "the old days" and regaling young staff and other interested novices like me with dramatic tales from his tenure. He described himself, proudly, as "part of the old boys club," recounting tidbits of breaking news or information that came from sources like a US official with whom he had a regular lunch date. On the other hand, he had invested two decades of his life trying to untangle the intractable problems of providing aid to people who were displaced in socially and politically complex environments. In that time, he seemed to have both identified and accepted some of the contradictions of this work.

In many conversations with Greg and others working in resettlement, the camp story emerged as a troublesome thorn in the side of humanitarian work and workers. Punctuated by tropes symbolizing pervasive fraud—"everyone was a single mother; everyone was from a minority clan"—the camp story idea framed refugees as figures always tainted by deception, which became a kind of treachery, biting the humanitarian hand that fed them.

On a Friday afternoon, sitting at a small table adjacent to his desk, Greg elaborated with an example:

> So in Mombasa, Kathy Donovan was taking a case history and a woman described—this is graphic—but she'd been beaten in the stomach by gun butts and she'd miscarried. Kathy started to cry. And, you know, by the end of the week everyone had lost a baby. I remember another guy who messed up; he slipped off the camp story and started to tell his real story. And what had happened to him is [that] he was from a minority clan and he was standing outside and a woman from a majority clan, an old lady, came out and said, "You! Carry my groceries home!" And there were armed men around and he knew if he refused, he'd be shot on the spot. So because of his tribe, he had to carry the groceries home, and she's like, "You're lucky you're not a woman or I would have made you cook it. Get out of my sight!" Persecution, fear of violence was a great claim. And he was so upset that I was writing it down because I wasn't putting the camp story even though I'm like, "This is, number one, the truth, and we both know this, and number two, this is a better claim."

In Greg's recounting of these memories, he articulated his role as an advocate, guiding people in ways that would aid their resettlement cases: "This is a better claim." He articulated another idea that I heard often: if people were more transparent, it would better serve their own interests. Several case workers argued that by shaping their stories to fit humanitarian priorities—in other words, committing so-called fraud—people hoping for resettlement worked against their interests. In this way, interviewers constructed a framework that allowed them to see the interests of their clients and their own interests (revealing the truth and thus upholding the integrity, as they often put it, of refugee resettlement) as aligned.[5]

"Often, I think what they've heard from other people weighs stronger on their minds than what I say to them," Rebecca, a UNHCR staff member, said to me, discomfort in her voice. "If you say, 'This is not going to cause any problems; please just tell me [the truth],' you know, then they still won't come out with it because what they've heard [from community members] is stronger."

Greg put it this way: "Who gets hurt by fraud? Refugees often get badly hurt by it. And they're the most vulnerable. They're the ones the anti-fraud measures should be trying to protect. The government of America most of the time does not pay a price when an eight-year-old goes into America improperly. That eight-year-old, if they're put into forced labor, does."

Greg was referring to the often-cited fear of child trafficking, which was addressed by UNHCR through strict requirements around family composition and thorough assessment of children who were living with adults other than their biogenetic parents. Greg and others also noted that people seeking resettlement were harmed by fraud because allegedly false or fake stories enabled less deserving people to take resettlement slots from "the most vulnerable."

Implicitly, this logic rested on the idea that "the most vulnerable" could not also narrate or reformulate their stories to fit a legible script (tell a camp story), and that there was a clear dividing line between those who deserved resettlement and those who did not, even as this meant that a majority would live without the possibility of the rights conferred by citizenship, many incarcerated in camps, for the rest of their lives—a reality beyond the control of individuals screening refugees for UNHCR or the US government.

In his office outfitted with a large white board marking the organization's quarterly resettlement goals, Greg continued on camp stories:

> As a survival technique, refugees will present themselves in the most advantageous way they perceive possible and so—it's mostly faded out in Kenya, but especially six or seven years ago, every Somali was from a minority clan.

Everyone was a Somali Bantu but, you know, "we were the part of the family that looked more Somali than Bantu." And so we had disappearing husbands because everyone thinks single moms will get in. . . . This guy Sam had a rule: no bald teenagers—because I did demographic checks on the data at RSC, and there was always this huge bulge of ages 18–21, but then you go back 18–21 years and there was no corresponding reason there was a huge explosion of births. . . . Now, we get it. I'd do it, too. But um, you know.

With his refrain of "no bald teenagers," Greg's colleague referred to his suspicion that adults were being passed off as minors in a family, since only unmarried biogenetic children under the age of twenty-one are considered part of a single resettlement case.

Like Greg, many people who conducted interviews simultaneously articulated a sympathetic view of the so-called fraud they suspected, alongside an idea that it was morally intolerable and harmed the integrity of humanitarian programs. Their work, as well as current border regimes, relied on the idea that only the "most vulnerable" could be resettled. At the same time, many UNHCR, NGO, and RSC staff (who had interviewed hundreds of people in insecure refugee camps and urban neighborhoods) also understood the basic logic of presenting oneself in a way that would help in being identified as worthy of resettlement. These two ideas existed in tension with one another: "We get it. I'd do it, too. But."

Often left out of these discussions about the ways in which practices labeled "fraud" harm refugees is the role that the resettlement process itself has in producing camp stories and other similar practices. While many people like Greg acknowledged on some level that the system itself created the conditions for repeating stories that "worked," many also suggested, implicitly or explicitly, that fraud was a problem endemic to the communities from which refugees came—a result of the corruption of so-called failed and failing states and the work of members of refugee communities who encouraged people to tell fraudulent stories in their interviews. The camp-story concept facilitates this kind of "unknowing" the social structure (Moodie 2010), or "structural oblivion" (McIntosh 2016, 10–13) vis-à-vis the hierarchies and structural conditions of resettlement that produce practices labeled "fraud."

Organizational rules and norms prevent people trying to access resettlement from advocating for themselves, because UNHCR and other organizations have systems to identify people for aid and resettlement on their own terms. Being seen as pushing for one's own recognition is often viewed as meddling in a process meant to be controlled by the organizations, or even as fraudulent. Greg articulated that more vulnerable people can be overlooked for resettlement when more economically stable, physically healthy, or socially connected people use their knowledge and resources to jump to the head of the line or even buy cases (Jansen 2008). But such discourses cast those living as refugees as inherently suspect, and shift blame from a global framework that excludes millions from citizenship onto disenfranchised individuals attempting to make use of available resources to claim a right to mobility and ultimately citizenship.

Whether Greg and many others who worked for the US RSC, global North–headquartered NGOs, or UNHCR were aware of it or not, rhetoric about fraud in refugee resettlement also echoes deeply ingrained discourses about welfare fraud in the United States and elsewhere and about people who rely on welfare. These discourses and anti-fraud initiatives have historically stigmatized and criminalized poverty and survival strategies such as collecting welfare while also working low-wage jobs because neither could sustain a family alone. As with Greg's refrain "Everyone was a single mother," condemning women who posed as single to garner benefits like resettlement, campaigns to root out welfare fraud in the United States in the 1970s and '80s also focused on women who lived with husbands or partners while claiming single status. Surveillance of family structures has been a mainstay of both welfare and refugee resettlement (see also Briggs 2020). Discourses about welfare fraud among poor and racialized recipients of aid reproduce American notions of "deserving and undeserving poor," particularly through the figure of the "welfare queen"—the primary (raced and gendered) figure of the welfare defrauder (Kohler-Haussman 2007, 330). As in the focus on welfare fraud, attention on fraud in refugee resettlement obscures larger, systemic issues. As Kohler-Haussman writes about welfare in the United States: "the structure of the economy and low welfare grants made extensive fraud unavoidable" (2007, 329), yet "the focus on crime, sexual impropriety, and fraud obscured, if not completely expunged, the material conditions of struggling families from the public dialogue" (346).

At times, people working in resettlement articulated that refugee resettlement programs tied to a global border regime create the conditions for the practices it labels "fraudulent." As one former RSC staff member put it, the system "incentivized fraud." This was often cast as inevitable and unavoidable. After all, humanitarianism is often oriented toward relieving immediate suffering of a select group deemed most vulnerable or at risk. In contrast to "long-term structural responses," Miriam Ticktin describes this kind of humanitarianism as "a conservative management of social and political problems, one that works to retain what is already there, rather than to change it or to plan for a different future" (2011, 63). Likewise, Erica Caple James writes that humanitarianism focuses on "certain forms of victimization or victim identities": "Selective recognition practices frequently generate 'triage' interventions that remedy immediate or acute suffering rather than transform the structural political, economic, and social conditions that contribute to chronic forms of insecurity" (2010, 90).

Such "selective recognition practices" mean that people often do what they can to be recognized. Even when people who worked with refugees saw such practices as built into the system itself, combatting fraud often focused on individual refugees or reforming refugee communities—as in the information campaigns using cartoons and films that I described in the Introduction. But practices like adding a child or an adult relative (the proverbial "bald teenager") to a family's case or framing one's life story to meet bureaucratic requirements of worthiness are forms of action responding to a system that officially demands passivity and endless waiting. These are forms of action that people who were displaced from their home countries often deem necessary and morally legitimate.

That people repeated stories that were known to "work" was, in part, a product of moments such as the one between Grace at UNHCR and the woman who had lived in Kenya for twenty-three years. The woman saw herself as possessing a right to move to a place that would grant her a path to citizenship and opportunities for a more secure and stable life. In this and innumerable similar exchanges, people were told that there was no such right, nor did they qualify for the privilege of resettlement. If one's real story of violence, displacement, and insecurity elicited no sympathy or action, a story that had worked for others became a necessary tool. As interviewers often had a difficult time discerning the veracity of a narrative, they used a range of evidentiary norms to assess the teller's credibility.

No Fishing

Isaro was an elderly Banyamulenge woman from eastern Congo. She lived near her daughter and her daughter's young children in a small apartment in a Nairobi neighborhood where the Banyamulenge community had built a church and many had made a home in the sprawling outskirts of the city.

It seemed that every event that I attended in the community—a wedding, a church service, a memorial, a going-away celebration—she was there, a diminutive figure dressed in *kitenge*, the African print fabric, a sparkle in her eye. At home and around her neighborhood, she wore a loose-fitting *kitenge* around her waist, her small frame engulfed by an oversized sweatshirt. When I first met her, her arm was held in a soft sling across her chest.

When Isaro first arrived in Kenya, she was assisted by a Kenyan pastor, who took her up-country to stay with his mother, who farmed vegetables. There, she began to speak some Swahili. When the pastor brought Isaro and his mother to Nairobi for a medical appointment about two years later, Isaro found that there was a large Banyamulenge community in the city and decided to stay. Soon after, she learned that her daughter, Francine, had fled to Nairobi, too, with her three children and one on the way.

While I was visiting Isaro and Francine with André, a student from Rwanda who worked with me as a research assistant, we met two of their relatives, Patrick and Gerard. It was typical for people to have visitors in their homes, and at the time, the two young men made little impression. But a month or so later, I received a call from a friend working at a human rights organization in Mombasa. Two Banyamulenge men had arrived at the organization's office, alleging that they were being pursued after fleeing recruitment into the Rwanda-backed, Congolese rebel group, M23—a group that had formed in 2012 but that, with international pressure, had officially agreed to disarm in November 2013. It soon became clear that these young men were the two relatives, Patrick and Gerard, whom I had met at Francine's home. Struck by the story, I reached out to Greg at RefAid to see if he could offer any advice regarding their situation. Greg's response to my inquiry provided a window into the epistemological foundations of credibility.

Soon after beginning long-term research in 2013, I was counselled by Greg and others not to make inquiries about specific people, and that it was not good for either the organization or my research for me to be mistaken for a representative of the organization. I made it a rule not to contact RefAid directly about people I met. Instead, I tried to assist people with information, asked NGO contacts questions in general or hypothetical terms on behalf of people documented as refugees and accompanied these interlocutors to offices where I could sometimes be helpful. But because Patrick and Gerard reported that they were in immediate danger, I emailed Greg as part of a reply to an ongoing email thread from that week.

The next day, Greg called. He was skeptical about where the young men had turned up. It was very strange, he asserted, for Banyamulenge to be in Mombasa. I explained the story as I had heard it from my friend the previous day: one of the young men had been recruited by M23, witnessed violence, fled, and then had been followed. Greg responded that the scenario sounded implausible. He saw me as a naïve do-gooder who believed any story I was told. He asserted that a lot of people witness bad stuff, but that once they had left their home country, they were gone. They posed no threat to the people perpetrating violence or corruption. The Rwandan government, he continued, goes after "big fish. And these people sound like they are small fish."

Greg asked, "Have they gone to the police?"

I didn't know if they had approached the police, only that they had gone to human rights and legal aid organizations.

He replied that organizations required police reports for two reasons (see also Thomson 2018, 213–12). "First," he said, "it established that the person was serious. If they haven't approached the police, then maybe they aren't. Second, if there is a serious security issue, we want the cops involved." He paused and, like many other times, presented a contradiction: "We may not trust them, but we want them there. The Rwandan government will not tell you that they are looking for you; they'll just kill you."

I knew from other cases that high-profile assassinations had taken place in Nairobi and elsewhere.

"Like the genocidaire who was killed here in 1997 or the person assassinated in South Africa earlier this year," Greg went on.

"Okay, I see," I replied, unconvinced but combing through the logic that animated his reply.

"The Ethiopian government," he continued, "they actually try to scare people. They say they're going to kill people, and then don't. But the Rwandan government . . . the thing is they're not going to waste thousands of dollars on sending agents after people who aren't important. And if these guys are approaching refugee agencies, then they might be fishing for resettlement or benefits. But this just doesn't line up with Congo and the Rwandan government."

The proverbial camp story was deemed dubious because it appeared to be a copy—a mass-produced, fake replica of an original story that "worked." On the other hand, Greg deemed Gerard's story implausible not because it seemed to be a copy of a story that had worked, but because it *failed* to replicate what he already knew. The story needed to reproduce commonly held knowledge about the places, governments, and people in question. For example, the story should have replicated what Greg believed about the ways in which the Rwandan government pursued enemies or others who posed a threat and about the profiles of such individuals. Reporting about confirmed and suspected assassinations of Rwandans in exile focused on high-profile figures (McConnell 2014). Another part of Greg's assessment rested a colonial "ethnoterritorial logic, which linked African populations to specific territories" (Weitzberg 2017, 90). Banyamulenge, people of highlands Central Africa, Greg asserted, didn't belong on the Indian Ocean coast. Their presence in Mombasa departed from typical patterns, Greg asserted, although access to bus and car travel was standard and their story explained how they had ended up there.

Greg's response to the story reflected another logic of the system in which he worked: the young men's apparent intention to seek benefits appeared as "fishing," or seeking benefits to which they were not entitled. Maybe Greg was correct in his assessment. Perhaps his long tenure in the field told him something about the case that I was unable to discern. Not jaded by nearly two decades of listening to stories in this context, I was surely more trusting or more curious than he was. Yet Greg's response highlighted a moral logic that said that those who intentionally seek out assistance are often unworthy, dishonest, and undesirable recipients of help. That logic that unfolded in his response laid bare an ideology about refugees that has long been noted by scholars: "the institutional, international expectation of a certain kind of *helplessness* as a refugee characteristic" (Malkki 1996, 388), where the helpless refugee represents "an ideal figure of which any actual refugees were always imperfect instantiations" (385).

Even though Greg had closed the door on the case, so to speak, it remained open for André and me. A few days after I received the call from Mombasa and spoke to Greg, André and I met downtown to take a bus out of the city to visit his mother and nieces. At the station, I mentioned the phone call from my friend on the coast and my conversation with Greg. André replied that Patrick had been calling him, too, after they met at Francine's house. He pulled up a text message from Patrick in which he asked André to meet him. But before they had had a chance to get together, Patrick and Gerard had suddenly left for the coast. All André knew was that Gerard had some images pertaining to M23 and the murder of several young men and had asserted that he was now at risk. A couple of weeks later, the two young men returned from the coast, and André and I returned to Francine's home to hear from Patrick himself.

Patrick had been living in Nairobi for about four years when his cousin, Gerard, suddenly came to visit. Gerard had been living in Kigali, Rwanda's capital, where he attended university, when he and other Banyamulenge students were approached by men from inside the Rwandan government about returning to Congo for an opportunity. This was several months after M23's official disarmament, and the government officials told the young men that they could have jobs as part of a new M23 political party. To Gerard and thirteen or fourteen other young men, this sounded like a good opportunity for gainful employment in their home country, and they traveled across the border into eastern Congo. When they arrived, the opportunity was not as it had been advertised. Instead of being recruited into jobs within a political party, they were being recruited to fight in a rebel group that had officially been disarmed.

When some of the young men resisted, they were shot on the spot. The rest of the young men fled back to Rwanda. Upon returning to Kigali, they approached the men who had originally recruited them, but the men denied having had any involvement in recruiting for M23 and disappeared. Parents started to inquire about their missing children. And Gerard, at this point fearing for his life, fled to Uganda, where his sister lived. While he was out watching a World Cup game one day, some men came to his sister's home looking for him. When his sister reported this to him, he grew alarmed and decided to leave again, this time for Nairobi, where his cousin Patrick lived.

Movement du 23 Mars, known as M23, was formed by minority Kinyarwanda speakers in Congo, including ethnic Banyamulenge, out of an existing group called Congrès national pour la défense du peuple, which was incorporated into the Congolese national army (FARDC) on March 23, 2009. In April 2012, a group of FARDC's Kinyarwanda-speaking soldiers mutinied and began a new rebel movement, calling themselves M23 (Koko 2014). Although the group was officially disarmed in November 2013 due to international pressure on Rwanda and had been defeated by the UN-backed Congolese army, a UN report from January 2014 stated that M23's "remnants and allies are continuing to recruit in Rwanda" (UN Security Council 2014a, 5). The same report noted that M23 soldiers recruited in Uganda and Rwanda in 2012 and 2013 had been "forcibly recruited into M23, having accepted false promises of employment and volunteering" and that "M23 allocated funds for recruitment and the transport of recruits." In July 2013, less than a year before Gerard's reported travel to Congo as a recruit, the UN reported, "M23 was forcibly recruiting civilians—and shooting those who resisted" (10). The UN Congo experts also interviewed recruits from Rwanda, five of whom were Congolese nationals living in Rwanda, like Gerard.

A similar report by Congo experts to the UN Security Council on June 25, 2014, around the time of Gerard's arrival in Nairobi, stated that "reorganization" of M23 had taken place in Uganda, though this was denied by the Ugandan government. The report did not mention similar activities in Rwanda, though it stated that M23 ex-combatants had escaped from a camp and that "owing to scheduling conflicts, the [UN] Group was unable to visit Rwanda to discuss the issue" (UN Security Council 2014b, 17). As in Gerard's narrative, the UN interviewed men who had been promised noncombatant jobs, such as drivers or mechanics. Those who resisted once in Congo were "threatened at gunpoint" (UN Security Council 2014a, 11).

After Gerard arrived in Nairobi, Gerard's sister called from Uganda to say that she would join him. Gerard was at church when Patrick went to fetch her from the bus station. She arrived with two young Rwandan men, who introduced themselves as Gerard's friends from school. Patrick described bringing the three back to his home. Gerard's sister sat between the two young men, but remained strangely silent. The two men talked, and after a while asked Patrick to get Gerard, but Gerard's sister signaled to him not to.

At that point, Patrick explained, Gerard hadn't told him anything about why he had come to Kenya, but he was now beginning to understand that something was wrong. Patrick found Gerard at church, explained what had happened, and the two decided to head downtown and get on the first bus they saw—headed to the coast. They arrived in Mombasa, where they approached the NGO where my friend was working at the time. According to her, the organization had paid for a place for them to stay and inquired with two European embassies about expedited resettlement.

After a couple of weeks, Patrick and Gerard received a movement pass from the Kenyan Department of Refugee Affairs, which allowed them to return to Nairobi without trouble from police or military, which were arresting and extorting refugees traveling without government permission at the time. Because they didn't want to bring any risk to Patrick's wife and child, they decided to stay with a friend of Patrick's in a neighborhood several kilometers away. While staying with Patrick's friend, Patrick received a call about a job—he worked on computers—and when he went to the matatu stage to pick up the person offering him work, a bunch of men tried to drag him into a vehicle. Some bystanders fought them off and the guys sped away. After that incident, Patrick and Gerard stayed in hiding. Patrick's wife took their child to stay with her parents. Patrick and Gerard went to UNHCR, where they were interviewed and given a follow-up appointment for only a couple of weeks later—a few days after our meeting. But in the following months, nothing happened with the young men's case. A couple of years later, back in the States, I chatted online with Francine. A single mother and survivor of sexual violence, she had been resettled with her children to Canada. She was doing well, she said, and Isaro, her mother, would hopefully be joining her soon. Patrick and Gerard, however, were still in Nairobi with no foreseeable opportunities to leave.

Whether, which parts of, or how Gerard's story mirrored true events is unknowable. I can't know what he experienced, nor what he believed, or the intentions of the people in his narrative. As I argue in the following chapter, how people interpret and narrate their experiences when they have lived, long-term, in a climate of violence and insecurity that the people assessing their claims have typically never experienced makes the endeavor of sorting "true" from "invented" stories far more complex than notions of "fraud" allow. But Gerard's narrative and Greg's response to it illustrate the ways in which a person's testimony for asylum in Kenya or resettlement to the global North must strike a sometimes impossible balance of attributes: aligned with known facts but not to a degree that it appears a fake copy, and exceptional in its demonstration of special vulnerability but without the subject appearing to be trying to access benefits. No fishing allowed. The "real refugee," as scholars have consistently pointed out, should appear helpless and grateful (Besteman 2016; Malkki 1996). By extension, the person perceived as intentionally seeking benefits is deemed especially suspicious, as Greg put it:

> The general principle is . . . if you can make it all the way here [to our office], you're not the most vulnerable; you're well enough off to seek services; you should go and seek a job. I'm being blunt but—and it's not quite that black and white, but, um, we do accept the occasional walk-in, but it's gotta be pretty extreme, like the woman who collapsed in the stairwell trying to make it up the stairs. Like those are the sorts of walk-ins we will consider. And often [to] some of those: "We'll give you drugs today, but don't come back. You don't qualify."
>
> Who are the walk-ins? Typically, they're the young males because they're most able to seek assistance and move about safely or typically were able to get a couple days of work and then could afford the matatu to come over here. Therefore, they're also the best suited to become self-sufficient.
>
> We want to find the single mom who can't afford to take herself and the

three small kids on the matatu and can't, doesn't have the time to walk across town because she's too busy trying to survive. . . . Now that sounds easy in theory, but they're also the people least connected to networks, least able to navigate the systems. They're the hardest to find.

Greg's statement reveals predicaments and paradoxes. It is difficult to locate "the most vulnerable." The people that his organization wants to assist are, by definition, the most difficult to find. They are also difficult to locate because, when they know organizational priorities, people fit themselves into categories likely to garner resettlement or other forms of aid, which can discredit them. RefAid was engaged in trying to correct a wrong in the refugee aid and resettlement system: better connected, more knowledgeable, better resourced people were more likely to receive help—a reality that those seeking resettlement also spoke about. But in this logic, the very act of seeking assistance undermined the claim of being worthy of help. It reinforced the notion that real refugees—those worthy of humanitarian assistance—were passive victims. While RefAid assumed that savvier people, including those who might genuinely be eligible for resettlement, found their way through other agencies, it reproduced an idea that someone worthy of assistance should not be an active participant in navigating aid and resettlement systems—in advocating for themself or shaping their own life in that way. Actions, behaviors, or demeanor that suggested a person was intentionally seeking out or "fishing" for resettlement undermined them. Moreover, the logic that the less vulnerable could rely on their own (economic) self-sufficiency was belied by Operation Usalama Watch, which recalled Hannah Arendt's observation about human rights and the stateless: "The moment human beings lacked their own government and had to fall back upon their minimum rights, no authority was left to protect them" (Arendt [1951] 1973, 292). A global order in which citizenship has become a privilege, rather than a right for so many, begs questions about that order's future.

Stealth Approach

Controlling perceived fraud in refugee resettlement has become a persistent aim of the US government and international organizations alike. In his 2005 report on the US Refugee Admissions Program, published by the Washington, DC, think tank Migration Policy Institute, David Martin wrote that several of his interviewees who worked for the US Resettlement Support Centers discussed the need for less institutional transparency to garner greater transparency on the part of their refugee interviewees:

> [They] emphasized the need for what some called a "stealth" approach to resettlement. That is, preliminary work that will fix or record key individual characteristics or histories—such as detailed questioning as part of camp registration or a UNHCR population verification exercise—should be completed to the greatest possible extent well before any public mention of a possible resettlement initiative. At such an early time, the interviewer is far more likely to obtain a full and candid picture of the person's true situation, undistorted by his or her guesses about what will maximize chances for resettlement (or by the coaching of a third party). (2005, 6)

Popular views of humanitarian versus national security approaches to forced displacement might imagine two regimes animated by different claims and priorities. Yet both seek to extract truth and transparency from refugees. Many people working with people forcibly displaced from their homes believe that this can be best accomplished if organizations restrict transparency in return.

Greg reflected this sentiment, noting that his organization had once resettled seventy young men and publicized it widely, in hopes of confusing people's assumptions about who the organization considered for resettlement. Since single mothers were typically preferred candidates, along with families more generally, resettling young single men was intended to disrupt what people trying to access the system assumed about resettlement priorities. When I asked Greg how people could access his organization's programs, which included mental health counseling, medical assistance, and food aid, in addition to resettlement, he replied, "So, how to get access to our systems? If I was to put myself in the shoes of a refugee, I would not be very impressed with the refugee agencies. Because we're arbitrary; we are not clear and transparent—deliberately; we are probably often rude, partly because people keep pushing and pushing, and the squeaky wheel sometimes has to be told to butter off. Because being polite won't get them to move."

The emphasis on identifying and mitigating fraud brings together the twin imperatives of resettlement: identifying people deemed deserving of humanitarian charity and securing borders against those deemed undesirable, unworthy, or dangerous. Policies like DNA testing, which I address in chapter 4; practices in camps like "night-time invasions for accurate census taking," and marking people's skin with gentian violet to prevent them from collecting double rations, as Voutira and Harrell-Bond describe (1995, 219); and every-day interactions like those taking place in resettlement counseling produce the figure of the fraudulent refugee. But the figure is also a global one. Contemporary asylum regimes in the global North increasingly employ technologies and forms of expert knowledge to verify or disprove asylum seekers' claims. In France, physicians examine asylum seekers and provide medical certificates to validate claims of torture (Fassin and d'Halluin 2005). In the US and elsewhere, professional experts, including anthropologists, are called upon as witnesses on culture and country conditions (Moodie 2022). In 2022, the US introduced asylum text analytics, which uses algorithms designed to detect "boilerplate language" and "patterns and anomalies" that, according to USCIS, suggest plagiarism and fraud in asylum testimonies (Rud 2023). DNA testing is now used widely to verify family-based claims in the US and throughout Europe (Heinemann and Lemke 2014). As physical exams and algorithms take precedence over people's own accounts of their lived experience, these technologies reflect the increasing investment in purportedly objective methods of determining truth from falsehood, while a small chorus of voices raise alarms about the use of these technologies in asylum and resettlement contexts (Barata et al. 2015; Rud 2023).

Borrowing from Jemima Pierre, discourses about fraud are part of a "racial vernacular" of refugee resettlement—a "discursive scaffolding" for the "unequal material relationships and processes that structure engagement between the Global South and the Global North" (2020, 86). Pierre demonstrates that development terminology reproduces "liberal ideologies through language that assumes the goodness of European liberal configurations (the rule of law, inalienable rights)—configurations that structure postcolonial African states' unequal relationship to the rest of the world" (95). Likewise, discourse about fraud and concepts such as "stealth approach," "camp story," and "fishing for resettlement" fortify the idea that people who have been forcibly displaced are problems to be managed. These terms naturalize an unequal global system that makes moving across borders a right for some but a privilege for most in the global South. They background the fact that living outside citizenship for years in camps has been deemed a solution and frames a core problem as "social and cultural behavior"—here associated with corruption or dishonesty (Pierre 2020, 93).

This chapter examined how the figure of the fraudulent refugee is produced through the resettlement system and the ways in which humanitarian and national security imperatives intersect in global refugee resettlement processes. The fraudulent refugee figure draws from various tropes and stereotypes of racialized subjects related to ideas about corruption in African societies, welfare fraud, and, as I describe in later chapters, Islamic terror. It emerges in the everyday work of classifying people as worthy or unworthy in a global system that makes citizenship an impossibility for the vast majority of the forcibly displaced in the global South. But how do people living with asylum seeker and refugee status make sense of accusations of fraud in their claims for asylum in Kenya or resettlement elsewhere? And how do they conceptualize the resettlement process and those who manage it? These are questions to which the following chapter turns.

TWO

Selling Cases and Eating Money

I AM SITTING WITH Asma and her mother, Halima, in their third-floor apartment in Eastleigh, which looks out at a large mosque. It is late afternoon and five- and six-story concrete buildings cast long shadows across the neighborhood. Rooftops glow, and drying laundry flickers and sways. Sunlight glints off megaphones sprouting from mosques. People move about busy streets, carefully stepping over small rivers of muddy water in the crumbling roads, as they make their way back from afternoon prayer and do errands before sunset. These days, few people are out after dark.

Halima is the head of the household that includes her seven children plus Asma, who is her much younger half-sister from their father; a nephew; and two grandchildren from her older daughter who no longer lives at home. Everyone calls Halima *hooyo* (Mom). She runs a tight ship to keep the family of twelve fed, clothed, schooled, and out of trouble. She has been trying to get her family resettled abroad through UNHCR for many years, and they moved to Nairobi from a smaller city a couple of years back so that they could travel more easily to and from the UNHCR office.

Asma recently finished high school and operates as Halima's right-hand woman, helping her manage the ten younger children in the house. Because of her language skills, she takes the lead dealing with appointments, documents, and following their resettlement case more generally. Asma describes recent visits to the UNHCR office:

> We went twice last week, and twice the week before. So, when we got there on Friday, I called and I reached someone who knows us and knows our case. So,

I told him, "I'm here outside. Can you meet us to speak to us?" He said, "Sure, no problem. I know you—I know you by face. I'm coming in ten minutes." But we waited for three hours! Until they closed the doors and everyone had gone. When I called again, it was someone else on the phone. They said they can't connect us back to the same person. We send an SMS [text message] every night, but they never reply. We don't even know where that SMS goes.

Halima says that she thinks someone has stolen their case.

"How would we know if they had?" I ask.

"You put your fingerprints," Asma replies. "Then they see. 'We thought you had already gone. Why are you still here?' That happened to someone we know. The woman went through the [UN's] doors by force. And when they looked up her case, they saw that someone else had gone in her place. They said, 'Didn't you already go to Canada?'"

Asma and Halima's description of their day at UNHCR reframes the narrative about fraudulent refugees by shining a light back on organizations and how they work. In my discussions about UNHCR and other agencies with people living as refugees in Nairobi, waiting and silence were pervasive themes. As I described in the previous chapter, people trying to access these organizations discussed waiting with little access to information about their case or inquiries they had made. In contrast to organizations' focus on fraud, often articulated in terms of problems with consistency and credibility, people living as refugees described UNHCR as secretive, arbitrary, and corrupt. The previous chapter shows that organizations that work with refugees invest considerable energy defining the parameters of a person who is eligible for resettlement and attempting to guard against fraud, defined by UNHCR most broadly as "the misrepresentation of fact for personal gain" (2011, 128). This chapter takes up two questions: How do peoples' lived experiences intersect with humanitarian logics of deserving and undeserving? How do people interpret and respond to accusations of fraud and to the consequent denial of their claims for resettlement to a third country or for asylum in Kenya?

Though often beholden to humanitarian assistance, particularly in the form of identification documents, people living as refugees in Kenya also point a finger back at refugee aid organizations. They criticize their difficult-to-reach locations, frequently changing staff, shifting rules, opaque regulations, unexplained judgments, endless waiting, and text messages that seem to disappear into thin air. Frequently, people described organizations and their staff as selling cases and eating money—accusations of corruption that draw on long-standing tropes criticizing misuses of power in many African contexts. By accusing humanitarian agencies of corruption, people living as refugees and asylum seekers in Nairobi rejected fundamental aspects of humanitarian work and hierarchies of power in which it is embedded.

"Not Credible"

I first met Yvette while working with André, a Rwandan student who had been introduced to me by a friend, Lucy, who worked at the NGO RefAid. André had worked as an interpreter at RefAid on a short-term project and had also received services there, as had his mother and two teenage cousins whom his mother took care of. Organizations often hired Rwandans as interpreters for Banyamulenge Congolese clients because of their shared language. Because he had done community-based work throughout the city, André had gotten to know the Banyamulenge community, and Lucy suggested that André could introduce me to some people. While I later benefited from research assistance from within the community, André was the first person to introduce me to members of the Banyamulenge community in Nairobi.

André rented a room in South B, a middle- and working-class area, while he studied media and film at a college in the nearby city center. He hustled to make money from odd jobs, including working with me, but also received financial support from a Swedish couple whose daughter had met André while working in Kenya, allowing him to pursue higher education. André and I typically met at Mwiki, a transportation hub in Kasarani—a large, working-class neighborhood several miles from Nairobi's Central Business District.

Departing from town in the morning, the bus to Mwiki careens down the Chinese-built Thika Highway, whipping past lanes jammed with commuters traveling in the opposite direction toward offices and businesses downtown and beyond. Turning off the smooth highway onto Mwiki Road, the bus bumps over roads in disrepair. It rumbles alongside open fields dotted with cows, machinery, and marabou storks pecking at garbage and past concrete apartment buildings, many still half built, with steel rebar rods shooting into the sky. Nearing Mwiki, the narrow road is clogged with buses and matatus making their final stop, waiting to pick up passengers for the fifteen or so kilometer journey back downtown. Touts in piecemeal uniforms mill about, shouting "Tao, tao, tao!" (town), beckoning passersby, and slapping their hands against brightly painted vehicles thumping with dance-hall or gospel music.

At Mwiki, André and I would transfer to a cramped, nine-seat matatu that travels on winding roads toward other neighborhoods. The gentle hills stretch out along the asphalt, the sky pierced by the occasional thorn tree. The suddenly rural landscape appears further from the city than it is, until the *mat* turns and we find ourselves on streets flanked by brightly colored clothing stretched over wire mannequins, crates of flapping chickens, tables stacked with cellophane-wrapped CDs, with the Jamaican singer Busy Signal or the Nairobi group Sauti Sol blaring from the salesman's player.

On the day we met Yvette in April 2014, at the height of Operation Usalama Watch, André and I had gone to visit a different woman, Maombi. After we spent the morning at her house, she had offered to introduce us to Yvette, who she thought I might be interested to know because UNHCR had rejected her asylum claim. André and I agreed, and Maombi led us to an apartment on the first floor of a building across the road. Unlike Eastleigh, which was vibrating with the anxiety of people under continuous police surveillance, Kayole, peripheral and primarily home to Kenyans, had so far been left alone by the anti-refugee operation.

Yvette's home was small and dark. In the sitting room, two couches with worn upholstery faced each other. A curtain hung in a doorway that obscured the kitchen and bedroom. In the corner sat a small TV, and by the door was a sewing machine. Above it hung a large poster featuring rows of dresses, varying by length, sleeve, neckline, and hem. Yvette herself wore a loose-fitting blue dress embroidered with gold-colored thread. Her chocolate-brown wig was cut into a bob reaching just past her chin, and a gold-colored chain lay on her chest. Maombi introduced us as Yvette welcomed André and me to sit down. To my surprise, she did not wait for my careful Swahili introduction, which I had come to expect. Unlike her neighbors, who typically said little until I had explained who I was and what brought me there, Yvette immediately began describing how she had been denied refugee status, then breaking into sobs.

Yvette had come to Kenya in 2010. When we met, she was living with her two daughters (one in her late teens and the other in her early twenties), one young granddaughter (the child of her older daughter), and sometimes other women who stayed in Yvette's small, rented apartment. Born in a village in South Kivu in 1965, she had completed secondary school in the nearby city of Uvira, making her uncommon among Banyamulenge women of her generation, who typically stayed in the rural highlands, married, and began their careers raising children and managing a household. Yvette had met her husband in Uvira where she eventually worked as a primary school teacher and businesswoman and later as a Pentecostal pastor. So, she explained, when her interviewers at UNHCR saw her with her earrings and her wig—unlike the stereotypical unadorned Banyamulenge woman with cropped hair and stoic disposition—they doubted her. Yvette cut a different figure from the stereotype. Her unconventional appearance—her sartorial and aesthetic assimilation to urban Congolese life, which made her look different from the majority of Banyamulenge women her age, helped her explain why she had been rejected as an ethnic imposter. However, over the course of the next year, Yvette added to the picture, suggesting other possible reasons for her exclusion from refugee protection. Her story centers the ways in which people understand and respond to being accused of fraud.

On the day we first met her, André and I sitting across from her in her dim living room, Yvette asked me to pass her a woven handbag that sat beside me on the couch. She opened it and began unfolding heavily creased papers and passing them back across the table: a police report filed after her twenty-two-year-old daughter was raped in Nairobi, the report of the medical examination her daughter subsequently underwent at the office of Médecins sans Frontières, her asylum seeker's document issued by UNHCR prior to its review of her case, the rejection letter from UNHCR, her letter of appeal, a letter written by Banyamulenge community elders to UNHCR on her behalf, and so on. Like many other women I met, who opened purses, plastic bags, even suitcases filled with documents, she laid out her evidence with care.

Yvette and her daughters had completed five interviews at UNHCR, the first four in Swahili, and the fifth and final interview in Kinyamulenge—the indigenous language of the Banyamulenge Congolese community and a dialect of Kinyarwanda and Kirundi (the national languages of Rwanda and Burundi). Because Yvette's and her daughters' national origins were called into question, the languages used were significant. In March 2012, Yvette received a rejection letter from UNHCR that noted that her original application had been filed in March of 2010. It mistakenly stated that she was a thirty-five-year-old woman, even though her UNHCR asylum-seeker pass stated that her birth year was 1965, which would have made her forty-five when her application was filed. The letter stated:

> We regret to inform you that after a thorough assessment of your refugee claim, and careful consideration of all available information, UNHCR has de-

termined that you are not eligible for international refugee protection under UNHCR's mandate. This decision is based on the following determinations:

Upon consideration of all of the available information, including explanations provided by you, the Office has determined that the information you have provided on these relevant and important points of your claim is not credible.

The information you provided in support of your refugee claim was vague and unclear in important areas. In particular, you were not able to provide sufficient detail to support your claim that you are Congolese national resident in Eastern Democratic Republic of Congo and suffered harm from the mai mai [rebel groups] on account of your ethnicity.

The letter concluded:

There were substantial inconsistencies within the information you and other family members provided in support of your claim. Specifically, you were not consistent with information on your identity, family background, and place of residence and account of flight.

You did not give a satisfactory explanation for these inconsistencies which relate to facts that are considered to be directly relevant to your eligibility for refugee protection.

The Office has further determined that there is no reasonable possibility that you would face serious threats to life, physical integrity or freedom resulting from generalized violence or events seriously disturbing public order in your country of origin.

A separate rejection letter addressed to Yvette's oldest daughter, who had to prove refugee status independently because she was no longer a minor and thus no longer a dependent, stated the following:

The information you provided in support of your refugee claim was vague and unclear in important areas. In particular, you were not able to provide sufficient detail to support your claim that you are a Congolese national of Banyamulenge ethnicity who was born and raised in [name of village], DRC. You were lacking in details about [village name] and the surrounding areas including the geographical features therein, which you would be expected to know. Besides, you claimed to be fluent in Kinyamulenge but when the language test was administered, you answered in Kinyarwanda.

Because Kinyamulenge is a dialect of Kinyarwanda, the distinction would have required the interpreter's analysis. "Maybe they lived in Rwanda for a while," André suggested to me after we had left Yvette's house, "and her daughter picked up the accent." But André, a native Kinyarwanda speaker, asserted that Yvette spoke the Kinyamulenge dialect, noting the subtleties of her speech. The community seemed to vouch for her, including Banyamulenge neighbors like Maombi and a group of elders who had signed a letter to UNHCR appealing her rejection. Later, Yvette confirmed that they had lived not in Rwanda but in Burundi for four years, in her daughter's early teen years. Had UNHCR known about their stay in Burundi during that interview? She clarified this in her letter of appeal.

In 2005, as fighting and targeted killings intensified in Uvira, Yvette became separated from her husband and sons. While being hidden by a neighbor, Yvette was repeatedly raped, and continued to suffer pain and problems with mobility years later, something she confided when I began visiting her alone, without André. Banyamulenge had come to be seen as a foreign, Tutsi enemy inside Congo, and members of the community were massacred by rebel groups and the Congolese army, including during planned deportations and in camps. Although people rarely shared with me the granular details of their exodus from South Kivu—a topic I never initiated in discussion—most people had witnessed and survived violence. Many had seen the massacre of family and other loved ones (see Stearns 2011). Eventually, friends who had provided protection to Yvette and her family called her and told her, "Run, hide, and cross into Burundi. If you don't, you will be killed. And don't say that you know us. If you say that you know us, we will be killed, too." Yvette and her two daughters fled across the border to Burundi, where they were aided by a Burundian pastor. After he died, they came to Kenya. "When we came here, we met problems," she reflected. "Problems up to this moment."

An Eligible Minority

For a community of a few hundred thousand at most, making up only a fraction of a percent of the Congolese national population (Stearns 2011, 59), the Banyamulenge have loomed large in the Congolese national imaginary, particularly since the 1990s. Historians date the arrival of Tutsi migrants from pre-colonial Rwanda to Congo's contemporary South Kivu province to between the seventeenth and late nineteenth centuries (Mamdani 2001, 247; Prunier 2009, 51). As Kinyarwanda speakers, Banyamulenge were originally called Banyarwanda (people of Rwanda). With their national belonging becoming a matter of political debate after Congolese independence in 1960, Banyamulenge were barred from running for office, and many were refused national identity cards (Stearns 2011, 65). During that period, Kinyarwanda speakers of South Kivu asserted their national belonging, rejecting the "new-comer" narrative by referring to themselves as Banyamulenge (people of Mu-lenge), the part of contemporary South Kivu Province to which they trace their origins in Congo (Thomson 2013, 99; Prunier 2009, 52). This name also served to distinguish them from the Kinyarwanda-speaking refugees from Burundi, Rwanda, and Uganda who began arriving during the postcolonial period (Thomson 2013, 99).

In the aftermath of the 1994 Rwandan genocide, the Banyamulenge community became embroiled in conflict as Hutus fled Rwanda across Congo's border. The perception of Banyamulenge as being of Rwandan and Tutsi origin became newly politicized in what Prunier (2009) calls "Africa's world war," given its vast international dimensions, as well as its length and the scale of its violence. Following the genocide, over one million Hutus fled to Congo fearing retribution from the new Tutsi-led government (Prunier 2009, 53). In 1996, the Rwandan Patriotic Front (RPF) declared war against Congo, pursuing genocide perpetrators and others who had fled along with them. In the intersection of Rwanda's military motives in Congo, a multinational initiative to overthrow Congo's President Mobutu, and domestic electoral politics, the Banyamulenge were cast as internal enemies. Because Congo was the world's largest producer of cobalt (used in cell phones and other electronics) and a major source of industrial diamonds, copper, uranium, and other minerals, foreign investors cashed in on the conflict, paying rebel groups and the government millions for access to mining, thus fueling the war (Stearns 2011, 288).

The RPF supported Banyamulenge, seeing them as co-ethnics in enemy territory, while Congo's President Mobutu stoked hatred against them among neighboring communities in his bid for reelection. In September 1996, the South Kivu deputy governor announced by radio that Banyamulenge should leave the country within a week or be imprisoned and killed. Hutu extremists and genocide perpetrators residing in Congolese refugee camps attacked Tutsi communities—both new Tutsi refugees and Banyamulenge. The RPF, along with a Rwanda-backed Banyamulenge rebellion, delivered retribution on Hutus in refugee camps and on Congolese citizens beyond (Thomson 2013, 100–101). While warlords may have become rich from mining contracts, many "part-time" rebels and combatants made ends meet by robbing and brutalizing civilians (Prunier 2009, 336–37). Yvette and her husband, who owned property and were well connected in Uvira, stayed until 2005, at which point their protection ran out.

Banyamulenge in Nairobi were survivors of attacks on their communities by rebel groups and attacks on refugee camps where they had sought safety across the border in Rwanda and Burundi. Many were survivors or family members of people killed in the 2004 attack on the Gatumba refugee camp in Burundi, just miles from the Congolese border. Some had also survived government imprisonment and torture. Many had been on the move for years—seeking safety in different parts of eastern Congo and in camps and cities throughout the region. The most fortunate had arrived in Nairobi with intact households, but most had suffered the death or disappearance of family members and friends. Many children and young men and women had been separated from their families. Some assumed their parents and siblings were dead, only to be reunited years later. Others searched and searched through the internet, organizations that helped with family tracing, and community networks and word of mouth but came up with nothing.

Widows, widowers, and orphans populated poor and insecure neighborhoods in Nairobi's outskirts like Kasarani and Kayole, where, in addition to the Somali neighborhood of Eastleigh, I spent the majority of my time in Nairobi between 2013 and 2015. Unmarried young people often lived together, taking care of each other and pooling limited resources to pay rent, buy food, and meet other basic needs. Moral standards demanded that people in their own precarious circumstances open their small, rented apartments to newcomers who would arrive at the bus station in downtown Nairobi and find their way to these neighborhoods in search of their community and lost family members. Reunions were made possible by the close-knit nature of the community and its popular spaces—including the offices of organizations like UNHCR and the churches that the community had established in the decade since they began arriving in Kenya's capital.

UNHCR and organizations like RefAid had identified Banyamulenge, along with other Congolese, as minorities who had faced persecution in their home country and thus candidates for resettlement (see Easton-Calabria and Lindsay 2013). When I began long-term fieldwork in 2013, this was a recent change. For several years after the conflicts in eastern Congo began, Congolese were ineligible for resettlement to a third country because of the relative stability of other parts of Congo—a country larger than Mexico that stretches from the lakes of East Africa all the way to the Atlantic Ocean. For most Congolese living in the easternmost part of the country—the site of the conflict—neighboring East African countries are far easier to reach than the capital city of Kinshasa, 2,400 kilometers away, and more familiar because of shared languages like Swahili and Kinyarwanda/Kirundi.

The change in Congolese eligibility was, in part, for expedient reasons. Somalis, who had long constituted a major portion of the Africa caseload for the US refugee program, were increasingly backlogged because of heightened security screenings required of Muslims—a trend that foreshadowed the near total shutdown for Somalis and people from several other Muslim-majority countries during Donald Trump's presidency. Security backlogs meant that agencies were constrained in meeting their target numbers and filling the slots offered by host countries. Congolese were deemed easier candidates for resettlement because, in addition to the ongoing violence and instability in their country, as a primarily Christian group they did not face the same security obstacles. In 2015, the US government agreed to resettle fifty thousand Congolese refugees over the span of five years. People working in resettlement in Kenya suggested that Banyamulenge were well represented among Congolese resettlement recipients because their minority status and continued persecution by other Congolese groups gave them a strong claim to being neither able to live safely in Kenya nor to return to Congo.

At UNHCR in neighboring Uganda, according to Sandvik, Congolese were stereotyped as "'wild,' 'dirty,' 'primitive,'" and as "tricksters" (2011, 21). In my research in Nairobi, however, I found that Banyamulenge were often regarded differently. Like the dominant narrative in Congo that placed them outside the national community, stereotypes in the aid world also characterized Banyamulenge as culturally distinct. Their identities as Tutsis meant they were often grouped with Tutsi genocide victims across the border in Rwanda. They were, in this way, seen as worthy victims who often conformed to the "social aesthetics of eligibility," the term Cabot uses to describe the co-production of eligibility between interviewers and asylum seekers based on narrative plausibility but also on "affect and the applicant's comportment" (2013, 454). Similarly, among UNHCR and other humanitarian staff in Tanzania, Malkki writes, "there was a pronounced tendency to try to identify and fix the 'real' refugee on extralegal grounds. And one key terrain where this took place was that of the *visual image* of the refugee, making it possible to claim that given people were not real refugees because they did not look (or conduct themselves) like real refugees" (1996, 384). With married Banyamulenge women usually dressed in *kitenge* and with a stereotypically reserved affect in public spaces, many Banyamulenge may have more easily fit into a conceptual slot of what Western and even Kenyan staff members imagined a real and "good" refugee to look and behave like.

The "bad refugee" and the "good refugee" are concepts that have been used by several scholars in refugee studies (Espiritu 2006; Sandvik 2011; Tang 2015). Sandvik uses "bad refugees" to point to "a particular form of bureaucratic memory" in which UNHCR staff in Uganda labeled individuals as "unruly or disobedient" and ultimately denied them assistance. Being connected to such people, she writes, "implied impurity—specifically, lack of credibility—by association" (2011, 22). Meanwhile, Cold War geopolitical imperatives and narratives of American exceptionalism made the Vietnamese "good refugees," as humanitarian objects of rescue from a so-called just war, Espiritu writes (2006; see also Tang 2015, 5). Some of my interlocutors were "bad refugees" in ways that are connected to both Sandvik's and Espiritu's concepts. They did not support a geopolitical agenda (and those who were Muslim provoked US anxieties about homeland security) and were deemed "unruly" in the specific sense of being seen as dishonest—as frauds.[1] On the other hand, Banyamulenge were often seen as "good" refugees. They did not trigger special security protocols, and their comportment and physical presentation seemed to align with an idealized expectation. Yvette, however, made a different impression. Neither her narrative nor her presentation compelled those who listened to her story.

Making an Appeal

As a widow, a mother, and a grandmother living in Nairobi's outskirts, Yvette had many things in common with Banyamulenge women who lived around her and who were documented by UNHCR as refugees. Her exclusion, therefore, not just from a resettlement case but from refugee status altogether tormented her. The year that Yvette's asylum claim was rejected, the rejection rate for Congolese asylum seekers in Kenya was 25 percent (Refugee Consortium of Kenya 2014, 16). That made her part of a minority (though a substantial one) of Congolese living without refugee status and documentation, yet likely one of fewer Banyamulenge widows and single mothers. Over the year following our first meeting, I spent time with Yvette and her teenage daughter, Françoise, as they continued to seek refugee status from UNHCR. In subsequent conversations, Yvette had different explanations for her rejection—an injustice she turned over in her mind over many long days and nights.

When I visited, we would talk about UNHCR and the status of their case, problems in the neighborhood or with her landlord, and Yvette's business ideas. A competent seamstress, she tried to sell clothing but had few customers. She was also a Pentecostal pastor—one of many in the community. At the wedding of a Banyamulenge couple, all the pastors were invited to bless the couple, and I was surprised to see around fifteen people, mostly men, rise and gather around the young bride and groom. Continual prayer to a God that offered eternal salvation, along with cathartic singing and dancing in packed Banyamulenge churches, allowed people to keep going in their state of displacement and grief. Yvette had a small group of followers, mostly Kenyans, who would come to her home, where she would lead them in prayer. When I visited, she would pray in her charismatic Pentecostal style, sometimes moved to tears, always including me and my work. This could feel like a protective blessing, but at other times like a warning: would I be a righteous person and help her? Yvette would sometimes watch me as I spoke, her eyebrows furrowed, seemingly turning over a thought or lost somewhere in the space of her mind. When she would come to, she would ask for some money or propose some other way I could assist her.

I doubted that the alleged inconsistencies in her UNHCR testimony, her obvious desperation, or her dramatic emotional style were evidence that she did not meet the legal definition of a refugee: "someone who is unable or unwilling to return to their country of origin owing to a well-founded fear of being persecuted for reasons of race, religion, nationality, membership of a particular social group, or political opinion," according to the UN Convention and Protocol Relating to the Status of Refugees. Rather, I suspected that those things reflected years of surviving violence, insecurity, and unspeakable loss. I wondered if her personality had an adverse effect on UNHCR case workers who were primed to doubt and often allergic to anything they perceived as manipulation.

After Yvette's first application for refugee status was rejected, she went to the Refugee Consortium of Kenya, a Nairobi-based organization that provides legal assistance to refugees and asylum seekers. Two months after receiving her rejection letter, Yvette filed an appeal detailing her life story and attempting to resolve misunderstandings. Her appeal letter stated the following:

I wish to appeal the earlier decision. As I stated earlier I am a Congolese national born in [village],[2] [zone] in [area]. This was in 1965. I got married in 1982 to [name]. We lived in Uvira in [neighborhood]. We later moved to [neighborhood] in Uvira. I got two children while living in [that neighborhood], [name] and [name]. The others were born in [another neighborhood].

I also mentioned that my tribe, Nyamulenge,[3] are targeted by the Maaimai. In 2005 my neighbor was attacked and his daughter killed. We were informed that they were headed toward our house. This was in 2004/2005. We fled in different directions. I do not know where my husband went to and he took two of our sons with him. We moved to Burundi with my two children. We lived there for four years and a few months. In Burundi, my daughter was defiled and conceived the child [who] is living with us. One of my sons lives in Kakuma. We were hosted by Daniel (pastor) who later died. We did not have anyone else to go to. We did not have security in Burundi and we always felt that he was providing security when he was living.

This was a very tense period because of the Katumba [sic] killings had just taken place [2004].

On my family background my father's name was [name]. Mother—[name]. My siblings were [name], [name], his wife was [name]. I had other siblings who were born by my father and other women. Some of them are [name], [name], [name], among others.

I feel that my life would be in danger if I went back to Congo. I am also scared for my children because of what I went through.

The war in Uvira was ongoing that we would be peaceful for two days then the third day we hear screams and people would be killed. My children and I sought refuge in my neighbor's house (Mbembe)[4] and he would rape me. I didn't tell my family because it was shameful and I am a pastor. I was a pastor and a teacher. I stopped teaching to become a pastor.

My husband and I owned property in Uvira. 2 houses in [neighborhood], 1 house in [neighborhood] where I once taught and two unbuilt plots. The property was later taken by Congolese.[5] I learned that my husband was killed when he went to take the property. This I was told by refugees who entered the country this year. I fear that I would be killed too.

I worked as a teacher in [name] primary then [name] primary school and [name] primary school. All these schools are in Uvira.

My parents named me [name], I gave myself [name]. I chose this name when I was asked my full names. My pet name at home was [nickname]. The government required all to have a Christian name. I was baptized and I included the name Yvette to my other names. I loved my pet name and I didn't want to lose it so I decided to put it in my school papers.

With the above information I hope I have been able to clear the questions that arose and to convince that I am from Congo and taking my family back to Congo now would be like signing a death warrant for my children.

> My parents told me that I was born in 1964 when I was joining school. Later on we had a discussion with my elder brother who was able to count backward and said that I was born a year later than the given date.

When Yvette returned to UNHCR with the letter of appeal, she contin-ued to be given new appointments for several months later. When we first met, it had been just over four years since her arrival in Kenya—four years since she had begun seeking refugee status. Yvette explained that she had a relative who had worked as an interpreter for UNHCR, who she asked to try to intervene on her behalf. But after he did, things became even worse, she reported. Instead of being given new appointments for three or four months later, UNHCR had given her an appointment that was seven months in the future. As she explained her situation, Yvette began weeping, "I've been here for five years, and they are just increasing the days [until my appointment]! Some people stay for one month and get a mandate [ID]. Why have I been rejected?" She described returning to UNHCR and encountering a Rwandan staff member: "We've rejected you! We've given you a response! You've gotten what you deserve!" she said the woman had shouted at her.

Drawing from Yvette's own narratives, Yvette was perceived as a "bad ref-ugee" in the sense that Sandvik describes from her research on UNHCR in Uganda: "Unruly or disobedient clients were blacklisted" and denied assis-tance (2011, 22). Yvette and her daughters seemed to be considered "unruly" and dishonest. Though I could not discuss Yvette with UNHCR staff—as indi-vidual case files were strictly confidential—she seemed to occupy the position that Sandvik describes: a person whose story did not add up by bureaucratic standards and whose demeanor made her difficult to help based on dominant (if unspoken) norms and expectations.

Her rejection troubled her deeply. It was troubling because living without documentation excluded her from scarce but available services predicated on refugee status, including medical care and counseling, rent assistance, and resettlement opportunities, among others. But it was also troubling because it constituted a denial of her history and experience. As psychiatrist and medical anthropologist Roberto Beneduce writes on asylum in Europe, "Denying the truth of their experience to a man or woman who has been tortured and hu-miliated is a real psychological apocalypse, which dramatically reiterates the traumatic experience of the past, and shatters any residual 'trust in the world' (Amery 1980, 28)" (2015, 558).

It was not simply a matter of Yvette's past. As Erica Caple James writes on humanitarian intervention in Haiti, "continuous traumatic stressors," or "routines of rupture," "multiple ongoing disruptions to daily life rather than single traumatic events"—constituted an interwoven past and present (2010, 132). Yvette's continued attempts to be recognized by UNHCR and granted a document enabling her to legally stay in Kenya were a central part of the "continuous traumatic stressors" in the aftermath of the violence that had brought her to Kenya.

"Look how I've been abandoned!" she once wept. "I've been thrown out [nimetupwa]![6] I don't have a place [mahali], I don't have refuge [kimbilio]. We don't have our rights as refugees. I've been thrown out completely!" Without the UNHCR identity document, she was "not under any government," she said. "I'm just there in space."

In addition to its material significance, she experienced the rejection as a denial of her suffering, of her claim to be a person who deserved protection and rights, and of her membership in a community.[7] Remarking on what Hannah Arendt ([1951] 1973) called "the decline of the nation state and the end of the rights of man," Yvette recognized herself as unprotected by either a government or the UN. Saying, "I'm just there in space," she pointed to the relationship between territory, borders, and rights. Without any official status, she experienced herself as ungrounded. Without an ID, she was doubly outcast—first from her country of origin, then from the agency of international refugee protection.

In October, I accompanied Yvette to the Refugee Consortium of Kenya (RCK), the Kenyan legal organization that had helped her file her appeal. Yvette had been given an appointment at UNHCR regarding the appeal for February, still four months away. She wanted to inquire with RCK about the appeal's status and try to harakisha (hasten things). The morning of our journey, Yvette reached downtown around 6:30 a.m. I had thought we had agreed to meet at 8 o'clock, so I raced out of the house when she called to tell me she had already arrived. People traveling to UNHCR or NGO offices like RCK usually leave home early in the morning to beat the notorious Nairobi traffic and give themselves the best chance at getting through the door. From Yvette's home, the bus to downtown Nairobi could take an hour or more. From there to Nairobi's western neighborhoods where NGOs and UN offices are situated can take another hour, depending on traffic. RCK is located in one of Nairobi's affluent suburbs, where elite foreigners from Europe and North America and members of Kenya's upper class reside. The trip there and back required around two dollars, a cost multiplied if one had to appear with a whole family. This was a considerable sum when a month's rent in Nairobi's peri-urban outskirts cost between $50 and $100 in 2015 and when most people with refugee or asylum seeker status were barely making ends meet.

Meeting downtown near the National Archives, Yvette and I boarded a bus that ascended the hilly roads of Nairobi's western neighborhoods to a quiet, tree-lined street where the offices of RCK were nestled in a small building behind a gate. On the bus, Yvette told me about her stress, her ulcers, and the thoughts—*mawazo*—that tormented her. She had been to RCK perhaps twenty times, she estimated. By that time, the guard knew me, too, and when we arrived, we entered through the gates without needing to explain ourselves.

In the yard outside the building, people sat waiting to meet with staff members inside. As the morning drew on, one by one they were called to enter the office. We passed time talking with other women who were there with their own troubles: a Banyamulenge woman who had just lost a baby and was waiting for the determination of her refugee status so she could join her husband, who had just been resettled to the US; a Burundian woman dying of cancer who had a giant bag filled with X-rays and medical reports; a Somali woman from Ogaden who had been tortured in an Ethiopian prison. Most carried bags of police reports, medical records, identification papers, appointment slips, letters—documents of all kinds from various governments, and from local and international NGOs, some of which would be treated as credible evidence (particularly local police reports and documents from major international organizations), and others would be dismissed.

At ten o'clock, Yvette was called inside but came out shortly after, having been told that she would have to wait for the lawyer to return from court. She complained about the cold in the shaded courtyard of the compound. Her knees hurt. We exited onto the sunny street and bought tea and snacks from a kiosk that a few Kenyan women had opened across the road. Yvette asked for milk, good for her ulcers, she said, though she rejected the first one offered—a brand she did not recognize. Having been on her feet since before sunrise, she unwrapped a spare *kanga*, the versatile regional garment, from around her waist, laid it on the ground by the road, and stretched out on top of it.

She rested, got up when a curious monkey approached her, and waited some more. Returning through the gates of the compound, we struck up a conversation with a young Kenyan man. Yvette described her situation, and he advised her how to put forth her case. "Don't say a lot of things," he told her. "Just explain the problem clearly." As he left, Yvette took his hand, "God will bless you if you help me." It seemed good luck to run into a friendly staff member. But when I asked a guard about the man, he told me that he was a driver, not someone who worked with clients. We sat, we talked, we waited some more.

In the late afternoon, when only a few people remained in the courtyard, a young Kenyan woman came out of the office to speak with Yvette. Her appeal had been submitted to UNHCR, she told us, and there was nothing they could do to inquire or hurry UNHCR to respond. In fact, she warned us, to do so could compromise Yvette's case further—they could even take away her asylum seeker's document, the temporary ID that showed she had applied for permanent refugee status.

"Why would they do that?" I asked.

"I don't know," she replied, "that's just how they work."

Before we departed, a Somali interpreter lingering in the courtyard explained that Yvette's file would have been dumped in the same pile as those of new arrivals—in other words, into a massive backlog. The only thing Yvette could do now was to describe to UNHCR the current problems she was facing—to let them know that she had extenuating circumstances right now, in the present, he told her. Yvette and I left the RCK compound and walked down the quiet street in the afternoon sun to meet the bus at the corner. "That is very helpful," she said, referring to the interpreter's advice. She would go to UNHCR's Protection Unit and "push" from there, she said. She was as determined as ever to be acknowledged.

Weeks later while talking in her home, Yvette pulled a photo from an envelope of letters. In the photo, she stood in front of a background of foliage—twisting vines and shiny green leaves. Her face looked younger. She wore a blue and white dress. Her eyebrows were drawn in thinly; a straight, chestnut-colored bob framed her face. She held an expression that was serious but relaxed. I had an uncanny feeling that I was seeing a different Yvette—the same woman but not the same. "That was when I was still okay," she said, regarding the photo. I wondered how Yvette's experience—her chronic physical pain and *mawazo* (thoughts, here painful and disturbing ones)—shaped what she could remember or say. How did continually recounting her narrative to a doubting audience and a powerful institution's denial of her experience further wound her?

By the time I was preparing to leave Kenya in the spring of 2015, Yvette was again waiting for an appointment, which was still six months away. When we met shortly before my departure, she echoed Asma and Halima, whose words open this chapter. "The UNHCR workers are eating money," she said. "They're taking money to send people, instead of those who are really supposed to go."

Reframing Fraud

Many people, like Yvette, countered accusations of fraud with their own accusations—that it was UNHCR, not people like herself, who corrupted a system that was meant to aid people. Statements about "eating money" exist in a deep well of idioms that tie political power and inequality, patron-client relations, and the antisocial accumulation of wealth to eating and "the politics of the belly" in African contexts (Bayart 1993). As Schatzberg writes, "Power frequently concerns the capacity to consume, or the ability 'to eat' as expressed both literally and figuratively in many African languages" (2001, 40); there is "a close correlation between the language of food and the language of corruption" (41). Describing UNHCR and NGO staff as "eating money," or taking bribes, people living as refugees and asylum seekers reframe a discourse that casts blame on refugees, puncturing the "moral untouchability" of humanitarian organizations (Fassin 2011).

Congolese and others documented as asylum seekers and refugees also echoed and drew upon discourses about UN operations in their home countries. In eastern Congo, for example, people have long critiqued the extraordinarily expensive but largely ineffectual UN peacekeeping mission (MONUSCO) as "a cannibalistic entity" (Shaw 2018, 199). There, people working in UN compounds that "comprise islands of extreme wealth in tantalizing proximity to sites of desperate poverty" (204) are understood to be "'eating' Congo's wealth, leaving nothing for local people" (205). As Shaw writes, local people perceive MONUSCO and other UN agencies as part of a long line of colonial, predatory actors, "manipulating what is now eastern Congo's most abundant commodity: suffering" (205). Discourses about UNHCR "eating money" and "selling cases" are part of this wider vernacular for explaining power and global racial inequality broadly and in relation to humanitarian aid in particular (see also White 2000).

Corruption by UN and NGO staff, as well as by people posing as UN and NGO staff, has been documented and reported by journalists, scholars, and human rights groups. A three-part investigative story published in 2019 detailed corruption and retribution against whistle-blowers at UNHCR in East Africa—primarily in Kenyan and Ugandan refugee camps. The story chronicles the practice of selling resettlement cases for as much as $68,000 in Kenya and suggests that corruption more generally is underreported due to a systemic lack of protection for and intimidation of both refugees and UNHCR staff. Staff whistle-blowers have accused UNHCR of downplaying accusations for fear of losing donor support (Hayden 2019). Ultimately, UNHCR often takes an ends-justify-the-means approach, with the logic that the good of their work should be protected, even if it requires harmful compromises (see also Redfield 2011).[8]

In 2011, I was introduced to Shamso and her elderly mother, Fatuma, whose case had been sold to someone who went abroad under a false identity. The mother and daughter had arrived at the International Organization for Migration center from which people were transported to Nairobi's international airport, only to be told that someone had already left under Fatuma's name. Years later, I met a young man, Libaan, who had left the Dadaab camp when he was threatened because of his knowledge about resettlement corruption. In 2014, he was attending university in Nairobi. He reported that there were UNHCR staff members who regularly took bribes and who refused to help people who failed to play the game. To buy a case, he said, a person could pay $50,000 for a family of seven. In Nairobi, he reported, you could pay $20,000 for a single person—facts corroborated by published sources (Hayden 2019). These were rare occasions in which I met people who reported firsthand knowledge of such corruption. But these stories are part of widespread knowledge that circulates in refugee communities.

Many people documented as refugees or waiting for refugee-status determination pointed their finger at local Kenyan staff, largely because of racialized ideas about the ubiquity of corruption in African societies, even among African communities themselves. Some of these ideas were also, as in Yvette's case, tied to mistrust of interpreters who spoke a common language but belonged to an ethnic, religious, or political group that had a history of conflict with the interviewee's community. This kind of mistrust of interpreters and Kenyan staff ran alongside ideas about white North American and European staff members as benevolent helpers (see Malkki 1995, 145–47)—though views on white staff members may have been more varied and complicated than what people shared with me, a white foreigner. Despite the circulation of ideas about good foreign helpers and corrupt local staff, according to NGO interlocutors in Nairobi, the most notorious case of resettlement corruption in Nairobi's UNHCR office involved high-ranking European staff members in collaboration with a German hotel owner. Together, they orchestrated a resettlement-for-pay and resettlement-for-sex scheme (see also Sandvik 2011, 24–25). A young European staff member blew the whistle on the scandal in the early 2000s. Many of the staff were fired, and policies were revised to protect against such abuses, though selling cases apparently did not disappear altogether.

Stories and personal experiences with sold cases, extortion, and the general inaccessibility and opacity of organizations circulate and structure the ways in which people living outside citizenship understand and speak about the humanitarian regimes under which they live. A Banyamulenge pastor I met in Canada in 2016 put it bluntly: "People who pretend to be service providers, they should change their name and just say, 'We are money makers.' Their staff members are corrupted. People tell lies, they sell documents, people are resettled under different names." I suspected the pastor felt freer to speak critically as a Canadian citizen than many of the people with whom I spent time in Nairobi, who relied on UNHCR for documentation and protection and who were waiting for resettlement cases to progress. But in Nairobi, still, people often spoke with frustration about the rules of the game being concealed from them and waiting for months and years with little opportunity to make inquiries or obtain information. They expressed that the resettlement process ended up benefiting the well-resourced and well-connected—a problem that people like Greg Brown and organizations like RefAid also identified and were trying to remedy but with complex effects, as the previous chapter described (see also Feldman 2018, 169). Halima, the Somali woman with the large family who opens this chapter, put it this way: "Nowadays, rights are based on money." Who gets resettlement? "People with money. That's what we've seen."

At the same time, some of my Congolese interlocutors described UNHCR as "our mother and our father." They used kinship terms "and the claims, obligations, and emotions they implied—to interpret and reinterpret their social contacts" (Geschiere 2013, xvi; see also Voutira and Harrell-Bond 1995, 216; Schatzberg 2001). This came with an implicit critique regarding what a mother and father were obligated to provide for their children and how the UN had failed to fulfill those obligations. Banyamulenge, whose identities were in part constructed through their exclusion from their country of national origin, saw

UNHCR as their only earthly institutional protector, but a protector that often fell short. For this community, UNHCR's failures in Nairobi were refracted through other histories, including through the massacre of 166 members of their community in the UNHCR-run Gatumba refugee camp in Burundi in 2004—an event that also shaped their view of the organization.

Still, many who put their hopes for the future in resettlement articulated the problem not as institutions or systems but individuals at UNHCR who perpetrated corruption and allowed greed or divisions from their home countries to infiltrate the organization's decisions. In discussing UNHCR's rejection of her asylum claim, Yvette stated that the problem was

> not the UN in general. The UN is helping people. It's just a few employees. The UN came here to help us. And RefAid came here to help us. In the UN, it's Rwandans who work there. When we come, they don't accept us, and they say we're Rwandans from Kigali. They tell lies. They say, "This is a Tutsi from Rwanda." That's where the problem comes. There is no Banyamulenge who translates. Someone just sees you as an enemy, from what they see on the outside . . . they see your long nose,[9] and they place you there. Many who get rejected, they call them Rwandans from Kigali. A pure Kenyan can't differentiate Hutus and Tutsis, but that person who is the translator, he stereotypes you right away.

The Rwandan (Hutu) interpreter, Yvette claimed, acted out anti-Tutsi hostility by conspiring to ruin her case. If UNHCR cast Yvette and her daughters as frauds, Yvette saw UNHCR and specific UN staff members as greedy, corrupt, dishonest, tribalistic, and vindictive. The denial of her asylum claim, the appointments scheduled for months away, and the sense that she was treated with contempt when she came to the office, produced a sense that UNHCR "played by their own secret rules" (Shaw 2018, 199), which were not primarily oriented around promoting refugees' rights or well-being. So, she looked for back channels, seeking information through unofficial sources, and continued to knock on doors outside of the appointments UNHCR gave her.

Writing on humanitarian aid throughout Palestinian refugee camps, Ilana Feldman argues that "circulating accusations of corruption are a fertile ground for making claims about obligations" and that "corruption accusations are a means through which different actors define what humanitarianism should be" (2018, 169). Yvette's and others' critiques of how UNHCR's refugee status and resettlement processes work, along with documentation of corruption by journalists and scholars, require a different way of understanding resettlement

and hegemonic claims about fraudulent refugees in refugee-serving organizations and beyond. Communities trying to avail themselves of asylum in Kenya
and resettlement opportunities beyond bring different actors and problems to
the fore as they talk about these processes. Those problems are structured not
only by a dearth of financial resources and resettlement opportunities produced by global North immigration policies but also by a system of aid and
"durable solutions" that casts people as "passive recipients of charity" without rights to "self-determination, mobility . . . or self-governance" (Besteman
2016, 59). Yvette refuses to be a passive recipient, resisting her rejection from
refugee status. Listening to her claims about her life and the organizations she
looked to for protection allows us to see the figure of the fraudulent refugee
as a category that controls access to humanitarian benefits and that, as it in-
evitably fails to capture the complexity of people's lives and identities, causes
new forms of harm that appear increasingly fundamental to the experience of
forced displacement.

How Stories Are Made

In February 2014, André received a frightening call from his teenage cousins
Charlotte and Rosine, who lived with his mother, Mujawaimana. They were
with her at the hospital, where two men had brought her after finding her
unconscious. According to the story that had been pieced together, she had
been hit on the head by an object that had fallen from a construction site. But
as André relayed the story to me, the construction accident began to blur out
of focus. Over the din of reggae and the rumble of the rough road beneath
our bus, André described how, after he finished high school, his mother had
moved to Kawangware, a neighborhood with a large Rwandan community.
There, she had been threatened, eventually forcing her to move to the town
outside the city, where she now resided. The threats had had to do with her life
in Rwanda, her identity as a Hutu, and the fact that newcomers from Rwanda
were often feared to be government spies—fear rooted in government surveillance both inside and outside the country (Thomson 2013).

What happened in Kawangware wasn't Mujawaimana's first experience
being threatened. After the genocide, one of her relatives had held a position
in the new government, and she had gotten a job as a secretary in his office.
After a conflict with the ruling party, her relative fled the country. Now associated with an enemy of the government and a political exile, André's mother
was abducted and tortured once, twice, then a third time. At that point, she

knew she had to leave the country. She arranged to pick up André from school and flee to Kenya. On the noisy bus in Nairobi, André told me he hoped that his mother's recent injury wasn't a repeat of a past pattern. "It must have been an accident," he concluded, as if shifting back into a different version of reality.

Months later, André and I were discussing a neighbor of his mother who purposefully injured himself in an attempt to create a more compelling resettlement case. Injuring oneself to gain political subjectivity or social well-being is described by Ticktin as "biological involution" in her writing about *sans-papier*, the undocumented in France: "The structural situation encourages and rewards sans-papiers for configuring themselves as 'sick'" (2011, 195) to the extent of exploiting their own biology, potentially to the point of death (see also Beneduce 2015). In addition to purposefully harming themselves to create the appearance of vulnerability that was legible to humanitarian organizations, people André knew also turned everyday injuries into evidence to support their claims. "Like that time something fell on my mom's head," André added in an offhand way.

Would it have been fraudulent if André's mother told UNHCR that she had been or might have been targeted the day she was knocked unconscious? Or that she was afraid of that possibility? André had suggested that it was likely an accident, but he also had doubts. He interpreted the event in the context of Rwanda's recent history and his mother's personal history, as well as that of many of her friends and family members—including her teenaged nieces' mother, who had been a *gacaca* judge and was mysteriously murdered in her home, which followed the mysterious death of their father in prison.[10] People occasionally reported insecurity in a bid to fit into the UN's category of vulnerability that required immediate protection from "threats which seriously jeopardize their continued stay in a country of refuge," in UNHCR's terms (2011, 247). But many people, even those who may not have been in imminent danger in the ways that organizations recognized, were haunted by real histories of profound insecurity and violence and interpreted their present circumstances in that context. This could have been true of Gerard (chapter 1), who, if indeed he witnessed his friends' murders, may have genuinely believed or feared he was being pursued, whether or not that was factually accurate. This interpretive work on the part of people living as asylum seekers and refugees can be described as rooted in "fear and paranoia" on one hand and "the knowledge that is needed to navigate uncertain landscapes" on the other, as Al-Bulushi describes it (2021, 4)—the knowledge about how violence works that has enabled them to survive.

How people living as refugees or asylum seekers narrate their past for bureaucratic audiences is rooted not only in the conditions of scarcity, uncertainty, and bureaucratic expectations but also in the complexity of people's real lived experiences of uncertainty and violence. Both complicate ideas about "fraud" as simple misrepresentation. People do misrepresent their situations in attempt to garner coveted access to life-saving legal status, sometimes hiding their real stories of persecution, which are more complex and less likely to fit in humanitarian categories (see Beneduce 2015; Jansen 2008). The "bureaucratic violence" (Beneduce 2015, 551) of questioning and the expectations of consistent, reproducible, "coherent narrative account[s]" come up against "silences and the fractured nature of . . . traumatic experiences or memories" (553). As André's question about his mother reflects, the line between "truth" and "misrepresentation" for people faced with the bureaucratic demands of asylum and resettlement systems is unclear.

André's recounting of his mother's accident and his uncertainty about what had occurred are refracted through her life history, which involved being subject to targeted, politically motivated violence—living through the Rwandan genocide and the political insecurity of its aftermath. (Though she was not a member of the primary victim group in the genocide, Mujawaimana and André's home area was subject to reprisal attacks by the RPF when they took over the country). How André talked about his mother's head injury, which he narrated alongside moments in which she had been subject to violence and intimidation, underscores the complexity of people's experiences of insecurity versus what insecurity means and how it can be evinced in the eyes of humanitarian organizations and immigration systems. In this sense, stories—ones told to oneself, to friends and family members, and to outsiders like me and staff at UNHCR—were produced in a tangled web of memory and its limits, meaning-making amidst violence and the exigencies of the present. That present was constructed, in part, in the insecurity of asylum-seeker and refugee-status and the uncertainty of a twenty-first-century postcolonial city and through the technological overload that linked Nairobi's stateless (and others) to images of "the West."

———

In 2019, I sent Yvette's daughter Françoise a message. Françoise was now married and had two young children. "How is your mom?" I asked. "Is she still in Nairobi?"

She wasn't in Nairobi, Françoise replied, but said little else about her mother. Only hours later, I received a message from Yvette herself, who was in a car somewhere in Arizona. I asked how she had arrived in the States. Invited by her son, who was now in the US with a new baby, she came on a tourist visa using a Rwandan passport. She had left her two daughters and her grandchildren in Nairobi and wished to stay in the US so that she could work and send them money. "Nairobi ni shida sana" (Nairobi is a big problem), she wrote. In 2022, Yvette moved to a small Northeastern city. She got a job working with an organization that served the Congolese community there and had a work permit, she said. How had it all transpired—the Rwandan passport and the visa, getting work authorization? Unwilling to be another person in a long line of foreign investigators, I didn't press for more details. Always casting a critical eye, never waiting to be rescued, Yvette rejected the twenty-first-century marriage (or kinship) between humanitarian aid to refugees and the securitized borders of the global North. In the end, Yvette had circumvented the resettlement system altogether.

THREE

Mending Broken Bones

IN EARLY 2014, my friend Mohamed's cousin Sadiya was leaving for Australia. Excitement surrounded her upcoming departure, as well as the bittersweet of bidding a life and friends goodbye. Sadiya came to Mohamed's home with fruit and drinks, and they and other young relatives talked late into the night before her flight. In July, Mohamed updated me. Sadiya was now in the midst of a family drama. She had gone to Australia as the supposed wife of her cousin—her *ina-adeer* (the son of her father's brother). This particular cousin, Abdirizak, was the only one of the right age and marital status to play the role of husband to sponsor Sadiya. His father was arranging the process, and the wider family was in support.

However, Abdirizak had a girlfriend who he had been seeing for six years, and the couple had been planning their own marriage. Abdirizak had resisted being involved in the plan, as his girlfriend was upset that their own wedding would have to be delayed and was anxious that he was being usurped into a real arranged marriage. But the family assured the couple that the whole process would take only a year, and as soon as Sadiya arrived, they could officially "divorce." Then Abdirizak and his girlfriend could proceed with their marriage as planned. When Sadiya arrived, however, an unexpected problem arose. The family learned that they would have to wait for at least two years before the divorce for Sadiya's legal status to be permanent. As Mohamed described the situation, he commented on Abdrizak's father's obligation to bring his brother's daughter. Abdirizak's girlfriend, Mohamed also commented, had good character, having gone along with Abdirizak's need to put the interests of his family first—supporting his father's responsibility to his brother and his brother's children.

As the previous chapter revealed, people living as refugees experience resettlement and immigration bureaucracies as arbitrary, corrupt, and unjust, informing the ways in which they engage with them. But the ways in which people navigate resettlement and seek to go abroad are also tied to longstanding and emergent practices of kinship. Officials who administer refugee resettlement regard one of their primary obligations to be separating true from false claims, thereby identifying those they deem to be the most needy humanitarian beneficiaries. People living as refugees, on the other hand, have moral obligations that supersede administrative categories and humanitarian ideals. In the Somali community, immigration opportunities are stitched into the fabric of cultural notions about moral behavior and obligations to support kin in ways that diminish hierarchical dependence and improve the well-being of family members. Resettlement is a resource that promises rights and opportunities that are mostly absent for people living as refugees in Kenya: citizenship, freedom of movement, greater possibilities for education and work, greater safety from insecurity and persecution, and the ability to send remittances and sponsor others. These are resources that families seek to share.

In this chapter, I argue that the moral claims of humanitarianism and the moral claims of kinship intersect and shape each other as international organizations seek to manage displaced people and as displaced people seek to move, claim rights, and find safety for their families. The chapter elucidates debates and decision-making within Somali families and communities about competing obligations, such as managing the financial and other stresses of life in resettlement countries on one hand and fulfilling obligations to send money back to family and facilitate migration opportunities on the other. Like the moral logics of humanitarianism that prioritize alleviating suffering (Fassin 2012), members of the global Somali diaspora are also engaged in a moral project of alleviating suffering. Unlike humanitarian programs, though, which target those deemed exceptionally vulnerable, the Somali ethic emphasizes distributing resources and responsibilities as widely as possible and sponsoring family members to go abroad who have the potential to assist others.

Centering the competing moral claims between humanitarian institutions and people living as refugees shows refugees neither as victims passively resettled and saved nor as criminals or frauds, but rather as active agents maneuvering through their own constrained mobility to assist networks of kin. This chapter demonstrates the moral logics of kinship through the stories of one person who is relatively well resourced through his kin networks and another who is poor and lacks family ties. Before turning to these protagonists, Mohamed and Fardowsa, I take a closer look at the differing moral logics that animate humanitarianism and a global Somali diaspora.

Competing Moral Logics

International humanitarianism involves a relatively recent set of ideas, institutions, and forms of action. Redfield and Bornstein trace contemporary humanitarianism to "Enlightenment rationality, secularism, capitalism, and colonialism" (2011, 13), linking it to responses to the Lisbon earthquake of 1755, the birth of the International Committee of the Red Cross in 1862, the international movement to abolish slavery in the nineteenth century, and European civilizing projects—often medical in nature—used to reform colonial subjects (16–17). In a postcolonial and post–Cold War era, civilizing projects are extended and reworked in humanitarian projects focused on biological life and death (Hardt and Negri 2000, 313–14), or what Georgio Agamben (1998) called "bare life." Distinguishing contemporary humanitarianism from earlier forms, Fassin describes "humanitarian government" of the twentieth century's end, following the fall of the Berlin Wall, the rise of neoliberalism, and the "supremacy of the Western world" (2012, 14). Humanitarian government, he argues, directs "moral sentiments" toward the management, regulation, and support of the "poorest, most unfortunate, most vulnerable individuals" (1–3). Ticktin, likewise, distinguishes the object of current humanitarian compassion, the universal figure of "the morally legitimate suffering body," from the more politically and historically situated subjects of earlier movements, such as "the worker" or "the colonial militant" of the 1960s and '70s (2011, 11).

By historicizing humanitarianism and its objects, scholars denaturalize a hegemonic approach to human suffering that has shaped both domestic and foreign policies and programs worldwide, particularly from the twentieth century on. The moral sentiments and moral actions of humanitarianism—what Fassin (2012) calls "humanitarian reason"—have largely been oriented toward "immediate suffering, usually understood as bodily or psychological anguish" (Redfield and Bornstein 2011, 6). UNHCR and other organizations involved in refugee resettlement have prioritized people with medical conditions, survivors of torture, and people facing immediate threats in the country of asylum. The figure of the real refugee as recognized by international humanitarian organizations or governments is "free from desire, will, or agency" (Ticktin 2020; see also Malkki 2010). Thus, their need "requires evaluation and confirmation, being weighed in a moral balance that abhors any suggestion of fraud or corruption" (Redfield and Bornstein 2011, 13). As Ticktin writes, "valorizing refugees as innocent, vulnerable, naïve, and lacking responsibility for their circumstances, the category [of innocence] enables the criminalization of all those who want to change their circumstances, who see better lives and refuse to accept inequality or its accompanying forms of violence" (2020). Alleviating suffering amidst crisis situations, as opposed to orienting responses toward political solutions, justice, reparations, and long-term structural change, has come to appear self-evident and natural—a largely unquestioned moral good (Fassin 2012, 8).

Indeed, war, mass displacement, and natural disasters require life-saving interventions—the distribution food and water, medical care, evacuations of unsafe areas, and other humanitarian responses to urgent needs. Yet often, such responses rest on racialized, geopolitical hierarchies that structure who can demand political rights and solutions and who must rely on the whims of charity. Certain kinds of suffering are privileged, while others are deemed outside the domain of humanitarian concern. The "illness clause" in French asylum policy, for example, grants asylum to people with illnesses that can be treated in France, while people fleeing other kinds of unlivable conditions at home are deported (Ticktin 2011). As Ticktin asks, "Who gets to embody this paradoxically privileged position as the most disenfranchised, the most wretched of the earth, the most worthy of care?" (2011, 11–12). She answers that "one's suffering must be configured as a particular biological form with affective resonance—enough to compel moral action" (13).

If the individual suffering body is the primary object of compassion in contemporary neoliberal humanitarianism, what of the collective in which the individual is embedded, whose lived experiences are shared? Who fled their home with others? Who cares for and is cared for by kin—often beyond the biogenetic nuclear family? And what of those seeking political rights and solutions to statelessness, whether or not they are deemed "most vulnerable." For many living as refugees, distinct moral logics operate beyond the moral logic of international humanitarianism and at times conflict with and contradict humanitarianism's demand for the innocent individual of exceptional suffering. One such moral logic emphasizes mobility as a right rather than a privilege, as well as collective responsibilities.

Like humanitarianism, kinship is suffused with moral standards pertaining to what members of a family are expected to do for one another. Such obligations are especially evident when they are breached. In multiple African (and other) contexts, witchcraft accusations, for example, act as a "powerful leveling element . . . a constant reminder to overambitious leaders how dangerous it can be to disrespect the egalitarian ideology by refusing to share with their relatives" (Geschiere 2013, 41). As more people from throughout the African continent migrate to the global North, such "leveling elements" are also globalizing. People from African countries living in Europe and North America, Geschiere writes, anticipate "the telephone calls from home with their endless demands," demonstrating the "remarkable elasticity of kinship claims—bridging completely novel inequalities and distances" (22).

Other idioms and terms conjure the morality of sharing among kin. For example, writing on sex tourism in Kenya, Meiu writes about the "money of wrongdoings" that could "lose its polluting qualities" if "directed toward the good of the wider community—rather than consumed individually." In this context, elders compelled younger men who amassed wealth through sex work to "demonstrate their commitment to local values by sharing their wealth with others" (2017, 3–4). In sum, a powerful ethic of redistributing resources among kin and community prevails amidst changing economic and social realities. Refugee resettlement and the opportunities that it creates, including for making money, is part of this widespread moral framework.

For Somalis in particular, Islamic obligations of charity are central to "a profound commitment to sharing resources" (Abdi 2015, 97). Powerful and long-standing norms of familial obligation compel diasporans in the global North to send remittances. These norms involve the maintenance of "familial harmony," "dignity," the avoidance of "shame" and "disgrace," and pressure to alleviate "the disparity between the relative position of sender and recipient" (Lindley 2010, 129–31). The obligation to redistribute wealth among kin is part of a fundamental ethic and economic principle in the Somali community in Nairobi and beyond. Where there is a "commonly expressed view that hoarding capital is neither sensible nor moral, . . . there is a moral imperative to redistribute wealth" (Carrier 2016, 187). In addition to the important role of sending remittances in fulfilling this wider moral imperative, initiating

family sponsorship and helping to facilitate resettlement is a critical way, perhaps a more perfect way, to relieve the "novel inequalities" (Geschiere 2013, 22)
within the Somali and other African diasporas in a global age.

How a Bone Is Healed

Mohamed and I sit on the balcony at Hamdi, a Somali restaurant in downtown Nairobi, eating lunch. Mohamed recognizes some of the men at nearby
tables—political leaders from the Somali community. A blue-and-white
awning shades us from the afternoon sun as we look out at storefronts on a
quiet side street off Kenyatta Avenue. Mohamed is anxious about his alien
card, the government refugee ID, which he is trying to retrieve today. He needs
it immediately because he has been cleared by the Canadian government to
join his uncle in suburban Toronto. Only this one last document stands between him and authorization to leave Kenya. But the government employee he
was put in touch with by his old friend, Amina, who is now in the US, is not
returning his calls. So, we are eating *pilau*, anxiously waiting for the contact
to pick up his phone. Mohamed has barely left Eastleigh since the police occupied the neighborhood and began arresting people on the street. He is eager
to get back before dark.

Over the previous decade, Eastleigh had become a site of surveillance
and had been associated with people perceived as dangerous newcomers and
temporary residents. But Eastleigh has a long history, as do Somalis in Nairobi, who were there as early as the late 1890s—nearly the founding of the city
(Whittaker 2015, 122–23). The area of Eastleigh was established as a residential
neighborhood in the early twentieth century, designed for white settlers in
accordance with British "hygiene-related racial anxiety" of the nineteenth and
twentieth centuries (Carrier 2016, 29). Due to lack of road access to central
Nairobi, however, white settlers had no interest in the area, originally named
Nairobi East. By 1913, it was advertised as "an 'Asiatic' estate" (33). People from
South Asia, many of whom had come to Kenya around the turn of the century as merchants and laborers, eventually settled there.[1] In smaller numbers,
Somalis from British Somaliland also put down roots, having come to Kenya
as guides recruited by British explorers. Eastleigh has always been a "shifting
and super-diverse 'ethnoscape'" (Carrier 2016, 54), populated by migrants and
refugees from many parts of Kenya but also the African continent, the Indian
Ocean world, and beyond. Because of the early Somali presence, Somali-

Kenyans from the northeastern region settled in Eastleigh after independence, particularly following government policies that restricted pastoralist livelihoods in the 1980s (51). By the 1990s, when Somalis from the Republic of Somalia first started arriving—driven by the war and drawn by family, community, religious, and linguistic links—the neighborhood was emerging as a major Somali diasporan enclave. Its demographic makeup and religious and commercial landscape today mark it as a Somali place.

By the time Mohamed moved to Eastleigh in the early 2000s, it had become a major commercial center of Nairobi and of East Africa—in large part due to Somali entrepreneurs' business links between eastern Africa, the Middle East, and China (Carrier 2016). It was also becoming a target of anti-terror operations, which converged with anti-refugee and anti-Somali operations, increasingly in the wake of Kenya's military invasion of Somalia in 2011. When Mohamed and I sat at Hamdi in April 2014, police, including the paramilitary General Service Unit, had terrorized Eastleigh residents for over a month in a campaign of mass arrest and detention.

In the wake of Operation Usalama Watch, which began a matter of days after a directive was announced for all refugees to vacate cities and go to Kenya's UN-run camps, police extorted untold amounts of money from Eastleigh residents. People lived in fear of nightly raids on their homes; being stopped at random on the street; and the possibility of arrest, extortion, detention, and deportation to camps or to Somalia. Several months prior to the operation's official start, Mohamed had broken his leg on a street near his home during a police chase in his neighborhood. The police—known for their shoot-to-kill practice—sent bystanders running to avoid the fray. Mohamed had been among them and fell, badly injuring his leg—an injury likely made worse by a bone ailment he had had since birth and that had brought him to Kenya in the first place.

We finished eating. Mohamed looked agitatedly at his phone. I ordered coffee, trying to stay alert. I asked him how his older sister, Zamzam, felt about his leaving Kenya. He reminded me that the family had originally planned for her to be included in their process before she decided to return to Somalia with her husband. When they discovered Kismayo was too unsafe, they returned to Kenya, but by then it was too late to add them, as the paperwork had already been submitted for Mohamed, his cousin Ahmed, and Issa, the brother of his uncle's wife. "It's just missing," he said, brushing off the question. Of course, she will miss him, but that's the nature of life. People are stuck. People are on the move. Family sponsorship also separates families.

I have never met Zamzam, who now lives in Dadaab with her husband and children. Mohamed has told me that she treats him like a child, although he is in his twenties—"as if she gave birth to me!" Their mother became paralyzed when Mohamed was a young child. "If you saw her while she was sitting," he said, "you couldn't tell." She could use her arms and hands but not her legs. She had fallen into a well when Mohamed, the youngest of six brothers and one sister, was small. He was close with his mother—the baby of the family, always by her side. But Zamzam had helped raise him, especially after his mother's injury.

Mohamed had been born the year the war began, in a coastal village south of the port city of Kismayo. Throughout his childhood, as different factions fought over the city and the wider area, his family moved between Kismayo and their coastal home. As we wait at the restaurant to hear from the government official, Mohamed recalls the village he has not seen in more than a decade. Over the past month, the police have come to his door demanding identification. Strangers have called him "al-Shabaab" as a slur. Just weeks after our lunch at Hamdi, he would be arrested on the street by plainclothes police. In this environment, Mohamed says he dreams of eating fish and sleeping on the white sand beach of his village, where he could not be harassed or intimidated. In reality, though, this is only a dream. The Indian Ocean village of his childhood is not the place that he longs for, as he knows. His home region of Lower Juba had been devastated by violence for decades, most recently by al-Shabaab, US drone strikes, and the African Union Mission in Somalia (AMISOM). His village had been taken over by al-Shabaab, and in a matter of months, it would be the site of fighting between the militant group and US-backed AMISOM troops.

Mohamed had finished high school in Eastleigh in 2012. At the time, he had asked his uncle Ali in Canada, who had supported his education and living expenses for several years, to send him to university. Mohamed had been hoping to study biology and someday become a doctor. But his uncle, who supported a large number of family members in Kenya and Somalia, had broken down his monthly and yearly expenses, calculating that over 50 percent of his annual income went to family in Africa. University tuition for Mohamed was beyond his financial capacity, and anyway, he hoped Mohamed would be leaving Kenya soon.

For several years, Ali and his wife had been arranging to sponsor Ali's two nephews, Mohamed and Ahmed, and his wife's younger brother, Issa. Canadian citizens and permanent residents could sponsor any people documented as refugees, including family members beyond their nuclear families (Government of Canada 2023). Ali had submitted the paperwork in Canada in 2011, and in June 2012 the young men had gone to the Canadian embassy on Limuru Road, a few miles from their home in Eastleigh, to file their part of the application. Now, in April 2014, the young men had passed two interviews at the embassy and hoped to leave Kenya later that year.

Meeting Mohamed

In the summer of 2011, while studying Swahili in Mombasa, I had sent emails to several people listed on the UNHCR Kenya website. One, a resettlement caseworker from the US, agreed to meet me when I arrived in Nairobi a month later. When I returned the next year, she connected me with Amina, a Somali interpreter, who tutored me in Somali in the summer of 2012. We would meet downtown in the evening after she had finished working at UNHCR in Westlands for the day. She accepted my modest grad-student payment and extended her workday three nights a week to help me learn kinship terms, greetings, numbers, and so on. We would meet in an empty classroom at Mount Kenya University on Moi Avenue, where she had recently been a student, and became fast friends. Between my leaving Nairobi that August and returning one year later, Amina had been resettled—after many years of waiting—to the US, where she quickly started working for a local resettlement agency and later as a home health aide. I emailed her in August 2013 when I arrived to begin my long-term dissertation fieldwork; she replied that none of her former UNHCR colleagues had responded to her message about tutoring an American PhD student, but her friend Mohamed was willing. She nudged me a few days after her first email: "Did you get my email?" Copying Mohamed's phone number again, she wrote, "He's a good friend of mine."

Later that week, and only days before al-Shabaab's attack on the Westgate Shopping Mall on the other side of the city, Mohamed and I met at a restaurant near the apartment he shared with Ahmed and Issa. Ahmed and Issa, who had finished high school before him, were taking university classes. Issa was boarding at his campus and came back occasionally. Ahmed commuted to his school downtown but was busy studying and organizing a Somali youth association, which had a small space in an Eastleigh business. Many of Mohamed's high school classmates had scattered after graduation. The Kenyan citizens, many of whom had been boarders, returned to other parts of the city and country, some beginning university. Many of the Somalis with refugee status had left through resettlement and family sponsorship. A few had left on government-sponsored scholarships to China or Turkey to continue their studies. Some of the young women had married men in Europe or North America, and some had gone to neighboring countries to wait for resettlement processes—Ethiopia or Uganda, where they hoped the process would be faster. Others had married in Nairobi but were no longer "around," as Mohamed put it; they were at home, now wives and mothers with a new kind of all-consuming work. Others, like Ahmed and Issa, were continuing their studies. Mohamed, on the other hand, was "around," waiting for his process to come to fruition, with little organized to occupy him. He had a romantic interest, but she was busy finishing high school in a different neighborhood. This left him with time to help relatives and neighbors who needed assistance with their own resettlement and family sponsorship processes—translating documents, making phone calls, accompanying people who spoke neither Swahili nor English to various offices—and also time to hang around with a foreign anthropologist.

Growing up between his coastal village, a major Somali city, the Ugandan and Kenyan capitals, and shorter periods in Mombasa and the refugee camps, Mohamed had developed an eclectic and cosmopolitan worldview. He was passionate about the future of Somalia's peace and progress and had taken on, at least in discussions with me, the language of international rights around issues such as female circumcision, or FGM, and forced marriage. He occasionally submitted questions to be read on air on the journalist Julie Gichuru's program, *Africa Leadership Dialogues*. He attended events and talks to which I invited him on the other side of town at places like Amnesty International and the British Institute in Eastern Africa, while he invited me to organized events in Eastleigh.

Mohamed, Ahmed, and Issa were all well informed about Somali, Kenyan, and world politics and loved to debate. Mohamed and Issa were often at odds, with Ahmed mediating. "If Issa says this is a door, I will say it's a window!" Mohamed would proclaim, laughing about their constant disagreements. In the afternoon, when I would meet him for language lessons on the second-floor restaurant in Eastleigh, above shops selling clothes, perfume, and jewelry, Mohamed would often tell me that the three had been up all night debating. Whether it was Somali federalism and the best path for power sharing, the civil war in Syria, the banning of a book in Eastleigh shops, or various principles of Islamic law, through years of discussion, reading and watching the news, formal education, and listening to positions voiced at the mosque or in tea shops, the three were skilled in the art of argument. Issa, in particular, could talk at incredible length, boring his opponents into submission by using extraordinary levels of detail. "The professor," his friends called him teasingly.

When Mohamed broke his leg, I began coming to his house for Somali lessons, as the flights of concrete stairs in his apartment building and the crowded and uneven, often flooded streets were inaccessible on crutches. I started meeting his friends and neighbors, getting to know Ahmed and Issa, and listening to and participating in their conversations. Amidst a particularly lively round of debate, Mohamed would declare, "All we're lacking is the media!" pointing out that their discussions were worthy of circulation beyond the walls of the small apartment. His worldview had been shaped by his exposure to a wide range of people and places. Growing up relatively independently, in three countries, including in a village, four cities, and a refugee camp, he had many influences and a cultivated curiosity about the world. His transnational upbringing and the role of his diasporic family, as well as the constraints on his mobility, are paradigmatic of a global Somali diaspora and the workings of transnational kinship.

Leaving Somalia

Mohamed grew up during the civil war that began in 1991, though almost never spoke to me about the war in the context of his own life. Once, he shared a story about an uncle who was murdered in front of his son, who later went crazy. Another time he explained that one of his brothers had been shot and killed. But he did not contextualize these events in relation to the political dynamics of the war, except in the most general way. When I once asked him why he was surprised when he saw a Kenyan soldier for the first time—hadn't he seen soldiers in Somalia?—he said that everyone in Somalia had a gun, but they were not dressed in uniform. As Kapteijns writes, "even the *concept* of civilian noncombatant had been completely abandoned by all sides" early in the civil war (2013, 179). The insecurity of the war was the condition of everyday life from the time he was born but was not a common topic of conversation among young Somalis living in Nairobi.

As a young child, Mohamed sometimes heard the name Nairobi. His uncle Abdiqani, his cousin Ahmed's father, who worked for an international organization, occasionally went to Nairobi for work. At the time, as a young boy educated at a madrasa, he was unaware that Nairobi was in a different country, where people spoke different languages and practiced different religions. He was familiar with the city's name only as another place within a known realm. When Mohamed was ten, his family decided that his uncle Abdiqani would bring him to Nairobi to seek medical treatment for the bone problem that he had had since birth. When I recorded Mohamed in 2014 at my apartment in Pangani, he told the story this way:

> Just a week before my departure is when dad told me that Abdiqani was coming, and we'll be going to Nairobi. And the Nairobi I have in mind is like, I don't even know if it looks like the sky. I just used to hear, "Oh, Abdiqani is in Nairobi, Abdiqani is in Nairobi." I never even knew if it was part of Somalia, or whether it was anywhere else. We traveled. I remember it was morning. Very early in the morning. We never passed Kismayo. It was my first time to travel with a car.

"Had you traveled by bus before, or never a vehicle?"

"[Only] by boat," he said, his eyes narrowing.

> It was my first time to travel by car. It was very unusual to me. . . . The road was *so* rough. Then I vomited very badly. We were four. One was the driver, the uncle, I, and one was a soldier. There's no peace in the country, so if there is something, maybe a roadblock, we needed someone. Then we traveled, we traveled, we came to a place called Badhaadhe. It's part of Somalia. We rested there. My clothes had to be washed. We had to rest there. Have lunch.

Mohamed snapped his fingers, emphasizing their onward motion.

> We departed again. At six evening we were at the border of Kenya. This place is called Hulugho. Then Hulugho, what I remember was that the guy [soldier] was carrying a gun—in any case, to defend us. Then what they did, they had to bury the gun somewhere before we reached—a very short distance from the border, we buried the gun somewhere, so the Kenyans don't catch us with that. So, then we entered the border as civilians. Then the Kenyan soldiers came. For me, I'm very young, [but] they asked some questions to the uncle. For me I was wondering, this looked like a movie to me. The other thing that really made me wonder was when I saw the Kenyans. Because I believed that all the people that exist around the world are only Somalis. . . . We talked, they talked, everything was okay, we entered.
>
> In Hulugho, we stayed with someone who the uncle knew. I started asking some questions: "Uncle, who are these guys?" He told me, "We're in Kenya." I said, "Kenya?" "Yeah." Then I just kept quiet, still having some questions, like "What is Kenya?" but I couldn't ask far more. I just kept quiet, kept quiet. Then later I asked, "Who are these guys?" He said, "These are Kenyans." I said, "I have never seen people looking like this." He laughed. He said, "Oh, you'll see them more."
>
> In the morning, again we [left for] Garissa. At around four, we came to

Garissa. In Garissa, things were normal. It just looked like Somalia.[2] . . . We had a hotel. Then the hotel had a balcony. I stood there. I started watching the city. Cars were moving, very busily. Then I asked, "What are these cars moving like this?" He said, "This country is very peaceful. People are just running their duties." "Oh," I said, "Okay. I see."

Mohamed snapped his fingers again.

In the morning again, we had to travel to Nairobi. That's when I realized that now we're in a different world. Completely. Everywhere I look, I don't see the people I knew, the faces. Now things look very different. I'm wondering! So many questions now in my mind. In Nairobi, I remember some cousins came to see me: the son of So-and-So. They only know [my] dad, but no one knows me. "The son of So-and-So was brought for medical," [they said].

Mohamed was taken to Kijabe Hospital, where he would stay for a week. Following his hospital stay, he and his uncle stayed in a hostel in Eastleigh for several months. About six months after his treatment, his uncle had to leave for work, traveling to Mombasa, Tanzania, and Uganda, while Mohamed was left in the care of others.

Before, his aim was for me to be treated in Nairobi and then sent back to Somalia. When he went to Uganda, he decided that I and his son should go for studies. He liked it there. Then he came back and asked me, "Mohamed, do you want to go back to Somalia?" I said, "Yes!" I was missing the family so much. . . . Then he started discussing with the young aunt [in Seattle]: "How do you see if I bring Ahmed, and Mohamed is already here, and they go together for studies?" She said, "It's very good." For him, he had the idea, but financing was these people who were outside [of Africa]. He couldn't just make his own decisions because he was not someone who could just be around all the time—he was traveling. He had to inform these people so they can at least know where we are. He was like, "What could this young boy be doing in a country that is so violent?" Everyone's carrying a gun. Even people of my age were carrying a gun. So, he said, "Let him be at least safe from that." Later on he told me, "You're not going back. You'll go to school." Then the preparation of bringing Ahmed started.

With no end in sight to the insecurity at home, Abdiqani brought Mohamed and Ahmed to Uganda's capital, Kampala, where they lived with the family of a Somali man who drove a commercial truck that Abdiqani owned. He hired a Ugandan tutor to teach the boys English for three months until they had enough basic skills to begin school. While the truck driver was on the road, his young wife looked after the two boys. Mohamed described the relationship as one of frequent conflict. The boys were stubborn and noisy, and she had no control over them. Furious one day, she threatened to poison them. After that, they refused to eat the food that she cooked, and over time, they left the house altogether and lived on their own. They ate at the small restaurant of an elderly Somali woman, to whom Abdiqani sent money for their meals and other necessities. He sent their school fees to a sheikh he knew and trusted. The boys made friends with their schoolmates and quickly learned both Luganda and English. They became close friends with their Somali and Ugandan peers. Without the oversight of their parents or close relatives, perhaps they experienced the world around them with fewer boundaries.

A Family Matter

Abdiqani has six siblings. He is actually Mohamed's cousin; their fathers are brothers. But Mohamed, the last born of his family, is a year younger than Ahmed, who is the firstborn of Abdiqani's children, so he calls Abdiqani "Uncle" on account of their age difference. Mohamed's parents and their siblings all remain in Somalia. But Abdiqani's siblings are spread out all over the world, from Seattle to Stockholm to Toronto. Only Abdiqani remains on the continent, working for an NGO and traveling between Somalia and various parts of East Africa. Abdiqani and his siblings were planning for Mohamed and Ahmed to leave, too. They should go abroad where they could support themselves and carry on the obligation to assist relatives back home. Their family abroad could not sustain them forever. It would eventually be up to them, two capable and educated young people, to sustain others.

Over the years that Mohamed and Ahmed lived in Kampala, several plans were raised and abandoned. When they were still young, the family had considered sending them to the US as if they were the sons of the truck driver and his wife, who had a resettlement case. Ultimately, their family was uncomfortable with them going to the US at such a young age. They should stay among the Somali community, where their cultural and religious values could be molded. About seven years after they first arrived in Kampala, another uncle—one of Abdiqani's younger brothers who was living in Europe—traveled to Nairobi to marry. Their aunt in Seattle, a mother of five with a powerful voice in family decisions, had never been comfortable with the two boys living so independently in Kampala.

"I got a call one day at school," Mohamed said. "It was the aunt. She told me, 'Pack your things. You're going to Nairobi.'"

The boys finished the school year and traveled to Kenya. Mohamed had not been there since he had left the hostel in Eastleigh where he had recovered from his treatment at Kijabe Hospital seven years before. That was a different lifetime—before they had gone to school, before they had learned to speak and think in two other languages, and before Mohamed's mother had passed away in Somalia. He had not seen her since his journey to Kenya as a ten-year-old boy. The trip that had been planned to be a matter of months had turned into years.

By the time they left Uganda, Mohamed's Luganda was so good that he could practically pass as a Ugandan boy, telling the border guards on his way out of the country that he was just visiting Kenya on holiday. His Luganda was so good, he would say proudly, that when he met Ugandans in Eastleigh, they insisted that he must have a Ugandan mother. He shocked them by telling them which part of Uganda they came from by listening to their accents, and he made friends with the Ugandan ladies who worked in people's homes and in small restaurants around Eastleigh. Swahili became his next language to master, and he delighted and took refuge in his ability to get along with people through his knowledge of languages and the realities they encompassed.

Now in Nairobi, Mohamed and Ahmed moved in with their young uncle and his new wife. But the teenagers had become accustomed to living on their own and struggled to take orders from their new guardian, who they saw as more of a peer than their senior. After several months, they told their relatives at the command centers in North America that they could no longer live with the uncle. Mohamed recalled: "Then the aunt in Seattle and the uncle in Canada decided for us that we should go to the camps. They told us, 'You know, go to the camps, we're doing some programs for you guys. It is easier for someone to come [to North America] from the camps.' Then we were interested in going to Canada. They told us that it's just a matter of two months. But two months turned into eight months. I had never been to the camps before."

"What did you think the camps would be like before you went there?" I asked.

Mohamed answered:

The camp, the word *camp*, the camp—the word we use in the Somali language gives you an explanation that that place is not good. *Xerada* is like "camp," refugee camps, so *xerada* is like "fence," so you're in a prison which has an open roof.[3] You see? So, you can understand. We arrived there. We had relatives there. We lived with them a couple of weeks. Then my sister came. Then, when the sister came, we lived with her. They [she and her husband] were supposed to be part of the program to be taken to Canada, but because the process was taking so long, they couldn't wait. They moved back to Kismayo. That was when I saw my sister after eight years. When we came, we went to the UN to register ourselves. We got the ration card number; we were fully registered.[4] Then my sister and her husband moved back to Kismayo. Then we remained there, both of us, I and Ahmed there, in that same house. *Alone.* Again. Then later on we decided we'd leave. We called Ahmed's dad. We said, "We cannot be here anymore." They told us we had to stay, but later on they agreed.

"So, day to day, you woke up and what did you do?" I asked.

"You woke up and just walked around. There was nothing to do. *Nothing* to do. You fetch water. You fetch water. You fetch water, go and collect firewood. Yeah. That's a life which we were not used to. The temperature is like forty degrees Celsius. You drink like a whole jerry can of water in an hour. We even got sick! Very demoralized to be in the camps."

"Sick like how?"

"Mentally, disappointed. We *couldn't* be there. You lose appetite, cannot eat, you don't even talk. You're just depressed."

Returning to Nairobi, the boys insisted they live on their own. "We never wanted anyone directing us. We just wanted a free life," Mohamed explained.

Ahmed's father refused, but Ali, their younger uncle in Canada, agreed to take on their living and schooling expenses. From near and far, Abdiqani, Uncle Ali, and their siblings weighed in on the boys' lives. Their aunt in Seattle wanted them to attend a boarding school outside Nairobi, a common practice even for the working class in Kenya. But they refused and enrolled at Eastleigh High School, a short walk from the room they rented. Now formally registered as refugees, Mohamed and Ahmed knew the goal was to leave Kenya, though Mohamed would spend the next six years there, and Ahmed seven.

While in Nairobi, several ideas about leaving the country percolated within the family. Someone suggested they go to Egypt. Another had a plan to bring them to Sweden. But none of these ultimately came to fruition. Although the goal of having Mohamed and Ahmed access resettlement from the Dadaab camps had not panned out, a new idea emerged at the time Ahmed was finishing high school. Mohamed recalled:

When Ahmed finished, he was supposed to go to China for university, to do medical [training]. Then Ali called [from Canada] and said, "Calculate, make the budget and see." When we did, it was very expensive for the uncle to pay for that. This is when the process was arising. Then [Ali] said, "Instead of now doing this, if Ahmed goes to China, he needs accommodations for himself. Mohamed is again finishing next year, and he cannot just be around here. He has to go somewhere, too. And this money, I cannot afford." Then he said, "What if I sponsor them so they come to Canada and start university here? With loans, there are so many ways." Ahmed's dad said, "That can be very good if you do that." That is how the process of Canada started.

In this conversation and many others, Mohamed narrated his life through stories about the ways in which his relatives from around the world had shaped his journey. Mohamed's parents could not provide safety, medical care, or education in Somalia or outside. But Abdiqani and the flock of aunts and uncles spread throughout the world had taken Mohamed's future into their hands. Their investment in Mohamed and Ahmed—through the boys' education and eventually bringing them to Canada—was part of fulfilling their obligations as the members of a family who were capable of assisting their kin. They were also investing in the future: Mohamed, Ahmed, and Issa would be the next generation to continue assisting others. In this way, sponsorship was also a means of spreading the responsibility to support those in Africa who had less means of securing a livelihood. Mohamed's life embodied fulfilling the moral obligation to distribute both opportunities and responsibilities in order to uplift many. Resettlement, family reunification, and sponsorship programs were treated as valuable resources in fulfilling these moral duties.

A Broken Bone, Unhealed

On an evening at the end of April 2014, as the Kenyan police and paramilitary General Service Unit were deployed to Eastleigh under the banner of Operation Usalama Watch, Ibrahim was stopped by soldiers on his way home from class. I had known Ibrahim for six months or so; he was a young man who had grown up in the Dadaab camps and now went to university in Nairobi and worked with me as a research assistant. The firstborn in his family, he was a leader, an organizer, and an observant Muslim. He was ambitious, with a senator's smile. Having stopped downtown for a cup of tea on his way home that evening, he was returning late, past when most people in Eastleigh had locked their doors for the night, praying not to be awakened by police. Ibrahim was scrupulous and principled and refused to give a bribe to avoid arrest. He was taken to jail in Pangani and later deported to the Dadaab camps, where his parents and siblings still lived. With NGO connections and university student status, he managed to return a couple of weeks later. But it involved much hand-wringing and anxious communication among his friends in Nairobi and strategic negotiating on his part, as he raced the clock to return to the city in time for his midterm exams.

While being held at Pangani Police Station, Ibrahim befriended a young mother named Ayaan. Later, they were both transferred to Kasarani Stadium, the sports arena being used as a detention facility during the operation, and then to Gigiri Police Station near the US embassy. In Gigiri, where there were separate cells for women and men, Ibrahim was held with seventeen others in a cell so crowded that, while sleeping, you couldn't even turn your body from one side to the other. From there, Ibrahim was deported to Dadaab, where he stayed with his family. When he left Gigiri, Ayaan was very ill—in a critical situation, as he put it. Returning to Gigiri after coming back from Dadaab, he asked a police officer about Ayaan. "Amekufa" (she died), he told him. "We had accepted that Ayaan has died. Because she was very critical, in a coma," he said, gesturing to Ayaan, now seated next to him. "So when I saw her— actually it was she who called to me—I was passing here on the street, I said, 'Is that Ayaan?' I was shocked!"

When I saw Ibrahim about a month after his arrest and deportation to Dadaab, he was very much the same young man—pious, idealistic, smiling; slender, bespectacled, in pressed pants and a button-down shirt. But when Ibrahim introduced me to Ayaan, taking tea on the rooftop of the hostel where he rented a room, I could see how he had passed through something life altering. "It's strange to see someone you met in there outside," he commented in a rare, introspective moment, referring to his days in detention. "In there, we became like family. We would eat from one plate. When there was no plate, we would eat from a big piece of plastic." Ayaan nodded in agreement.

Ibrahim's time in the overcrowded jail cells of Nairobi and then in a mass detention center had led him into community with people who had not been family before. Ayaan had lived a difficult life. She left Somalia in 1991, at age seven, and ended up in the Kakuma camp with her mother and siblings. Her father, who went to Nairobi with a different wife and children, called her mother to bring the children to the city when he became ill. When he died soon after, conflict ensued between the two families. At a young age, Ayaan became responsible for her three sisters. The death of her father, the conflict between his two wives and their children, had resulted in the end of any kind of childhood, and all four girls were vulnerable to abuse and exploitation as Ayaan tried to make ends meet and keep a roof over their heads.

If the moral demands of kinship among Somalis living as refugees draw upon resettlement and family sponsorship programs to promote the distribution of resources, opportunities, and responsibilities, kinship, nevertheless, is not uncomplicatedly good or altruistic. And while the real flexibility of kinship arrangements in this context enables life-saving care and support—material, psychological, and otherwise—this fact does not preclude exploitation and violence in the domain of the family (Collier, Rosaldo, and Yanagisako 1997).

Mohamed's kin had the resources to access humanitarian and immigration programs to support young family members and ultimately enable them to support others. The following story, by contrast, demonstrates the ways in which those cut off from kin networks, particularly women, can be disempowered from making use of humanitarian resources and migration opportunities. The woman about whom I write next highlights the power of kinship through its absence and its violence.

Meeting Fardowsa

After meeting Ayaan, we made our way down from the rooftop of Ibrahim's hostel—a peaceful spot away from the fray, where laundry is hanging and young men come for prayer or to catch a bit of news or football on the small TV in a kiosk that sells tea. We exited the building on Ninth Street, making our way toward Second Avenue, flanked by tables with faded umbrellas shading clothes, shoes, fruits and vegetables, snacks. Behind them, four- and five-story concrete buildings house apartments, shops, restaurants, pharmacies, and other businesses—a contrast from the newer, shinier shopping centers and hotels around First Avenue. On Ibrahim's block, people sat along the street, selling tea, chewing khat. A woman typically dressed in a black *jilbaab* that covered her from head to ankle stuck her arm out of a ground-floor window across the street. Ayaan and the woman called to each other.

"She's my friend. From Kakuma," Ayaan explained.

Fardowsa burst out of the building, crossing the street diagonally to meet us, waving her hand above her head.

"The people you find there, you find here," Ayaan said, remarking on the movement of people between the camps and the capital.

Fardowsa's teeth were stained, maybe from khat. The ends of her fingernails were dyed orange with henna, which must have been done some months before, leaving white half-moons at the base of her nails. She wore one gold bangle and a watch, along with a gold ring. Her voice was soft and gravelly. Ayaan wanted us to go to Fardowsa's apartment, where Ayaan introduced me to the man sitting in the entryway. (Most buildings in Eastleigh have someone on duty to see who is coming and going.) Standing in the hallway, Fardowsa told me something about her daughter's leg injury and her husband, who had changed his name, but I didn't fully understand, and we arranged to meet soon.

Over the next months, I met with Fardowsa periodically, first with Ibrahim on his hostel's quiet rooftop. When she began to explain her problems to us, her eyes were glassy and her mouth shook. Later, I accompanied her to UNCHR, RCK, the Hebrew Immigrant Aid Society (HIAS), and other offices, trying to find resources for her many problems. Once in a while, I went to her home—first, a place where she was shut in by her former in-laws, who paid the rent but refused to pay the small expenses required for her children to go to school—for books, uniforms, and so on. She was there with five children, day and night. "They are trying to make us crazy," she said of her ex-husband's family. Later, after conflict escalated between her and the in-laws, I visited her in a new apartment—a room with a bed and two mattresses on the floor for her children and a small TV playing cartoons. Knowing her situation, a neighbor downstairs contributed money for her rent and entreated their landlady not to throw her out. Fardowsa showed me places in Eastleigh, as well, like the office where UNHCR ID numbers were posted each week for resettlement counseling.

Like Ayaan, Fardowsa was a child when the dictatorial regime of Siyaad Barre—a regime supported by US funds—was overthrown in 1991 (Besteman 2020, 4). Born in Mogadishu in 1982, Fardowsa was nine when warring factions began raping and murdering communities imagined to have benefited from Barre's rule and others they could simply take advantage of (Kapteijns 2013). She had moved from Mogadishu to Kismayo, to Afmadow, to Nairobi, to Kakuma, and back to Nairobi, where I met her in 2014. Her situation exemplified the ways in which people displaced by violent conflict vacillate between immobility and flight. While Mohamed's moves were primarily compelled by the pursuit of safety and things destroyed by the war, like medical care or education, Fardowsa's were motivated by the immediate threat of death and unremitting abuse. In 2009, in the Kakuma refugee camp, she and her family had been identified by UNCHR for resettlement, and their case had been referred to the United States. After completing several interviews, however, conflict with her husband caused her golden ticket to go up in smoke.

The Absence of Kin

In 2015, I interviewed Fardowsa, together with Ayaan, in the room where she lived at the time on Twelfth Street in Eastleigh. Her five children were also there, including the young daughter, Star, with the leg injury, caused when her in-laws pushed her from a window. I typically did not record people in Eastleigh because of widespread anxiety amidst a surveilled community, but Fardowsa welcomed being recorded. The only people to do so, Fardowsa and Ayaan requested that if I ever write about them, I use their real names, which I have. As I hit Record on my small digital recorder, Fardowsa waited for me to wrap up my introductory spiel describing my project and the purpose of recording. "Is that it? Are you done?" she asked when I finished. The rhythm slows and the tone shifts on the recording as I stopped talking and she began. A beat passed as Fardowsa took a breath.

"Me, I'm alone," she began.

I came here. I don't have a father or a mother. I'm alone. I don't have another family. Now . . . I don't want to remember . . . my family. I'm alone. Because I was in school when the war came. So, everyone ran. Even my family. Everyone went. The teacher told the students not to go outside. The war was heavy in my family's area. Every family ran. So, when I finally reached home, my whole family, all my neighbors—there was no one. My father was living in a different area at that time. My mother had fled. Me and another girl and a boy, when we reached the place, we saw that everyone had left. We went to our neighbor— another mother. She helped us. That mother took us up to Kismayo. I told her I had lost my family. She said, "I know you. I know your family. Come with my children."

Because the war was coming up to Kismayo, people were going to Ras Kamboni and to Mombasa by boat. People were screaming, "Get in, get in!" They were loading children in. The mom and her mom, who was blind, me, and the older daughter, we were standing on one side. The father said, "First take these [other] children." Then they would take us next. There were guns everywhere. And the boat just took off. So, me and the mother and her mother and the daughter, we returned to Kismayo. We stayed two weeks . . . no, one week. After one week, the mother heard that the boat had crashed. Her husband, her children had all died. So, the mother, her daughter, and her mother were left. And me. When the mother heard about her children, she lost her mind. Now it was her, her blind mother, and her daughter. There was no possibility to look after me. After the mother lost her mind, her stepfather came to take them all. I was left behind with neighbors. I lived there with the neighbors. I stayed there until I was grown.

Left with strangers, Fardowsa was raped by one of the sons in the household and eventually gave birth to a daughter and then a son. She stayed in that house for over a decade with her attacker's mother and sisters, enduring abuse and later taking care of two babies. Years after she was taken there, they went to Afmadow. Fardowsa explained, "I didn't have a family. I didn't have a mother. I didn't have a father. I didn't have a family. Then that man, he married a different girl. He left. There was nothing. [In Afmadow], there were some neighbors. Every day I was beaten. Those neighbors gave me a little money, and they took me along with them to Nairobi."

In Nairobi, Fardowsa searched for relatives but found none. "I had no mother. I had no father. I had no one to protect me. Up until this moment. I have no one. This is how my life has gone," she said.

The people who had taken her in told her, "Your people, they're not here. You're a mom with kids, and we don't have money. We have a guy of ours who can marry you and will take you to the refugee camps."

"So," Fardowsa said, "I was taken to Kakuma."

After marrying, Fardowsa gave birth to three more children, and after four years or so of living in Kakuma, the family was selected by UNHCR for resettlement. UNHCR referred their case to the United States. They finished interviews at RSC, and their case was presented to USCIS—the final stage of government vetting. However, around that time, Fardowsa's husband divorced her. He decided he did not want to be resettled with Fardowsa and the children. Instead of continuing with their resettlement case as a family, he leapt at a different opportunity. Though he had always maintained that his mother was dead, he now told Fardowsa that she was living in the United States and would be sponsoring him through a family reunification process without her. He planned to bring two of her older children, one of whom was his biological child and one of whom was not. Fardowsa was baffled.

> At the time we married, even to the UN, even to JVA, he told everyone, "My mother died." He said, "And my father died." When he came to JVA, he said, "My mother's friend is in America." But then he changed it to being his mother. To the UN, he said, "I have no mother." To JVA, he said, "I have no mother." To INS [USCIS] he said, "I have no mother." But then, he changed it. He said to INS, "I have my mother in America." When they asked the name of his mother, he said the name he had given of his mother's friend. They put that in the computer. Now, he finished INS, he said, "This is not my name."

Fardowsa's ex-husband was being sponsored by his mother under a different name—his real name. The name she had known him by, the name on his documents, the name that had been recorded for their resettlement case was not his real name, he maintained. His real name was the one his mother was using to sponsor him.

"Why did he have a different name?" I asked.

"I don't know," Fardowsa replied. "From the time I married him, from the time I had the children, his name was [full name]. Then he told me, 'My name isn't my name. My mother is in America. And me and my mother don't want to bring you.'"

Because Fardowsa's husband revealed he had a different name and identity, their resettlement case was stopped. Ayaan and Fardowsa maintained that DNA had confirmed that the woman in the US sponsoring him was indeed his mother.

"He started to hate her. That's why he changed everything," Ayaan said.

"Because he left me. You know, I have no family," Fardowsa added.

"Like a bastard. You have no father. You have no family. So people—they take advantage of that," Ayaan said.

Fardowsa filed a Request for Reconsideration (RFR) regarding the case. She received the following reply from RSC Africa / the US Refugee Admissions Program in 2013:

> Thank you for your inquiry regarding the above mentioned case. An update is provided below. We acknowledge receipt of your letter. The RFR response is attached. Please note that we will not send you any further response since your case has been closed and RSC Africa will not take further action.

The attached letter from USCIS, under US Homeland Security, stated:

> Subject: Rejected RFR
>
> Please note that we have rejected this RFR because it was submitted by Fardowsa [last names], the spouse on the case and not from the PA, [full name].

Because her husband had been the primary applicant (PA) on the case, and Fardowsa and her children dependents, she was not authorized to appeal the decision.

With their resettlement case cancelled and his sponsorship case with his mother in the United States beginning, Fardowsa's ex-husband took off with the two children he planned to take with him so that he could attend to the business of the case from Nairobi. It was a friend of his who informed Fardowsa where he had gone with her children. Although she tried to report the kidnapping to UNHCR in Kakuma, she said that waiting for their response would take too long. She headed for Nairobi herself.

"And you brought the other kids?" I asked.

"Yeah. I couldn't leave them. I have no one to leave them with. I have no family," Fardowsa replied. Once in Nairobi, she said, "I looked, I looked, I looked. Finally, I found them."

Her ex-husband was furious that she had come. Fardowsa asked her daughter to repeat what her father had said to her. The young girl replied matter-of-factly in her small voice, "Leave me alone. I'm not your father, and your mother is a dog. And don't call me your father again."

"Mama yako ni mbwa. Takaka" (Your mother is a dog. Trash), Fardowsa repeated in Swahili, her voice shaking. Her eyes filled with tears, and she wiped them with a pale yellow scarf that was draped over her head.

By the time she arrived in Nairobi, her husband was moving along in the sponsorship process. Complications surrounding his two names had arisen because of his child's birth certificate, where his recorded name was different from the one recorded on his new case. But somehow, he seemed to have moved beyond that hurdle by paying bribes to people who doctored documents, Ayaan claimed. Meanwhile, UNHCR—involved at the child-protection level—was asking Fardowsa if she would sign for her children to leave the country with her ex-husband. In a different conversation, I asked Fardowsa what she planned to do.

Tears ran down her face, "I have no choice. I can't provide anything for my children. But he's gone about it in a bad way. Forcing me. Not asking me. If he'd gone about it differently . . ."

Back in her apartment, she continued to remark on her disconnection from networks that could have helped her. "Me, I'm alone. Me, I'm alone. And UNHCR doesn't know me. You die useless. They don't know me. Maybe one day I'll be helped. Maybe one day I'll be helped by UNHCR. If they see all my problems, if they see all my issues, they'd have to help me and my kids. My first future was spoiled. And then again, the next one was also spoiled," she said, referring to the loss of her mother and father and then her marriage and the abrupt disruption of her long-awaited resettlement case. "He knows there are no people or family who can help me and support me, to talk to him and say, 'Why are you doing this to her?'"

Fardowsa began narrating her life not at her birth or her arrival in Kenya or any other point in time, but at the moment she was separated from her parents, which left her vulnerable to exploitation and abuse that stalked her through life. The protective power of kinship was a present absence—something she thought about, discussed, and grieved. She felt its absence acutely when her "own" people were not able to intervene on her behalf, when strangers or in-laws abused and mistreated her. She was kin poor. By contrast, Mohamed, though he had been separated from his parents and siblings for years, was kin rich. Even Fardowsa's ability to access humanitarian programs—programs that sought to assist especially vulnerable people like her—was hampered by exclusion from the kinship networks that often helped facilitate resettlement, after her husband divorced her and pursued migration through a different avenue, leaving her behind.

Fardowsa's experience reflects that often in Somali society "a married woman (always known by her maiden name) retains her natal lineage affiliation and is still, after marriage, regarded as a member of that lineage." Throughout life after marriage, agnatic kin (that is, kin of the woman's natal family) "are very much concerned with her well-being," rooted in the fact that historically, "marriage is . . . an insecure relationship in comparison with the binding and irrevocable character of agnatic affiliation" (Lewis 1994, 61; see also Lowe 2019, 195). But Fardowsa's kinship network was destroyed by a war. Fardowsa spoke to the power of ties with agnatic kin (through their absence) when she and Ayaan described her as a "bastard," a term they used in English to indicate the value judgment placed on being parentless. Had Fardowsa been adopted by either kin or non-kin, as many were during the civil war, she might have had a different fate. Instead, being raped by the people who took her in, she became not an agnate (like a daughter) but an affine (like an in-law, through the birth of her children) of the most violated kind.

After we first met, Fardowsa and I took her daughter Star to UNHCR to try to get a referral for medical assistance for the leg injury that had not healed. Star could not walk, and the pain kept her up at night. Fardowsa prevailed, instinctively and skillfully employing my presence to her advantage. The following week Star was transferred to Kijabe hospital, where Mohamed and his bone ailment had been treated a decade before. Two injured legs, two Somali patients at a missionary hospital outside Nairobi: One person, Mohamed, for whom the moral obligations of kinship, tied to gender and class, provided an advantage, starting with his departure from Somalia's civil war for medical treatment. For the other, Star, gender and dislocation from kin disempowered her and her mother, Fardowsa. Fardowsa's comments on the absence of kin in her life highlighted kinship's work. Mohamed's successful sponsorship to Canada and Fardowsa's inability to leave Kenya illuminate how the moral ideals of kinship intersect with global humanitarian and immigration programs and how kinship norms and their moral scripts make use of such resources—to the benefit of some and not others.

Still, Fardowsa's existing kin—namely, her children—were valuable on many levels. "My family are my children," she said. Somali women in Eastleigh value bearing many children. This value is rooted in long-standing notions of womanhood but also as part of a strategy for onward migration, as Lowe (2019) argues, and for benefiting from adult children's remittances. In a context in which many are separated from their families of birth, there are new pressures for women to bear children in order to secure their marriages and a place with their husband's kin (Lowe 2019). Though their loss was devastating, Fardowsa reasoned that if she allowed her ex-husband to take two of her children to the United States, they would someday be able to support her and their siblings. Ultimately, he did take the two children, and they settled in a large Somali community. When I spoke to Fardowsa at the end of 2023, she and the other children were still in Nairobi. Star, whose leg did finally heal, had turned fifteen. Ayaan had gone to Kampala, and Fardowsa heard that she had a resettlement process there. Fardowsa still had none.

Family Obligation and Moral Redistribution

Kinship facilitates access to resettlement and sponsorship programs, as Fardowsa and Mohamed show. Sponsorship, through family reunification programs or otherwise facilitating resettlement, is embedded in cultural ideas about the morality of familial obligation and the ills of inequality in a world of growing disparity. Sowdo, a sharp young woman who grew up in Kakuma and was now finishing high school in Nairobi, clearly articulated this ethic of redistribution, describing an aunt in Norway who sent money to her sister and niece but refused to sponsor them. Sowdo described the aunt's assistance as morally unacceptable, contrasting it with how she helped her brother in Somalia:

> Every month I send money, and I tell him, "How are you doing? How's your life? Is everything good?" That's helping, and the person I'm helping will feel

good. [He'll say], "At the end of the day, I have my sister. I don't need anybody."
But what if I send the money and the month is about to be over, and she [the
aunt in Norway] doesn't even ask how they are? There are some people when
they get money, they help more people. They give them jobs. They change the
lives of many. And some, they want to *rule* the lives of many. What if she sponsored her sister to Norway? [Then] she wouldn't be needed. Her sister would
get a good job, would get a house. She would be an individual. That's what
she doesn't want. She wants people to say, "Oh, Khadija helps her sister every
day." . . . You know, if she was a good sister, she could have sponsored her sister.
To Norway, to live a life just like her. You know, be an individual, instead of
sending money to her.

Sowdo's remarks reveal notions of good and bad assistance, good and bad
relatives, and the role of sponsorship or otherwise facilitating resettlement.
She distinguished between assistance that creates a patron-client hierarchy
and assistance that raises the person being assisted to a level where they are "an
individual." They know they have someone on whom they can rely or can rely
on themselves. In her account of the way that she sends money to her brother
each month, her generosity and investment in their relationship alleviates a
sense of bad dependence. Her brother can say, "I have my sister. I don't need
anybody." By contrast, her aunt in Norway maintains control over her sister
and niece through her financial support and produces dependence that she
could alleviate if she chose to, or so Sowdo imagines. So the moral logic goes,
the aunt's financial support without sponsorship (or emotional care) benefits
her pride and reputation but denies her sister substantial life improvement.

Somali discourses around wealth and inequality in the age of resettlement are suffused with moral claims about obligations of those with resources
and opportunities to spread them to others. These norms of obligation run
alongside and sometimes run into the moral ethos of a securitized humanitarianism oriented around bureaucratic rule-following and aid to the most
vulnerable. In 1990, 850,000 Somalis lived outside the Republic of Somalia,
the majority in three neighboring countries with indigenous Somali populations: Kenya, Ethiopia, and Djibouti. As of 2015, that number had increased by
136 percent, with two million Somalis residing outside the country, nearly a
quarter of whom were living in Europe and North America (Connor and Krogstad 2016). Decades of civil war have created a global diaspora with both real
and imagined material inequalities between people living in Somalia, those
in neighboring countries, and those living with greater material resources in
the global North (even though material differences are often imagined to be
greater than they are) (see chapter 5; Abdi 2015; Besteman 2016).

In the context of global inequality amplified by social media and the internet, as well as music, film, and TV, prioritizing assisting kin and other community members ignores the distinctions that humanitarian institutions impose between those deemed worthy and unworthy. Assisting kin, even if it subverts or collides with bureaucratic regulations, is a refusal of one moral framework and the insistence on abiding by a more familiar ethic, whose pull emanates from more intimate sources, as in the case of Sadiya at the beginning of this chapter, brought to Australia as if she were her cousin's wife.

Many people documented as refugees in Kenya seek to access migration opportunities in ways that fit with long-standing moral codes. They seek out stability and mobility, not waiting to be rescued but rather using humanitarian programs as a scaffold upon which to maintain kin relations, rebuild communities, and disperse resources across national and regional borders. But, as Fardowsa's story shows, such processes—which rely on kinship ties and the resources that flow within kin networks—can lead to the exclusion of the less powerful, as people inside humanitarian organizations themselves are often aware.

From the economic changes brought by colonialism to the effects of structural adjustment programs and neoliberalizing economies of the twenty-first century, communities across the world (in both the global South and North) struggle to manage shifting material conditions and growing inequality. Changing economies give birth to new social relations between women and men, across generations, and within families (Cole 2004; Geschiere 2013; Meiu 2017). In many African contexts, people like Sowdo seek to reinforce norms surrounding moral ways of consuming wealth that value redistribution. Shifting material conditions and transforming social relations give rise to new ways of critiquing wealth accumulation, as well as to a desire to take part in the seemingly fantastical wealth in distant parts of the world (or across the city).

Kikuyu[5] moral thought of the late colonial period, for example, distinguished between "laborious civic virtue and barren sorcery among men of means"—"virtuous wealth was encumbered with public debt; immoral wealth had no known social ties" (Lonsdale 1992, 440). To be moral, wealth derived in unprecedented ways in a changing economy required redistribution through existing networks of obligation. Contemporary Somali discourse around wealth and inequality in the age of refugee resettlement—a ticket to the global North for 1 percent—similarly insists that the wealth presumed to follow resettlement should be redistributed among kin back home and that those resettled should help kin to join them if they can.

These norms of obligation have major effects for those arriving in places like the US, as well as those who remain in camps and cities throughout Africa. Somali case workers at the resettlement agency where I conducted research in Columbus, Ohio, (chapter 5) held the government funds initially distributed to new arrivals that would be needed for food and rent. Otherwise, they said, new arrivals would send the full amount back to relatives, leaving nothing to live on in the months before they found work. "We will always be poor," a Somali woman who had arrived in the US as a teenager noted, because there would always be needs among relatives in Somalia and beyond. Finding ways of sponsoring kin to join them in global North locations accomplishes multiple goals: it enables the person to access citizenship rights, while simultaneously positioning them to contribute to the project of assisting kin (rather than being among the assisted), as Mohamed and Ahmed were expected to do. When Sadiya's family brought her to Australia as the wife of a cousin, they acted out a form of kinship (husband and wife) that is legitimate in the eyes of global North immigration policies to fulfill the moral obligations of kinship that those policies do not recognize. The family circumvented the kinship norms of immigration regulations to fulfill a different set of kinship obligations.

Within the moral regime of refugee aid and resettlement, lying "hurts the integrity of the program, and then people who may really need the benefit don't get it," as a former US RSC employee put it. Indeed, Fardowsa's story shows the ways in which working outside bureaucratic rules (as her ex-husband did) can do exactly that. Yet this humanitarian logic is but one set of moral ideas. It rests on a notion of moral action that privileges emergency response over structural change (even when an emergency has lasted for decades) and attention to particular forms of suffering. It is structurally linked to immigration systems that open doors to a very few. The moral project of refugee aid and resettlement intersects and often conflicts with the ways in which resettlement has been woven into the fabric of the social worlds of those subject to humanitarian governance. Not only do members of the Somali community in Kenya often reject the notion that mobility and citizenship should be available only to the few, but they also integrate humanitarian programs into existing norms of social obligation, ideas about "good kin," and moral social relations.

FOUR

Testing DNA and Transforming Kin

SOMALI-BRITISH WRITER NADIFA MOHAMED'S novel *The Orchard of Lost Souls* tells the story of an orphaned girl, a woman who deserts the Somali army after the death of her lover, and a paralyzed widow who is traumatized by the death of her only child. The three characters—unified by their marked social dislocation—are brought together as war breaks out in Somalia's north-west in 1988.[1] At the end of the novel, the three characters flee together by truck across the Ethiopian border. The orphan, Deqo, waits at a UNHCR tent to be registered. The novel concludes with a UN worker addressing Deqo: " 'Who did you come with?' Deqo pauses for a second to explain the situation, but then tells the lie her heart wants to tell. 'My mother and grandmother.' " The novel's final lines read: "[Deqo] is back in her familiar world; the war and all that time in Hargeisa just a complicated trial to achieve what she has always wanted: a family, however makeshift" (Mohamed 2014, 333–34).

For orphaned Deqo, the "familiar" world is not the world of an orphan-age or the streets that she has always known but the world of "a family"—the social ties that Mohamed's novel deems necessary. It is a "makeshift" family, as Mohamed calls it, which her young character maps onto a normative, bu-reaucratically legible, biogenetic family (daughter, mother, grandmother) when presented with the administrative system of UN registration. When Deqo crosses the border and is registered by the UN, she is produced as a new subject—as a refugee and also as a member of a presumed genealogical family. She has an opportunity to make herself anew, repairing the ruptures of her previous life. Her kinship with the two women is produced and made legible through the bureaucratic ritual of documenting the three individuals as a family unit. "The lie" in this story restores a social and moral universe; it mends the alienation wrought by violence and orphanhood.

After September 11, 2001, the US refugee program and refugee resettlement globally underwent systemic changes, with new and increased security measures. In 2008, motivated by reports about family composition fraud by Resettlement Support Center (RSC) Africa staff, the US refugee coordinator in Nairobi demanded action. Several years later, his former colleague, Greg, described his motivations: "What happens to my career if I'm the guy who sent a terrorist to the States?" The refugee coordinator, Greg explained, was concerned that people were taking advantage of a humanitarian program meant for the "most vulnerable." But he was also alarmed that this space could be taken advantage of by terrorists. Charting emotion from the Cold War to the War on Terror, Joseph Masco writes that Americans have been primed to "attune themselves to the possibility of terroristic violence as an unlimited daily potential" (2014, 19). The refugee coordinator's sentiments exemplify how "national security affect" played out in the refugee program, and how "the potential of catastrophic future events" shaped new plans and policies (19).

After the refugee coordinator sent a formal statement to his boss, RSC Africa was directed to conduct a DNA-testing pilot program. If kin relations could be verified, the logic went, dangerous strangers could not infiltrate the cases of refugees who had been appropriately identified for resettlement.[2] In the years leading up to the pilot program, refugees from African countries made up 95 percent of applicants to the Refugee Family Reunification Program. In a span of five years, thirty-six thousand people arrived from African countries through the program, while only four hundred came from other parts of the world (Bureau of Population, Refugees, and Migration 2009). Kenya was chosen as the initial location for the pilot program because RSC Africa was headquartered there and it was home to communities under scrutiny. Starting in Nairobi, DNA tests were conducted for five hundred people from Somalia and Ethiopia who had been identified for resettlement. The pilot program then expanded to include three thousand individuals throughout the continent, primarily of Somali, Ethiopian, and Liberian origins—the nationalities that had made up "the vast majority of P-3 [family reunification] cases" (Bureau of Population, Refugees, and Migration 2009). The anti-fraud pilot program turned African refugees into suspects in new ways.

The results shocked US government and NGO employees working in the refugee field. Of the cases tested, over 80 percent were deemed fraudulent in the reporting that followed. Amy Jacobs, who had worked in the United States with a local resettlement agency before coming to Nairobi to direct the reopening of the Refugee Family Reunification Program in 2012, took issue with labeling 80 percent of cases fraudulent. As she put it when I interviewed her over lunch, "What's more accurate is that [on those cases] at least one relationship was found to be different than what was indicated on their application." Refugee advocates in the US questioned the pilot program's methods and the analysis of results—including the fact that even though people were told the tests were voluntary, those who declined were counted among the fraudulent cases (Holland 2011, 1649). Nevertheless, the program was suspended for nearly four years. When the US reopened the program in 2012, DNA testing was a mandatory part of reunifying separated refugee families, as it was in several European countries already (Hautaniemi 2007; Heinemann and Lemke 2014; Helén 2014).[3] What are the consequences of DNA testing for the people seeking to come to these countries?

Employing DNA testing and using the biogenetic nuclear family as the bureaucratic unit of case composition more generally often separates families, even as such programs work in the name of reunifying them. The US Refugee Family Reunification Program produces nuclear families headed for the United States, while severing more expansive kin networks rooted both in long-standing social practices and the necessary kinship configurations created by civil war and displacement. In the process, DNA testing also creates "fraudulent families": those whose bonds are deemed insufficient to merit reunification, particularly when people present themselves in ways that do not conform to bureaucratic definitions. Kin and communities are separated as "relatives in transnational families must reshape kinship structures" to suit bureaucratic rules (Drotbohm 2020, 65). DNA testing in refugee resettlement invites examination of how the Global War on Terror and emerging technologies employed in immigration control shape kinship in the twenty-first century. Policies that uphold "the family" as integral to humanitarian aims and that employ DNA testing to verify family relations provide a case through which to study how genetic science works in new domains.

In one sense, this chapter begins where Nadifa Mohamed's novel ends— taking as a starting point the complexity of social ties and the diverse kinship formations that intersect with humanitarian programs that focus on "the family" as a central object of concern. What happens to people like Deqo and her "makeshift family" after registering at the refugee camp? This chapter charts forms of kinship and belonging among Somalis living as refugees in Kenya and the ways in which their lives converge with government and NGO categories. How are the demands of counter-terror goals, bureaucratic classification, barriers against migration from African countries, and hegemonic kinship norms braided together in the motivations and effects of DNA testing? How do the many "makeshift" families composed of people living as refugees interact with bureaucratic definitions of family used by global North governments? How do people respond to novel technologies and incorporate them into their ways of seeing the world?

Traveling Genes and the Logic of DNA Testing

Greg and I sit at a round table next to his desk. RefAid, the organization where Greg holds a director position, assists refugees in countries of asylum, while working with governments like the US and Canada to facilitate resettlement for a select few. Greg's office is on the top floor of a commercial building in an upscale Nairobi neighborhood. As I described in chapter 1, Greg had spent much of his career, about fifteen years, working for RSC Africa, the agency contracted by the State Department to screen refugees referred for resettlement to the United States. Having been charged with running the DNA pilot program, Greg reflected on it as practical and even inevitable. He saw it as the result of US-based resettlement agencies' resistance to implementing more elementary security measures for which he and others working in Africa had advocated, such as documents with better security features. Greg implied that the DNA pilot program was a we-told-you-so moment—perhaps unfortunate, but also the result of naïve domestic agencies that ignored the on-the-ground knowledge of the RSC staff working in camps and cities across the continent. Greg told the story like this:

> A new guy [State Department refugee coordinator] came in and he looked [the Family Reunification Program] over and he talked to his boss a couple times and said, "Look, I'm hearing that the process is thoroughly corrupt." "Yeah, yeah, yeah, it's okay," [his boss said]. And he's like, "You know what, if something goes wrong, and"—now this is a few years post-9/11—"what happens to my career if I'm the guy who sent a terrorist to the States?" . . . So the ref. cord. [refugee coordinator] wrote a memo and sent it to his boss saying, "Hey, I'm receiving multiple reports; they do seem credible. I don't have any evidence, but this is an area of real concern." So he has now covered his ass.

And it's his job to do that; it's his job to see that we're sending a good group of people over. And so, Washington sat on it for about a year. But because it was formal, they couldn't ignore it. . . . They said, "Okay, how do we actually test it?" Family reunion: DNA. So they anted up quite a bit of money and tasked RSC and said, "Okay, draw something up, guys." And it was literally, like, "We don't know anything about DNA. Can you give us a proposal?" And I was like, "Okay, that's kind of fun, cause I'm kind of a science-y geek." So, we looked at various sampling methods and decided let's just do everyone who is scheduled this week. Let's not try to randomize or anything; let's just do it for everyone.

Greg explained that when they looked at the numbers that came back, they excluded some of the "fraudulent" results—for example, if a child turned out to be the biological child of the mother but not the father. But despite such attempts to categorize the data in ways that more accurately reflected what they were trying to locate—relationships that had been knowingly misrepresented—the numbers were overwhelming. Greg continued,

Still, the number of cases that had at least one fraudulent person on it was staggering. Now here's the thing: if we are a real family unit, we all know that that one person on our case is not who they say they are. We know that that's not our brother or sister, and it's in fact our cousin or someone who paid their way onto a case. We know that, so that one person on the case actually implicates everyone on the case. Short of young children—and even they know it's not who they say it is—I've never been able to find any logical way to say that I accept that sort of thing. They know!

Underlying Greg's statement is the idea that DNA tests can show two things. First, they reveal biogenetic kinship relations, which are central to the resettlement case since the claim of each dependent—spouse and unmarried children under twenty-one—is derived from their relation to the primary applicant. Second, DNA tests detect lies, or fraud. Relations presented one way by the applicants but that are found to be something else reveal, according to Greg, deception and fraud. The applicants' moral character, also important to the resettlement application, even if implicitly, is discredited.

The pilot program that Greg oversaw and its reported results of fraud in over 80 percent of cases, led to the complete suspension of the Family Reunification Program for four years and its reopening with DNA as a required component four years later.[4] In 2015, when I arrived in Columbus, Ohio, to begin research with a local resettlement agency, the cost of the first relationship tested was $440, plus $220 for each additional child. A parent trying to reunify with multiple children would spend a considerable amount for someone newly arrived in the United States with no savings, trying to make ends meet in a low-wage job and working to pay back a US government loan for airfare, while also sending money back to help the family left behind. If the tests came out positive, the family member in the US could apply for reimbursement from the government. If one or more dependents had a negative result, the parent would carry the full cost, and the whole case would be rejected.

In 2013, near the beginning of my long-term fieldwork in Nairobi, I met with John, the US RSC Africa public information officer, who gave me a tour of RSC's building on Lantana Road in Westlands. Westlands is a tree-covered neighborhood dotted with upscale apartment complexes, fine-dining restaurants, and the offices of large corporations and international NGOs. The offices in high-rise buildings loom over *dukas*, small kiosks painted in Coca-Cola red or M-Pesa green that sell things like airtime, biscuits, and soda. In RSC's expansive building, the young American staff member showed me the high-tech library system in which thousands of refugees' case files were stored, each with an individual tracking device that made it easy to locate. These were all kept in a fireproof, flood-proof room on the building's ground floor due to the weight of the papers ("as heavy as two African elephants," John and Mwangi, the Kenyan librarian, joked). On another floor, John pointed out a room storing the large server that backed up RSC's files in Washington and at the US embassy several miles away; on a third one was a large, open room with small cubicles in which field staff worked quietly on computers. In the office of Amy Jacobs was the safe in which DNA kits were stored. John explained that once the "anchor" relative in the US sent his or her DNA kit, it would be kept here. Amy or one of her team members would accompany a physician from the IOM to collect sample cells through cheek swabs from family members in cities and camps across the continent. The kit would finally be sent to an accredited lab back in the United States. Negative results would trigger the case's rejection, and positive results would be used as one major piece of evidence to grant reunification.

DNA reveals the ways in which "the family" has become a central location of anxieties about undeserving people or criminals and terrorists taking advantage of a humanitarian program. It demonstrates the ways in which counter-terror and anti-fraud measures, trust in biomedical technologies, and a normative conception of "family" combine in a transnational humanitarian and immigration program. DNA testing rests on a hegemonic vision of the family as the biogenetic nuclear family. The supposed objectivity of the DNA test as an anti-fraud measure also reinforces that vision. But certain kinship formations directly contradict what is socially acceptable or legal in resettlement countries like the United States. UNHCR, for its part, states its commitment to accommodating the legal and cultural family norms of the countries from which its refugee clients come, aiming to "respect the culturally diverse interpretations of family membership and ensure the protection of members of polygamous families" (UNHCR 2011, 207). Yet they are heavily constrained by the laws of resettlement countries.

Polygyny, in which a man is married to multiple women simultaneously, is legal in Somalia, for example, but illegal in the United States and other resettlement countries. The United States, therefore, will not resettle or reunify a polygynous family as a single case. At times, polygynous families have been resettled as two separate but cross-referenced cases (which can receive different final determinations) when resettlement is seen as the only possible solution. In other cases, polygynous families are denied eligibility for resettlement, or families are separated either by the rules that govern state resettlement programs or by families' own efforts to make themselves eligible for the resettlement process (Besteman 2016, 94–95; UNHCR 2011, 207–9). Besteman's ethnography of the resettlement of the minority Somali Bantu community from Kenya to the United States in the early 2000s describes these kinds of separations, where polygynous families were resettled as separate cases. One would come as the legally recognized spouses with their children, and the other as a single-mother-headed household—"an enforced separation that was often a great hardship for cowives who depended on each other for support and for children who were separated from their father and siblings" (Besteman 2016, 94).

"Add-ons" beyond the nuclear family are sometimes considered, but such people should have resided with the family prior to fleeing their home country. This excludes those familial relations that have been formed precisely in the aftermath of people's departure from their home countries and their arrival in a place of asylum. In his report on the US Refugee Admissions Program, David Martin writes that his interviews

> produced many comments that the refugee program should make better provisions for functional family relationships in the chaotic aftermath of refugee flight. . . . When I inquired about making such a change, DHS officials explained that such a rule would be too open to fraud. Requiring that persons

in question have shared life together in both settings provides opportunities for questioning about both locations that is more likely to expose outright imposters. If imposters only had to present consistent stories regarding camp life, it would be easier to carry off fraud. These officers candidly acknowledged that the existing rule will unfortunately bar from being considered as part of the same case some persons who have formed genuinely close family-type affections through perhaps many years of life together in the refugee camp. (2005, 53–54)

Martin's research suggests that US officials and other decision-makers do understand the complexity of family composition among communities living as refugees. However, according to DHS officials, prioritizing the unity of "functional" families would offer people too much freedom to access the program in ways that support their own needs and undermine states' efforts to regulate the program's beneficiaries. A narrow definition of family that can be easily tested supports the goal of controlling access to resettlement. Martin's language about "imposters," presumably derived from the DHS officers he interviewed, reveals a view of people trying to access resettlement as adversaries of the state, which obscures the complexity of their lived experiences, histories, and social worlds.

In the 1990s, Jennifer Hyndman wrote about the "transnational politics of mobility" and relations of power that grant and deny access to borders, examining the ways in which large flows of capital have traveled from Europe to the Horn of Africa precisely to contain and immobilize the supposed beneficiaries of this aid. She writes, "What is clear is that the availability and mobility of money corresponds inversely to the relative poverty and confinement of refugees in Kenya" (1997, 171). In an age of new and globalizing forms of security, the fact that borders are porous to genetic material precisely in order to secure those borders against the people from whom the genetic material has been extracted invites new ways of thinking about the transnational politics of mobility. Not only do US dollars (and euros and pounds) support the containment of refugees, as Hyndman argued, but these dollars now fund corporeal extractions of cellular material in order to grant or deny access to places like the United States.

Unlike in asylum, in refugee resettlement the procedures that grant or deny access to residence take place outside the country in question. US officials and their partners conduct interviews for resettlement abroad—in places like Kenya, or Turkey, or Jordan—rather than after people have crossed US borders. But now, cellular material travels ahead, for analysis in US labs, in order to decide if the people from whom cells were taken will be allowed to follow. How do these novel techniques of governance intersect with both long-standing and emergent norms of family life? Next, I draw on the stories and commentaries of young Somali women and men that illuminate how they conceptualize DNA testing and other norms around family composition and how these aspects of refugee resettlement shape peoples' lives and communities.

DNA Meets Diasporic Kinship

Many people I came to know in Eastleigh, Nairobi's Somali neighborhood, were young women and men who had grown up between Somalia, Kenya's refugee camps, Kenya's ethnic Somali region in the northeast, and Nairobi, as well as cities and camps in Uganda, Tanzania, and Ethiopia. They were the generation born at the start of Somalia's civil war—their "destinies indissolubly chained to those of [their] country," (Rushdie 1991, 3). Most held refugee identity documents from UNHCR and the Kenyan government. Because Somalis had been among the initial group subject to DNA testing in the US pilot program, people I met in Eastleigh—most of whom were linked to diasporic kin networks—possessed intimate knowledge of DNA testing. The young people I talked with between 2013 and 2015 held well-formed opinions on the subject. They had already observed how DNA testing worked—how it came to bear on the intimate domains of their lives or the lives of people they knew. Never without contesting visions or debate, conversations illuminated how DNA testing had been taken up in collective imaginations and how it had shaped diasporic communities.

In my early efforts to discuss genetic testing in family reunification, I found that it was an issue that many were reluctant to talk about. I assumed that this reluctance stemmed from unease talking about an unpopular US policy with an American. And unwittingly shaped by the logic behind the policy itself, I imagined that discussing personal experiences with DNA testing could reveal transgressions against rules that people felt uncomfortable sharing. But as I continued talking with people subject to these policies in Kenya and later in the United States, I learned that DNA testing was a challenging topic perhaps more centrally because it could expose family histories that were often painful and fraught.

It was late June 2014. April and May had seen Operation Usalama Watch terrorize people living with refugee documents throughout the city. An estimated four thousand people had been arrested, either to be extorted and released or to be detained and forcibly relocated to distant refugee camps at the country's borderlands (Human Rights Watch 2015). The operation had targeted the Somali community in Eastleigh, filling its streets with police and its paramilitary wing, the General Service Unit, their green uniforms and maroon berets becoming a visual fixture of the landscape. By the end of June, the operation had calmed. Mohamed had invited a few friends who lived in his building to talk with me about the past months, as well as the ever-present issue of resettlement.

As a foreigner in Kenya, I was now required to carry my passport when I left the house. That day, since I was carrying a bag of sodas in glass bottles, I took a taxi instead of walking the two kilometers through busy neighborhoods to Mohamed's place. On Juja Road, the main artery that separated my neighborhood and Eastleigh, the taxi was stopped near Mlango Kubwa. Focused on making all things visible in the aftermath of Westgate and other recent attacks, the government had banned tinted windows. As a young officer approached the car, the driver asked me in a low voice not to mention that his car was functioning as a taxi. The driver lowered my darkened window, and I greeted the officer, handing him my passport open to the page with my picture. He handed it back and asked the driver for his license, returning it, too. Despite the windows, he nodded and looked up at the street as the car pulled back onto the congested road. We continued to Mohamed's place, tucked in Eastleigh's grid of busy streets. Stepping out into the hubbub of the neighborhood, I greeted the man seated on a stool outside the building watching people as they came and went. I climbed three flights of the open stairway to Mohamed's apartment, passing by the unmistakable scent of *uunsi* (incense of frankincense and other aromatics) and onions frying with cardamom and coriander.

Mohamed, whose life I described in the previous chapter, was born in southern Somalia and left as a ten-year-old child, growing up with his paternal relative, Ahmed, whom he usually referred to simply as his brother. Now in their early twenties, Mohamed and Ahmed still lived together, along with Issa—the brother of their uncle's wife—in one room of an Eastleigh apartment, sharing a kitchen with the apartment's other occupants—a mother with her teenage daughter, another mother with a toddler son, and others—many of whom were waiting to join family members elsewhere. Their room contained three single beds, a desk with a desktop computer (purchased with money sent by their uncle in Canada to support their studies), and an office chair on wheels. By the door was a green plastic hamper filled with clothes and a coat rack on which hung a jacket and a white *qamiis*, a garment often worn to the mosque. Sitting in the desk chair, I was reading to Mohamed some questions I had prepared for his friends, when a young man came striding, bouncing into the room. He unbuttoned his shirt and picked up a green prayer rug that was folded on the desk, laying it on the floor. I expected him to pray, but instead, he spread his shirt on the rug, pressing it with a heavy iron as he began to talk animatedly. A young boy, around one and a half, toddled in through the now half-open door, moving around the room, pulling the lid from the laundry basket, tottering a bit too close to the hot iron.

Soon, Mohamed's other neighbors arrived, sprawling across the three beds. Farhiyo and Khadro were sisters, and Najib—who had now finished ironing and put on the shirt, was their cousin. Khadro, the older sister, wore a leather jacket over her long, black *cabaaya*, and Farhiyo, an outspoken young woman who wrote poetry, wore a red scarf draped loosely over her head, the glint of a gold earring visible behind it. Farhiyo and Khadro's mother was in Dadaab, while they lived in Nairobi on their own. Hassan, another neighbor, also lived with relatives in the building. Issa, Mohamed and Ahmed's relative, joined us, too. Those assembled ranged in age from twenty-one to twenty-eight. Other than Issa, who had come to Kenya from Somalia in his early twenties, they were all either born outside Somalia or had left as young children. They spoke Somali, Swahili, and English—even Issa, who had only been in Kenya for a few years.

The group, in a familiar place with friends and relatives, had no trouble digging into my questions. They discussed how the war and resettlement had changed Somali families. They shouted over one another, illustrating their points with stories and jokes. Najib, imagining a hypothetical Somali wife in the US, shouted, "When I come home from work, she'll tell me, 'What you provided, cook it!'"—commenting on what he understood to be transforming gender roles in the diaspora. Everyone laughed. "I don't know how to do this stuff!" he exclaimed, to which his cousin, Khadro, replied, "Google it!"[5]

Unlike talking with people about their own individual cases, which often mirrored being interviewed by UNHCR or foreign government officials—an experience laden with anxiety—discussing resettlement as a group in general terms, in a familiar place reflected a more comfortable social idiom. When I asked about DNA testing, Najib began, gesturing to Khadro and Farhiyo.

Najib: We are cousins. So, if we are tested, they'll look the same, but they'll discriminate against me. They'll let them go, and I'll stay here.

Farhiyo: There are a lot of kids who a mom adopted during that time, and we don't have any system of formal adoption. You're just running, you see a child, you have sympathy, and you take that child. When the mom came to Dadaab, she won't say, 'This isn't my child'—she doesn't want the child to feel negatively. So, if resettlement comes and they're carrying the names of those parents, if you tell the UN the truth, they won't believe and will cancel the case. So, people don't say anything.

Najib: They say "child trafficking"!

Farhiyo: Once DNA comes, they won't accept [the case]. And then you have to tell the child.

Khadro: Also, DNA brings disbelief between the husband and the wife. Say there are five kids, and two are not from the husband. Then big problems will come. That's why people fear DNA.

Farhiyo: Yes, and some women are raped and get pregnant. Maybe she herself even didn't know. Even my mom adopted two kids—two boys; they were Somali Bantus. After Mom and Dad separated and Mom moved, they found some relatives and went to live with them. Now they're in Kakuma. But the boys saw Dad once in Kakuma, and they were asking about Mom.

Sophia: How long were they with your family?

Farhiyo [*looking at her sister for confirmation*]: Five years. They were very malnourished when Mom found them. After they recognized our father [in Kakuma], they asked, "Where's Mom?" So, they communicate with her.

Najib: This kind of thing brings mental problems to people.

Farhiyo: With DNA, problems come.

Najib: People even become street boys because of it. [*Laughter*]

Farhiyo: They should have a consultation first—separately—and be able to disclose any secret.

Najib: The man may even lose confidence. It's like the wife is saying, "My man was not able to satisfy me."

Hassan: If it is true, though, it's very helpful. It can make the case quicker.

Najib: But there are more problems than benefits.

Farhiyo: It's only good if it works for them. In the camps, people pray DNA won't be taken.

In the conversation, the group noted that DNA testing could cause a resettlement case to fail. But more centrally, they discussed the effects of DNA testing on family relationships—on feelings of trust and belonging among kin. While the group spoke about these issues without apparent restraint, a few weeks later, Mohamed invited another group of friends to discuss the same topics. This time, the issue of DNA testing provoked discomfort and debate over whether the topic should be discussed at all.

Back in Mohamed, Ahmed and Issa's small room, I asked the new group what a "typical" Somali family looked like. Samira answered without hesitation: "One parent is missing. For example, mom remains here, while dad has gone abroad. That's a typical Somali family—one parent is not around." Samira herself lived in Nairobi with her divorced mother and siblings, while her father lived in the United States. Mohamed, Ahmed, and Issa lived on their own and had done so for several years. As children, Mohamed and Ahmed had lived with a family that worked for Ahmed's father, then with an uncle and his new wife, and later with Mohamed's sister and her husband. More recently they had convinced their uncle in Canada to rent them their own place (the room where we were currently assembled). Mohamed's father lived in Somalia, and his mother had passed away when he was a child. Ahmed's mother was in Somalia, and his father was based there but traveled throughout the region for work. Abdirahman, who had also joined us, had been living with his brother in Nairobi for the past five years. His mother and eight siblings lived in Somalia and his father had died. Jabril's mother, father, and ten siblings all lived in Somalia, as well. For the past six years he had lived with his paternal cousins (the sons of his father's brother) in a room in an Eastleigh apartment while the four of them went to school. Khadija's mother lived in the US and her father lived in the United Arab Emirates. She lived with her grandparents and her aunts and uncles, but she referred to her grandparents as "Mom and Dad" and to her aunts and uncles as her sisters and brothers. It was important to her, she emphasized, that they introduce her to others as a sister, too. The group's lived experiences reflected Samira's notion of the typical Somali family as one separated by distance and by death.

The group spoke animatedly about the challenges of resettlement to the community, families, and individuals: the trials of waiting, family separation, and plans put on hold—education, marriage, and other aspirations deferred.

Abdirahman: There are still families in Somalia, and if the father goes to the UK or the US, for example, he might bring the family here or to Uganda, and start the [resettlement] process. But the problem is waiting.

Samira: You waste time.

Abdirahman: You might waste four, five years. Instead of going to school, you just say "I'm going to America"—you get *buufis* in your head.

Samira: We call it *buufis*. It plays with your psychology. You're always wondering, "Am I going?" You have anxiety. And then you might start making plans and then it doesn't happen. They just tell you, "No, sorry, come next year."

Abdirahman: Then there are people who just decide, "Forget it. I'm not doing this process." After two years, just forget it.

Samira: And then another problem comes if DNA shows that a child isn't a man's.

Khadija: You might even get to know that someone is not your father.

There was a silent pause.

Abdirahman: That's not something that should be discussed here.

Samira: What are you talking about? Why can't that be discussed? It's something that happens!

Abdirahman: That shouldn't be discussed here. Are you getting me?

Jabril: Yes, yeah.

Abdirahman: Are you getting me?

Khadija: I'm getting.

Samira, who had introduced the subject, didn't answer. I put down my pen on the notebook where I had been jotting notes, remarking that I had heard about how DNA testing was used and that I'd be interested to hear about how it affected the community. Abdirahman sighed.

Abdirahman: Disaster. Look, if you have an uncle or something who is like your father, then when DNA comes, that will ruin it—that's what we're talking about. The DNA thing came up because they knew some families were lying.

Samira: They were applying for other people who aren't their family. They made up "This is my child." But if you say that the person is not your child but you're caring for them, it can work.

Khadija: But they'll say that you can't be responsible for that other child.

Jabril: The problem is that then the child is going to feel different.

Samira: Yes, and you've been raised by those parents the whole time.

Jabril: The agencies know this, though.

Abdirahman: But if you say that it's another child [not "by birth"], they won't allow.

Mohamed, who had been quiet, mentioned child trafficking—one of the UN's and governments' stated reasons for vigilance about family composition and extensive measures for assessing whether a family can take a child other than a biogenetic daughter or son across borders.

Samira: If you have documents—adoption documents—then it's not a problem. If you can prove. . . .

Jabril: Do we have those documents?!

Abdirahman: We don't go by documents. We go by tribe. "This is my fifty[eth] grand cousin."

Sophia: So, do these institutions and the Somali community understand "family" in the same way?

Abdirahman: No, no, absolutely not. They don't. Family to us is different than Western culture. My aunt's son is like my brother. My grandmother is like my mom. My uncle is like my father. Even your second cousin is your brother.

Samira: Anyone who is your mom's friend is your aunt.

Abdirahman: Like my father, he adopted three cousins at a young age to educate them. They become part of the family. They identify with the family. You will move with them. That's where DNA comes.

Samira: It's cruel.

Jabril: The main point is that when a family lies, that brings problems.

Abdirahman: It's not exactly lying.

Jabril: But hiding it.

Abdirahman: But also the person doesn't want to be called out.

Khadija: Like I call my grandmother and grandfather "Mom and Dad," and I call their kids, who are my aunt and uncle, my sisters and brothers.

Mohamed: So, they're close in age to you?

Khadija: Even if they're not! I want them to say I'm their sister. I don't want them to introduce me in another way. We were all supposed to be taken abroad as a family. There was no DNA at that time, but we failed something. Now my mom [in the US] is trying to take me, but the problem is

that when she went, she never said she had another daughter. So DNA
may help.

Abdirahman: Well, DNA let me down.

Sophia: Would you be able to say how DNA affected your case?

Abdirahman: I had a case and DNA made it fail.

Samira: But *how* did it?

Abdirahman began to explain that he was living with his aunt and the
rest of her family, and that they were supposed to go to Sweden together: "I
was never told in the interview that there would be DNA. Later, we learned
that DNA would come, so we just pulled out of the process. So, they went to
Sweden. Now we just communicate by phone."

Abdirahman did not elaborate further, but the anger in his voice betrayed
his pain. He did not expand on the fact that in order to save the case and not
be caught "lying" or "not exactly lying," in his words, the family had to "lose"
Abdirahman—either to reveal to the Swedish government their genealogical
relationship or to create a story as to why he would no longer be part of the
case. The policy's work of defining Abdirahman as separate indeed separated
him in a dramatic way—dislocating him from the family to which he had
belonged.

Khadija and Abdirahman emphasized that to make a family member,
particularly a child, feel separate or different was a painful transgression,
which DNA testing and the logic of the biogenetic nuclear family required for
many families trying to access resettlement and reunification. They had been
marked as separate by DNA testing in Abdirahman's case or its underlying
logics in Khadija's case, making her wonder if her difference caused the case's
failure. The specter of genetic tests and the biogenetic nuclear family produced
unease about her place in her family and why their resettlement case had been
denied. In contrast, within the community, expansive notions of familial obligation and care were crucial to the moral workings of diasporic Somali society
and the repair of fragmented social worlds in sites of refuge from a decades-
long civil war.

In addition to separating families physically, DNA exposed relations that
were not as they had appeared: the revelation of a woman's infidelity or rape, a
"fatherless" child (that is, a child without a known biogenetic father)—a stigmatized position, or a sibling who is marked as different from the rest. Classifying the cousin, the niece, or the orphan as one's child or sibling works to

negate differences born of deaths, disappearances, and migrations of the civil war. Using kinship terms and carrying a family's father's and grandfather's names, according to Somali naming convention, naturalizes and publicly marks one's belonging. This is similar to how parents in other contexts who adopt children from different countries "kin" those children—socially "planting" them in their own ancestral places and family networks (Howell 2003, 472). For many, it was important to use kinship terms that negated genealogical distance, such as Mohamed calling Ahmed his brother. When he called Ahmed his brother, Mohamed reflected the practical and affective dimensions of a relationship between two boys who had grown up together, without either of their biogenetic parents or siblings, who all remained in Somalia. Khadjia pointed out the importance of calling her grandparents "Mom and Dad" and her aunts and uncles "sisters and brothers."

Mohamed and his friends reflected how multiple kinds of scenarios could cause DNA testing to disrupt a case: One or both parents who did not know that a child was biogenetically unrelated to the father, those who knew but never revealed that to the child, or families where all knew the "genealogical truth" but where the child's difference was minimized so that the family could be resettled together and the child could maintain his or her identity and sense of belonging. The logic and effects of DNA testing disrupted more than just local concepts of kinship and obligations of care. They interacted with imperatives to mend a social fabric ruptured by war. The "lie" of genealogical relations—calling the niece a daughter, for example—was not done solely for immigration purposes or for profit, though that did occur. Practices of healing social wounds of familial dislocation was central to Somali life and transnational families in the decades of Somalia's civil war and political instability.

Different Genealogies

Mohamed once told me a story of a family who lived in an apartment below his. The husband and wife had multiple sons, including one who—now a young man—had been taken in as an orphan when he was very young. The young man and his father were extremely close. When his father became ill, elders and sheikhs in the family urged him to tell the son about his true origins, but the father could not bring himself to break his son's heart, as Mohamed put it. When the father died, though his mother and siblings were willing to share their inheritance equally with him, the sheikhs insisted that he could not receive an equal inheritance to his brothers, in keeping with religious law. The son was distraught, refusing to believe that he was not the person he had always known himself to be. The young man married and was given one of his father's shops. He needed something to sustain his family, Mohamed recounted, though the shop was not equal to what his brothers had been given.

As Mohamed and I discussed the story, he explained his views about the matter of inheritance and how things might have been different had the news of the son's origins come from his father himself before he died. Mohamed paused. "But he couldn't even speak of the issue," he added. The story and Mohamed's memory of it years later illuminates taboos around genealogy and what can and cannot be spoken. The fact that DNA tests were so disruptive in the Somali community was not because genealogical relatedness is unimportant but precisely because it is central to identity and belonging (Lewis 1994; Lowe 2019).

While he was sipping tea at my home in Pangani, with my husband listening from the kitchen as he put away dishes, Mohamed told me, "Somalis, they hate one thing. There's something called 'wecel.' It's like, a kid without a father. An unfathered kid."

"Why is that hated?" I asked.

"Ayayay, they *hate* it. It's a *shame*. You can't call that man who raised you a father. To be born as *wecel*, without a father, your mother being impregnated without being married—that's the one that is a shame. It's like inheriting shame."

"What is their clan?" I asked.

"They have no clan. You'll just be photocopied onto the mother's clan."

"Why do you say 'photocopied'?" I asked.

"It's like something which is not true. It's not the original one. The *wecel* causes a very big problem."

In Mohamed's reflection, a child without a known or publicly acknowledged father is shameful because the child represents a transgression on the part of their mother that, as in many places, is highly stigmatized (see also Besteman 2016, 250–57). But the "fatherless child" also suffers social stigma because he or she cannot be placed correctly within a lineage.

The story of the young man after his father's death and Mohamed's comments about "fatherless" children give insight into the fear caused by DNA testing—something that can expose destructive or taboo secrets and unravel a social universe and a person's sense of belonging within it. "People pray DNA won't be taken," Farhiyo says. We see this unraveling in other contexts, too. In the US and elsewhere, genetic ancestry tests that reveal family secrets around race, ethnicity, and parenthood have also upended people's sense of self. A whole range of books, documentaries, and podcasts trace such stories and the emotional upheaval that often follows (Copeland 2020; Shapiro 2019). Some of the effects of genetic testing in a global age are broadly shared, while others are rooted in socially and historically specific contexts (Abel 2021).

In Somalia, as in other African societies, people have long been incorporated into genealogical lineages through systems of child fosterage, patron-client relations, servitude (Besteman 2016, 39–40; Evans-Pritchard 1940; Weitzberg 2017, 29), and creative practices that help solve a family's need for descendants when death or infertility interferes (Evans-Pritchard 1951). In other words, genealogical membership and identity can be derived in many ways—not only through birth and shared genetic material, as scientific conceptions of genealogy would have it. In the Somali context, genealogical knowledge has come to take on new significance in an age of global displacement and diaspora. As Keren Weitzberg writes, many Kenyan nationals of Somali ethnicity "saw lineage as an important tool for tempering the threat of linguistic and cultural change. . . . Knowing one's genealogy ensures that 'we never get lost,'" as one person explained to her (2017, 163). But the importance of knowing one's genealogy and where one exists in a genealogical lineage also intersects with other realities of life during a civil war—of kinship created in the context of orphanhood, violence, forced migrations, and the dispersal and separations of families. These forms of genealogical knowledge that create order amidst violent disorder at times clash with the kinds of knowledge that can be ascertained by a DNA test.

So, what happened after DNA testing was instituted in the US Refugee Family Reunification Program? On one hand, one might guess that many applications were denied, given the ways in which Somali (and other) diaspora families were often configured. But the opposite was true. When I left Nairobi for Columbus, Ohio, in early 2015, the US Refugee Family Reunification Program had restarted two and a half years earlier—in October 2012. Of the hundreds of family reunification applications filed in Columbus since then, resettlement agency staff were not aware of a single case that had been denied on account of DNA results. This fact reflected the stakes for those applying and their clear understanding of how DNA testing worked. Filing a case that they knew or feared would not "pass" a DNA test would result in the case's rejection and the US-based sponsor's inability to recuperate the large sum invested in genetic testing. It could also reveal painful histories that people managed by incorporating others into their households and lineages.

From "Makeshift" to Nuclear Family: Before and after DNA Testing

In late 2020, weeks before the US presidential election, I spoke to Marissa, the director at Ohio Refugee Assistance (ORA), the resettlement agency in Columbus, Ohio, where I had been based in 2015. Since the election of Donald Trump in 2016, the US Refugee Admissions Program had been reduced to a paltry version of what it had previously been. In 2016, the Ohio-based agency (one of three resettlement agencies in Ohio's capitol) had received 1,400 people through the refugee program. In 2017, they received only 600 people, and that number had been approximately halved each year since. Several Muslim communities, including Somalis, had been barred from entering the United States by Trump's Executive Order 13769, titled "Protecting the Nation from Foreign Terrorist Entry into the United States." Somalis and many others attempting to come to the US, including the thousands of people awaiting family reunion, were stranded, with no foreseeable end to their waiting. So, although there was little data to go on from after 2017, there was no indication that DNA tests were responsible for the denial of many cases since the Refugee Family Reunification Program had reopened in 2012. The families allowed to reunify under the program were, by and large, biogenetic nuclear families comprising a married couple or single parent with their unmarried biogenetic children under twenty-one.

By contrast, in the 1990s, people had commonly added people from outside their nuclear families to their cases. At times, these families reflected the composition of a household, including both related and unrelated orphaned or separated children, as well as adults. Social and moral obligations or financial incentives compelled people to include individuals from outside their households, too—whether relatives, friends, or acquaintances. In writing about the resettlement of Somali Bantu refugees from Kenya's Dadaab camps in the late 1990s and early 2000s, Besteman notes that "refugee families figured out ways to turn extended families into nuclear families while trying to avoid having to lop off those family members who could not fit into the new model, . . . turn[ing] cousins into siblings, nieces and nephews into children, orphans into family members, and family members into orphans in order to present family structures that were legible and desirable to American interviewers while also being as inclusive as possible" (2016, 94).

These practices were so common that resettlement interviewers who had doubts about a family started asking if children were "wa tumbo moja" (Swahili; from the same belly). In Somali, interviewers would ask older children, "Ma isku hooyo iyo aabo ayaa tihiin?" (Are you from the same mother and father?) One RSC staff member's "no bald teenagers rule" (see chapter 1), a snide joke about people's attempts to pass adults off as their dependent children, demonstrates how many people working with refugees conceptualized such practices. Despite such practices being stigmatized, there was more leeway to add people to cases in order to more widely distribute resettlement as a resource. Buying cases, of course, primarily enabled better resourced people to access resettlement, though it was often minority communities and other disadvantaged groups originally identified for resettlement who might have benefited from selling a spot.

Recounting his work with RSC Africa, Greg described the 1990s as a time in which it was simple for people to present a large family for resettlement or reunification, with little scrutiny of relationships and scant documentation to keep identities straight:

> The ration cards had a photo which was grommeted on—you know those little round grommets, a bit like an eyehole on a shoelace? A little metal ring. That was the security feature. How hard would it be to pry that off, put a new photo in, and bend it back? Then there was a rubber stamp that said United Nations High Commissioner for Refugees. Well, one day I noticed—this was the first time I'd ever run into fraud—they'd spelled *United* wrong. So, the quality of the documentation was very poor. The [Family Reunification cases] were a mess because—I don't know if you've ever seen the old AORs [Affidavit of Relationship forms]? You put down everybody you'd wanted to have come to America. Can you imagine how long that list was? There was no photo, no DNA—DNA was also in its infancy in those days—but there was nothing except "I swear" before a notary public somewhere in the US. . . . There were never any empty spots. Because here the thing is my little brother dies but I have a spot to go to America? It gets filled."

Greg portrays this time as a free-for-all, where nearly anyone could come to the United States. Unremarked upon are the motivations, conditions, and moral logics of the people making choices to commit what officials defined as fraud. Nor are the structures of the resettlement system itself or the nature of vastly unequal access to mobility between people of the global North and global South that create the conditions for such practices. For the most part, Greg focused on administering a triage-like system that decided who did and did not merit resettlement. He oversaw a process that considered truth telling an absolute and that took for granted that truth would be ascertained primarily by people who were foreign to the communities seeking resettlement, through bureaucratic interviews in an environment of mistrust. By contrast, many of the people who had come or were trying to come to the US through the refugee program used a different set of priorities, where the bureaucratic rules of UNHCR or a foreign government were subordinate to fulfilling social and moral obligations to kin and community, as I discussed in the previous chapter.

Habiba's parents, for example, had prioritized such obligations. In the course of my research in Columbus, I came to know Habiba through my time at ORA, where she had been a staff member for several years. Habiba had grown up first in Somalia, briefly in Kenya, and later in Ethiopia, before arriving in Buffalo, New York, as a teenager, later moving to Minneapolis, where she married, then to Pittsburgh, and finally to Columbus, where she moved her family for a job. In 2015, she was the mom of two kids, working full time assisting new arrivals. She wore glasses and practical shoes. Sometimes Ikran, a Somali caseworker, would bring lunch back from her apartment, cooked by the mother of six with whom she lived—and some of the women staff would gather around Habiba's desk to eat together. Other times, a staff member would pop out to the Somali restaurant down the road to get tea in the afternoon, and we would hover around Habiba's desk, sharing gossip over Styrofoam cups. People seemed to gravitate to her corner—a center of sociality in the office. She was liked and respected by staff and clients alike.

Habiba's own family had been aided by an aunt in Buffalo when they first arrived, and her father then began working as a caseworker at a local resettlement agency. She remembered him going out at midnight to receive families at the airport. She was inspired by how he helped other families, and she later followed in his footsteps. While attending community college, where she majored in an interdisciplinary social sciences program, she volunteered as an interpreter at the local resettlement agency, and years later followed this path to a career at the Columbus-based VOLAG. "It's a really good place," she said of ORA. "Otherwise, I wouldn't be there. When I go home and I'm going to bed, I think about the day. If I didn't help someone, that bothers me. But anyway, this is what I know," she told me.

At the office, Habiba talked about her family often. Her sister had gone back to Somalia for a short time and complained about the food. Her father had gone back for good; an older man, he was more comfortable there, despite the challenges, and wanted to contribute something to the country while he still could. Her mother stayed in the States. Her siblings lived in various cities around the US. She talked about her husband and her young kids—the funny things the children would say or the difficulty of meeting their expectations for things like an iPad or a pair of Nike shoes. One Friday afternoon in the summer, she and I headed out in her minivan to a nearby Tim Horton's. Over iced coffee and a donut, she recalled her memories of leaving Somalia as a child and about the struggles of supporting family back home.

"When did your dad go back to Somalia?" I asked, picking up a thread that had been left dangling from earlier in the conversation.

Habiba laughed a little, perhaps uncomfortably. "Actually," she said, "I should go back and change my story."

In the sun-streaked booth in the mostly empty fast-food café, Habiba told me about her other family. Like many, she has two: the mother and father who she refers to regularly as Mom and Dad, with whom she fled Somalia, who brought her to the United States, and who raised her from the time she was six. She also has a biogenetic mother and father in Somalia, whom I hadn't heard about in our casual conversations in the office.

Habiba was born in a village in northern Somalia in the 1980s. Because her grandmother (her mother's mother) had only had three children, including only one daughter, she was alone by the time Habiba was a young child. At age four, Habiba was sent to live with her grandmother several hours away. "My grandma was lonely, I guess, and she needed someone to help . . . not help, but she was lonely. She wanted someone around. So, I was the one who was chosen," Habiba said, reflecting on this fated decision that altered her life in greater ways than could have been imagined at the time. In 1988, fighting between Barre's government and the opposition Somali National Movement, along with government targeting of civilians in the north, forced Habiba and her grandmother to flee to Mogadishu. Her parents and siblings, meanwhile, stayed in the village where they lived several hours away. When violence erupted in Mogadishu in 1991, her grandmother chose not to flee south and leave for Kenya, as many were doing at the time. "She said to my uncle's wife, 'I'm not going, but take Habiba.'"

"So, I was raised by my mom's brother, and my brothers and my sisters are actually my cousins," Habiba said. "That's the family I know." Habiba explained that she had not seen her biogenetic parents since she was four years old. "But I am supporting them, and I talk to them," she added. Most of her biogenetic siblings were still in Somalia, but a couple had come to the US. "That was actually one of the reasons I went to Minneapolis," Habiba said. "I had two aunts and cousins, and when my sister arrived there, I wanted to get to know her and help her. We weren't raised together, but we get along fine. She was there at my wedding," she added, her voice rising to an upbeat tone.

Now that Habiba had clued me in about her two families—her two sets of parents and siblings—she switched back and forth between referring to her mother as "my mom," "my aunt," and "my uncle's wife" as she dipped in and out of different parts of her past and present. She recalled that "my aunt's father" knew about sailing and convinced them not to take a boat from Kismayo to Mombasa, and that "my mom" must have paid a bribe to get them out of the Nairobi airport, as they had arrived without documents. Meanwhile, she spoke of "my parents" who had never left their home. Which parents she meant could be deduced by context. Both couples were parents—one set by virtue of her birth and early childhood and her enduring efforts to support them financially, the other by virtue of having been raised by them for the majority of her life.

I asked, "In your resettlement case, did the fact that you weren't the biological child of your parents ever come up?"

She replied,

> It was never mentioned. I mean—my [last] name Omar is my [maternal] grandfather's name. And even when I came to the US and got citizenship, I never changed it. It didn't matter to me if it was that grandfather or this grandfather. I mean my real name should be Ali but I really don't care. And my parents raised me as their own—really and truly. And there was no DNA at that time, so there was no need of telling stories. The man I married also has the wrong name. So, our own kids' names are even wrong. We choose the wrong one for legal purposes. So, there are sprinkles of the past on the kids here, too.

I asked how she thought DNA testing and a stricter set of guidelines about family composition affected families now.

She replied,

> Other families raise kids for many reasons. When people come to ORA, I hear all the time, "I'm leaving my brother's son or daughter, or daughter of my best friend who died." It's not fair. Is it fair? Sometimes no. Children who have no

place to go—and I'm one of those. My uncle said I'm his daughter. If he hadn't, I don't know if I would be here. In the US, your family is that—your family. The others are your relatives. In Somali culture, family is beyond your own family. I know many people who wish they could raise their brother's or sister's kids. Would they lie? Some would if they could. In war, people do things that are so wrong, but for so many different reasons.

I told Habiba about a young woman I knew in Eastleigh. I had met Yasmin, age sixteen, through Mohamed. Yasmin's uncle and his three children were waiting to be reunited with his wife, Yasmin's maternal aunt, in Europe. Yasmin was helping him by cooking and taking care of the kids. When they finally left for Europe, Yasmin was left behind. The last I had heard, she had headed for Mombasa, where she had relatives.

Habiba's head was turned to the side. She was looking out at something in her mind, seemingly lost in thought or memory. "If I weren't part of the [resettlement] process, what would I do?" she wondered aloud. "How would I support myself? And you're a child. Imagine feeling left out. Once they're gone, it's like living on the streets." She seemed to be considering her young self and Yasmin at once.

As a woman raised in Somali communities in multiple diasporic locations who graduated from a US university and now worked in the resettlement world supporting others, Habiba translated one set of moral imperatives and social norms into another: "In war, people do things that are so wrong, but for so many different reasons." She described how different norms, particularly around kinship, intersected and how they ultimately reconfigured families in a global Somali diaspora. DNA reassembled some families—primarily nuclear families—while often separating more expansive groups that sustained people in countries of asylum.

"The Natural and Fundamental Group Unit of Society"

The family holds an important place as a category of concern in the emergence of twentieth-century human rights norms. Article 16 of the Universal Declaration of Human Rights (UDHR) asserts: "The family is the natural and fundamental group unit of society and is entitled to protection by society and the State" (United Nations 1948). The 1951 Refugee Convention on the status of refugees draws on the UDHR's language, stating that "the unity of the family, the natural and fundamental group unit of society, is an essential right of the refugee" and advises governments to ensure "that the unity of the refugee's family is maintained" (UNHCR 1951). What did the authors—who imagined family to be "the natural and fundamental group unit of society"—understand "the family" to be? And how was this notion taken up by people interpreting human rights norms in the later decades of the twentieth century and first decades of the twenty-first?

Common visual representations of early human ancestors and nonhuman primates often depict a father, mother, and child, reproducing a notion that the heterosexual nuclear family is fundamental to human nature itself (Haraway 1997, 240–44). Yet, the nuclear family is a relatively recent formation to gain social prominence—a product of the eighteenth and nineteenth centuries that accompanied the rise of industrial capitalism, specifically in the US, for the white middle class (Stacey 1998, 6–8). Forces of the twentieth century, however, worked to naturalize this form: "an intact nuclear household unit" is a "form of family life that many mistake for an ancient, essential, and now-endangered institution" (5). US policies have often punished alternative family formations under the rationale that nuclear families prevent poverty and other social ills, while simultaneously criminalizing people of color (Briggs 2020; Cohen 2004; Kohler-Haussman 2007; Stacey 1998). While many working-class families and families of color in the United States never conformed or were foreclosed from entering the nuclear family ideal (particularly with a male breadwinner and stay-at-home mother), the nuclear family "represented this nation's culturally mandated gender and kinship system" and family arrangements that diverged from it "have been judged and found wanting when compared with it" (Stacey 1998, 7).

"The family" is important both ideologically and administratively to humanitarian and human rights work, but it has also emerged as a site of anxiety and an object of anti-immigrant discourse. The 1997 edition of the *UNHCR Resettlement Handbook*—a fourteen-chapter document on UNHCR's resettlement policies and procedures—discusses "the fraudulent misrepresentation of family composition during the resettlement process" (UNHCR 1997, ch. 7, 19). In the 2011 edition of the handbook, UNHCR used a new term for that type of misrepresentation, calling it "family composition fraud," which includes "marriages of convenience; fictitious relationships, such as when distant relatives are claimed as sons and daughters; adding fictitious family members; substituting children, which may occur for money or under duress; or "losing" or hiding a family member to get an improved chance at resettlement (such as when a woman hopes to qualify for the Women and Girls at Risk category by claiming that her husband is dead or has disappeared)" (UNHCR 2011, 130).

Technology that reveals the "truth" of family composition through genetic science makes the family unit even more central to twenty-first century anxieties about so-called fraudulent refugees. The truth revealed by genetic testing requires a biogenetic nuclear family that is consistent with normative US conceptions of kinship—that is, as David Schneider wrote, "whatever the biogenetic relationship is" (1980: 23; see also Helmreich 2001, 130)—even as lived practice in the United States and other places where DNA has been used for border security is far more diverse and complex.

Because families and keeping families together are important to the goals of both UNHCR and the US Refugee Admissions Program, being perceived as posturing as a family is met with moral anxiety or indignation. Displaying appropriate gratitude, which requires compliance with rules, is a prerequisite of humanitarian assistance. As Besteman writes, "Humanitarianism demands . . . an apolitical life of silence, docility, conformity, and unending gratitude" (2016, 164). The real or perceived instrumental construction of a family for the purposes of resettlement disrupts the aim of resettling the "correct" refugees—those seen as honest, compliant with rules, especially vulnerable, and composing bureaucratically appropriate units for entry into the United States and elsewhere.

The scientific testability of the family—given the "authority and hold that science is granted . . . in defining and naturalizing the modalities of human relations" (Franklin and McKinnon 2001, 15)—reproduces the biogenetic nuclear family as the natural and genuine family unit. In the process of using DNA to verify family claims, the family is produced as whatever is testable—a truth derived "from the body" by expert scientific knowledge (Fassin and d'Halluin 2005; see also Ticktin 2011). The tests reproduce biogenetic families as "real" and others as "fraudulent." Changes in the law and in social life, as well as the diversity of communities with various kinship practices, have expanded meanings of kinship in the United States and elsewhere in the global North. Yet, popular knowledge of genetic science and new reproductive technologies that have expanded possibilities for biogenetic reproduction have also worked to reinforce biogenetic kinship norms and to further naturalize the nuclear family.

Securing the Nuclear Family

As the stories and reflections of people who appear in this chapter reveal, reunification and resettlement of families in the United States and elsewhere often follows the disruption of familial bonds and networks in other places. That immigration regimes separate families is not new. Recently, it has been made dramatically visible through the separation of Central American children from their guardians and parents as a deterrence strategy at the US-Mexico border (Dickerson 2022). Asylum seekers often must leave children behind because of the extraordinary dangers they face on their journeys (De León 2015). For families able to seek prior authorization to move, bureaucratic regulations, application fees, and other costs often mean that they must migrate abroad in a piecemeal fashion, leaving spouses and children behind with plans to reunite when it becomes financially possible (Coe 2014, 87–114).

Using the nuclear biogenetic family as the primary or default unit of case composition in resettlement and family reunification is motivated by multiple imperatives. It purports to prevent fraud, child trafficking, and unwieldy chain migration in which people could continue to apply for more distant relatives. In addition to being motivated by these imperatives of immigration control, DNA testing produces nuclear families and reinforces a culturally dominant notion that the nuclear family is *the* family—or the "normal and natural" family (Coe 2014, 106)—while allaying fears about Muslim and other cultural Others. As Junaid Rana writes, "Illegal immigration, terrorism, and trafficking go together in this schema of interchangeable objects that ultimately work to control and regulate immigration through the rhetoric of anti-terrorism. In other words, uncontrolled border crossing brings not only dangerous people but also dangerous objects, ideas, and practices" (2011, 60).

While refugee resettlement is a legal form of border crossing, it is, as we have seen, fraught with mistrust about who might illegitimately access it and what people might bring with them. The imagined dangerous practices that Rana writes of include practices involving the family. Besteman notes that what her Somali Bantu interlocutors recalled most about the cultural orientation program they attended before leaving Kenya was the many aspects of their family lives—polygyny, earlier and arranged marriages, and various parenting norms—that would be frowned upon, pathologized, or criminalized in the United States (2016, 210). Viewing Somali practices such as polygyny, extended family cohabitation, or financial commitments to expansive kin groups as uncivilized or antithetical to white middle-class US norms (see Po-vinelli 2005) animates the exclusion of non-biogenetic, nonnuclear kin from family reunification. DNA testing reinforces a mainstream cultural norm and works to turn people arriving through US Refugee Admissions into more culturally familiar or seemingly culturally assimilable subjects.

Widespread US conceptions of kinship highlight love as an essential component (Schneider 1980)—for example, in the popular slogan championing same-sex marriage, "Love makes a family." Kinship formed for the purpose of worldly concerns such as immigration or money is stigmatized. As Collier, Rosaldo, and Yanagisako put it, in the United States "what gives shape to much of our conception of The Family is its symbolic opposition to work and business" (1997, 77). Yet here and with kinship the world over, love and attachment exist in relation with other motivations, needs, and desires. "US immigration laws are based on a myth or fiction of family life" in the US and elsewhere, writes Coe (2014, 106). Piot notes that "visa lottery kinship" (kinship instrumentally constructed for immigration purposes) in Togo is "cut from the same cloth as everyday Togolese kinship . . . satisfying concrete needs, both material and social, by whatever means possible" (Piot with Batema 2019, 73). Kinship practices that respond or exist in relation to immigration regulations are part and parcel of the ways in which kinship inherently works.

The proliferation of new technologies and architectures of border security is a persistent feature of the twenty-first century. These technologies are sometimes blunt and sometimes highly technical. They sometimes go largely unnoticed and other times are major topics of political discourse and debate—as in Trump's border wall. Algorithmic risk profiles use data like race and education to screen potential US border crossers (Besteman 2020, 80), and governments across the world use fingerprinting, iris scans, and facial recognition technologies in the production of "smart borders" (108–9). In 2022, the US introduced Asylum Text Analytics, which scans asylum seekers' testimonies for language that allegedly indicates plagiarism and fraud (Rud 2023), while France has long used medical exams performed by physicians to verify or dismiss asylum seekers' narratives about past physical harm (Fassin and d'Halluin 2005).

Genetic science has permeated the consciousness of individuals and communities through the now widespread availability of direct-to-consumer genetic-ancestry testing (Abel 2021) and the scientific study of specific communities' genetic origins (Abel 2021; Abu El-Haj 2012; TallBear 2013; Tamarkin

2020). Describing the ways in which a South African community put scientific findings to use, Tamarkin writes, "To understand contemporary power and politics, we need to understand the emerging political significance of DNA, and to understand the political significance of DNA, we need to attend ethnographically to the people from whom genetic samples derive" (2020, 25).

Tamarkin and others write about the ways in which genetic science has been used to make different claims about race, ethnicity, and origins, which have been used to advance a variety of political goals. As for using DNA testing to ascertain parentage, DNA has been used along with common paternity testing in efforts to repair and seek justice in cases of family separations. It has been used, for example, among Yemenite Jews in Israel who had children taken in the 1950s (Weiss 2001) and Argentine children abducted from their parents who opposed the military dictatorship in the 1970s and '80s (Smith 2016). Indeed, DNA is now employed in myriad political projects.

DNA testing as a tool of border control, in particular, sheds light on kinship as a locus of surveillance and control within a context of securitized, transnational humanitarianism. DNA testing has shaped diasporic families and altered the inherent flexibility of kinship to provide care in the face of mass death and displacement. Whether biogenetic or not, kinship does not simply exist; it is *made*—through social rituals of incorporation, both mundane and elaborate (Carsten 2004, 9). DNA testing in refugee resettlement demonstrates the ways in which science and technology are increasingly employed to bolster security regimes and how security and kinship are co-constituted in immigration policies.

After living in Nairobi from August 2013 to March 2015, I returned to the United States to begin conducting research at a local resettlement agency in Columbus, Ohio. There, I saw from the vantage point of my home country—which now appeared both familiar and strange—how nuclear family case composition looked from the other side and how technologies of surveillance continued to have a hold on people even after they had passed through the resettlement process.

FIVE

Resettled Families in
an Age of Global Security

DAHIR AND I SIT at Ginevra, a Somali restaurant on a strip of Columbus's Morse Road—a hub of the local Somali community. On the same corner sit African Paradise Restaurant and a branch of Dahabshiil, the global Somali money transfer company. Across the street, Somali-owned shops fill Global Mall, offering clothes, food, housewares, and electronics. Down the street is a Senegalese restaurant, a Mexican grocery, Fashion City, Arby's, and a pawn shop, making it an increasingly typical mélange of establishments on a Midwestern city's commercial outskirts. Two of the city's three refugee resettlement agencies are conveniently located in the area, accessible to the communities that have made this area home over the last decade or so, revitalizing it in the aftermath of its decline following the demolition of a once-popular destination mall in the early 2000s.

I try to eat slowly while Dahir ignores his lunch, telling me about how his mother and younger siblings still live in Kakuma camp in Kenya, while he and his older brother have managed a stressful existence on their own in Ohio for over two years while waiting for their family to join them:

> The biggest problem was that the money I received was so little, but I had to sit down with my brother and still cut a budget out of our budget to send Mom and kids to keep them alive. Because we did not come united. I'm living in this country for two years. I always ask ORA [Ohio Refugee Assistance][1] and they don't give me information. Same as the RSC [US Resettlement Support

Center]. Both are telling me, "Your mom is on hold." "What's 'on hold'? Can you please give me an explanation?!" They say, "We don't know that. Just be patient." I've been patient for two years now. They tell me, "Not our problems. It's Immigration, Homeland Security, the government—to make sure the case is clean." I ask them, "Okay, what are the security challenges that this case can have? What are the security challenges of a mother of fifty years old, who's sick!?" Our hands are tied. Our lives are not complete without our family.

Dahir speaks about his life in the United States not as an endpoint along a route but rather as one of several nodes that connect far-flung families, diasporic communities, and the transnational humanitarian processes of refugee resettlement between his home country, East African countries of asylum, North America, and beyond. His narrative "unsettles the assumption that the resettlement of refugees is an automatic solution to displacement" (Ramsay 2018, 2) and "challenge[s] the conception of refuge as relief or resolution, the end of the journey" (Besteman 2014, 427). Once in the United States, resettlement and family sponsorship processes remain part of many people's ongoing relationships with government security, transnational immigration bureaucracies, and international humanitarian governance as they manage new and familiar forms of uncertainty while hoping that their families will eventually come.

This chapter shows how transnational family networks between North America, Somalia, and its neighboring countries keep members of the Somali community in the US under the scrutiny of state security. People enact kinship obligations transnationally by sponsoring children, spouses, and parents through programs such as the US Refugee Family Reunification Program; waiting for family members who were not able to travel together because of US case composition regulations; and sending financial remittances to support families—about 1.3 billion dollars annually from the diaspora to Somalia alone (Oxfam 2015, 1). But for people with Muslim identities, post-9/11 security practices challenge access to humanitarian programs like the US Refugee Admissions Program (USRAP). The War on Terror continues to haunt people who hail from countries targeted by the United States once they arrive, including through their family members undergoing security checks abroad. Sending remittances through money transfer systems like *xawaala*, the only available method of sending money to Somalia, invites suspicion. In these ways, newly arrived Somali-Americans often remain entangled in regimes of securitization, even after having been vetted by multiple US agencies prior to arrival. The transnational family becomes a central, if overlooked category in the ways in which counter-terror practices operate and intersect with social worlds.

Surveillance of Somali communities in the US is directly connected to perceptions of Somalia and ongoing events inside the country. After the 1998 al-Qaeda bombings of the US embassies in Kenya and Tanzania and the 9/11 attacks (events in which no Somali people were involved), Somalia was increasingly viewed by the United States as a security threat in the Global War on Terror. Without a functioning central government, security analysts saw it as a prime locale where wanted international militant Islamists could hide and recruit (Ibrahim 2018, 22). Meanwhile, Hollywood movies of the post-9/11 era like *Black Hawk Down, Captain Phillips,* and *Eye in the Sky* portrayed Somalis as terrorists, pirates, and war lords—the ultimate villains in the global story of our times.

In the 1990s and 2000s across Somalia, local, neighborhood-wide Islamic courts emerged as seats of governance and dispute resolution in the absence of a central government. These courts were "an expression of organic forms of governance that were grounded in the practices, concepts, and norms of the historically rooted Islamic tradition of the community" (Ibrahim 2018, 26). The CIA saw the courts, however, as manifestations of radical, imported ideologies and ultimately backed a coalition of anti-courts warlords. The CIA-backed targeting of sheikhs from the Islamic courts led to a popular uprising and the creation of the Union of Islamic Courts (UICs), which further galvanized the United States to support an Ethiopian invasion to overthrow the UICs in 2006. From the rubble of the UICs emerged al-Shabaab, a militant group that opposed the new, weak, US-supported central government (Ibrahim 2018, 22–25). Ibrahim writes, "The story of the rise of the UICs and what came after it has all the elements of what has become a common enough occurrence in Muslim world: an economic and political crisis in a Muslim society, a local response framed in Islamic symbols and discourse, an ill-informed Western intervention that leads to a more radical and militant 'Islamist' response on the ground" (2018, 25).

Besteman, likewise, notes that despite its efforts to combat terrorism in Somalia after 9/11, the US "in fact enabled al-Shabaab to emerge as an effective anti-Western terrorist group" (2020, 5–6). The US- and EU-backed African Union Mission in Somalia took over as a military operation in Somalia for fourteen years, until 2022, and was then replaced by the African Union Transition Mission in Somalia, which, at the time of writing, aimed to transfer its responsibilities to the Somali Security Forces by the end of 2024. Ultimately, ordinary Somali diasporans' ties to their families and communities in Somalia have been viewed by global North governments through a counter-terror lens—a fact that surfaces in the story that this chapter tells.

As a Black Muslim immigrant community in the United States, the Somali-American diaspora is subject to the racializing discourses that position Muslims as suspects in a post-9/11 world. Suspicion is embedded in the community's "transnational relations with the home country" that "locate them within local and global discourses of America's War on Terror" (Abdi 2015, 200). In the United States, daily life often remains entangled with state security apparatuses through obligations to families abroad—regularly sending money and sponsoring family members through the Refugee Family Reunification Program and the similar "follow-to-join" Visa 93 program. The day-to-day experience of remitting money and dealing with the protracted process of sponsoring family members holds people like Dahir in anxious anticipation, waiting for a resolution to disjointed social worlds.

Growing African Diasporas in a Midwestern City

After living in Nairobi from August 2013 to March 2015, I touched down at 1:00 a.m. in Syracuse, New York, the closest airport to my hometown. My mother smiled, almost laughing, standing on a desolate carpet under the fluorescent lights of the nearly abandoned building. In the months ahead, I would witness many airport reunions between relieved and overjoyed parents and children who had waited for years, with no assurance that they would see one another again. Unlike the people with whom I worked, whose mobility was impeded by twenty-first century border regimes, my little blue passport afforded me the option of traveling with relative ease in Nairobi, the East African region, and around North America, enabling my multi-sited research. This fact was not lost on my interlocutors. "You can go anywhere with that golden dragon," Mohamed once said, mistaking the bald eagle emblazoned on my passport for a mythical monster.

With my mom at the wheel of her Toyota, we crawled along Route 92 and then inched along Route 20, the white fuzz of a March snow amplified by the headlights. A week later, I drove to Columbus, Ohio, a city I had never visited but where I had arranged to be based at a local resettlement agency for the next six months. From the hills of upstate New York, I drove west on Interstate 90, along Lake Erie—flat and gray—past Buffalo and Cleveland, where snow was still drifting down, and then south on I-71 and, nearly eight hours later, into the parking lot of my new home base. Columbus is home to the second largest Somali community in the United States (after Minneapolis), along with growing numbers of other African communities. The city also hosts several small and large organizations working with refugees, including three resettlement agencies at the time of my fieldwork, though one was forced to close its doors in 2017 after major government cuts to refugee admissions. In 2015, these organizations were bringing people through the US Refugee Admissions Program to central Ohio every week and nearly every day.

In early discussions about my interest in the US Family Reunification Program with Greg, the director of RefAid in Nairobi, he had mentioned Columbus, along with the name Marissa Thomson. Later Amy, who oversaw the Family Reunification Program through RSC Africa, mentioned Marissa, too. Marissa, a lawyer, had served as director of Ohio Refugee Assistance (ORA) for many years. Under her leadership, ORA processed large numbers of family reunification applications, accounting for a substantial number of those received by the RSC in Nairobi, which oversaw resettlement for most of the continent.

After being introduced to Marissa by Greg over email soon after meeting him in Nairobi, I spoke with her over Skype about the Family Reunification Program, its suspension in 2008, and the slow reopening that had begun just a year earlier, in 2012. Marissa seemed to be an experienced and knowledgeable advocate who was thoughtful about changes to the Family Reunification Program, including the introduction of DNA testing (see chapter 4). When I learned I had received additional funding to continue my research, I contacted her about spending time at her organization, and Marissa agreed. At ORA, I was made a volunteer and intern, with a badge, email address, laptop, and shared desk—a contrast from the research I conducted from the peripheries of the more guarded refugee institutions in Nairobi. In Columbus, I spent most of my days accompanying caseworkers on their many daily tasks with clients, sitting in on meetings, observing family reunification consultations, and working as a Swahili interpreter for the first Banyamulenge family that ORA resettled.

A Somali caseworker, Ikran, who had arrived through the resettlement program several years prior, generously located an apartment for me to rent in one

of the buildings where the organization regularly found homes for new arrivals. When I arrived at ORA fresh from the highway on a cold March evening,
Ikran had left for the day, leaving the apartment's keys with a colleague. I was
surprised to hear she was gone since we had planned to meet, but I quickly
learned that caseworkers oriented unpredictable schedules around their newly
arrived clients—juggling; trouble-shooting; managing the many appointments, requests, and needs of the people they assisted. Delayed flights, doctors'
appointments, a sudden need for a ride to a job interview, a long-awaited document that had to be delivered—resettlement caseworkers serve as the guides for
most people arriving through the US Refugee Admissions Program, especially
for those without existing social ties in their new home cities. The caseworker is
the tie—responsible for picking up people at the airport, providing first meals,
finding and furnishing first apartments, acquiring Social Security cards, applying for government benefits, enrolling children in school, setting up mandated
English language training, teaching people how to use public transportation
and how to navigate an American grocery store, and linking them with job
counselors, among their most immediate tasks. Three months after arriving,
people who have come through USRAP are technically on their own. The caseworker moves on to the next arrivals, though people like Ikran often stayed in
touch with their clients long after the three months had elapsed.

Columbus is a growing city compared to many others in the US Rust
Belt and Midwest regions. Its diversified economy, with the state capital and
government jobs, the state's flagship public university, and several corporate
headquarters including Nationwide Insurance and American Electric Power,
helped the city weather the 2008 recession better than many of its size (Glinton 2016). With a population of 850,000 and a metropolitan area population of
almost 2 million people in 2015, Columbus had the seventh-lowest unemployment rate among major metropolitan areas in the US (Bureau of Labor Statistics 2015a; Bureau of Labor Statistics 2015b). During the period I conducted
research there, the largest communities arriving through the Refugee Admissions Program were Somalis, followed by Iraqis and Nepalis from Bhutan. As
part of the US government plan to resettle 50,000 Congolese refugees over five
years, people from eastern Congolese communities were also beginning to
arrive. Estimates of the Somali population in the Columbus area range from
10,000 to 80,000 (Dachenbach 2015; see also Abdi 2015, 174). As of the 2015–
16 school year, Somali was the second most common home language of K–12
English Learner students in the Columbus metropolitan area, after Spanish
(Sugarman and Geary 2018, 3).

A small number of Somalis had come to Ohio in the 1980s, often as university students. Liban, one of ORA's longtime case workers, for example, came in an early wave of Somali migration to Ohio. In the 1980s, he had been encouraged to come by a friend who was a student at Ohio University in nearby Athens. Following the government collapse of 1991, Somalis started coming to the US in greater numbers, and Columbus's reputation among Somalis grew. People were attracted by the low cost of living and later by kin and a growing community, mosques, Somali businesses, and the increasing availability of Somali resettlement caseworkers, medical interpreters, and government resources translated into the Somali language.

Family reunification cases excluded, people who come to the US through USRAP cannot choose their destination. Rather, cases are allotted to cities based on the capacity and capabilities of local resettlement agencies, as well as the city's local resources, like available affordable housing. But this doesn't stop people from moving after they arrive in the US. Many who had first been resettled in either more expensive places like California or in places with fewer Somalis or less support for Somali communities came to Columbus or other major US hubs of the diaspora like Minneapolis. The availability of jobs in factories and warehouses enabled people who didn't yet speak English to begin working relatively quickly, and many Somali women, in particular, were employed in "pick and pack" warehouse jobs, where they find and package items for shipment. Inadequate public transportation, insufficient affordable housing, the instability and low pay of warehouse and factory jobs, and the limited nature of government support make life challenging for new arrivals, who often have limited language and other transferable skills for employment (see also Abdi 2015). But the relatively stable economy and the robust Somali community make Columbus a desirable location, nonetheless.

Just south of Morse Road sit apartment complexes with two- and three-story brick buildings flanked by large concrete parking lots and encircled by strips of green lawn. Few management companies will sign rental agreements with people who have no rental or employment history in the United States, so resettlement agencies like ORA have to locate housing for all their clients in a small number of buildings run by a few willing management companies. In 2015, some of these apartment complexes housed many Somali, Congolese, Rwandan, and Burundian families arriving from camps and urban neighborhoods across the East African region.

My own apartment was located in a small two-story brick building built in 1961 a couple of miles west of these complexes, in a neighborhood mostly home to small mid-century ramblers and a few other small apartment buildings. The two two-bedroom apartments above me were rented by a Somali family that included a wife and husband, his mother, and their seven children. In the building behind us lived three more Somali families. Two families—one that had come from Kenya and one from Ethiopia—rented the two apartments on the top floor. The two basement apartments were rented by a mother and her children who had come from Kenya, until they were forced to vacate when the apartments flooded after a week of heavy rain. In the spring and summer that year, neighbors lounged and visited on front steps and in the green yards that extended from their stoops to the curb. The kids often played outside in the late afternoon and evening, sometimes with children from other buildings or houses on the street.

Among those I came to know through ORA and in the Northland area neighborhoods, kin connections were reshaped through people's new obligations to send money and to navigate a new set of bureaucratic processes as they attempted to bring family members to the United States. In January 2014, just over a year after the reopening of the Refugee Family Reunification Program, a staff member at the RSC in Nairobi reported that 1,562 cases had been filed since the program's reopening, accounting for nearly 6,000 refugees waiting in African countries to come to the United States through Family Reunification alone. By mid-2015, at least several hundred applications had been filed in Columbus. After years of waiting, people who had come to the US through the resettlement program begin to wait again. And although all communities wading through refugee resettlement and family reunification bureaucracy face backlogs and long wait times, people with Muslim names and identities face a specific set of obstacles.

The US FBI has taken special interest in the Somali community throughout major US cities. Starting in 2009, Columbus was among five cities subject to the FBI's Specialized Community Outreach Team program, which used outreach activities to surveil and gather intelligence on the Somali community (Buhain 2015; Federal Bureau of Investigation 2009). The program ended a year later, but in 2015 the US Justice Department launched a new program, Countering Violent Extremism, which similarly recruits community leaders, teachers, and others as informants (Kimball 2015; Sheikh 2019). In the early 2010s, the Northland neighborhood's Columbus Global Academy—a public middle and high school focused on English as a Second Language for students of immigrant backgrounds, the largest group being Somali—partnered with the FBI. The Bureau ran an FBI Teen Academy to teach students about the organization's work, and in 2011, the school received the FBI Director's Community Leadership Award, which recognizes those making "extraordinary contributions to their communities in the areas of terrorism, cyber, drug, gang, or violence prevention and education" (Columbus City Schools 2012).

According to in-depth reporting by journalist Janet Reitman (2021), a former FBI agent, Terry Albury, described open racism and "unabashed hatred" directed at the Somali community in his office in Minneapolis, recalling a secretary suggesting that the Somali "problem" in Minnesota could be solved by bombing the housing projects where they lived. Remarks such as this one demonstrate the depths of dehumanizing anti-Muslim, anti-Black, and anti-Somali racism and the ways in which foreign wars against Muslim "others" and ideas about Muslim immigrant communities congealed in an American imagination after 9/11. Leaked documents show coercive recruitment of informants from within Muslim communities, endemic anti-Muslim racism in the FBI, and an FBI incentive structure that promoted opening investigations based on guilt by association or minimal evidence and keeping them open without cause. For millions of people, including many Somali Americans, any time they "applied for a passport, or a job that required a background check, or a driver's license, or simply had [their] name run through any sort of government database," an FBI record would appear, casting them in a suspicious light, even when nothing was ever found. The FBI directed agents to "instill fear and then generate this paranoia . . . so that [people] know that they're under suspicion perpetually," according to Albury (Reitman 2021). Members of the Somali community in Columbus and the family members for whom they were waiting were targets of perpetual suspicion, even though some of them were beneficiaries of a humanitarian program.

Waiting, Continued

The previous chapter described how in 2008, the US Refugee Family Reunification Program was suspended after a DNA-testing pilot program showed that over 80 percent of the cases tested (of primarily Somali and Ethiopian families) fell outside the program's standard definition of *family*. According to the US government, these findings demonstrated widespread fraud (Bureau of Population, Refugees, and Migration 2009). In 2012, the reunification program was reopened, this time with DNA testing as a permanent component.

Though they received no dedicated funding to support their work, local re-settlement organizations like ORA were responsible for submitting family re-unification applications under the new program. During the four years when the program had been suspended, people who had arrived in the United States through USRAP were unable to apply for family members who, for a wide variety of reasons, had not been included on their original cases.

When the program reopened in 2012, people who had been waiting for years for separated family members began sleeping overnight in ORA's park-ing lot to ensure they were at the front of the line to fill out paperwork the next day. For a whole year following the program's reopening, three staff members devoted almost two full workdays each week to filling out family reunification applications to make up for the years when the program had been closed. By the spring of 2015 when I arrived, ORA had caught up on the four-year back-log. Still, every Monday, when Marissa held an hour of walk-in consultations for the family reunification program, the hour was filled with people coming to begin the process. In these initial meetings, Marissa established whether the person's family members were eligible for the program. If they were, she sent them to meet with Kathryn, another staff member, to schedule an appoint-ment to fill out an Affidavit of Relationship (AOR), the detailed paperwork required to apply. On Tuesdays, Liban's office was filled with people checking on their cases, and throughout the week Kathryn held appointments to fill out the AORs, which would then be sent to the national voluntary agency with which ORA was affiliated.

Many of the people who came for a consultation with Marissa could not bring the family members they were hoping to sponsor for reasons such as the genealogical relationship, the family members not living in a country of asylum, or too much time having elapsed since the would-be sponsor's arrival. Others were stopped early in the process because of demands for evidence that they could not produce. For example, a woman who had applied for her husband came to ORA one day with a letter from USCIS requesting a death certificate for her first husband. The letter stated that in an early interview in Kenya, she had claimed that her husband had died in 1991. But in her paper-work applying for her second husband to join her in the United States, she wrote that her first marriage had ended in 2000. The woman said she had no way to procure a death certificate. Without it, the letter stated, her case would most likely be denied. In an effort to provide USCIS all the evidence they might request, Marissa had clients assemble not only marriage and birth certificates but also, as proof of the relationship, photographs and printouts of Facebook and WhatsApp conversations between the client and their spouse abroad. A staff member would then translate the conversations into English. The most intimate and private corners of people's lives became open to government scrutiny in order to prove they were a genuine family.

After working in the office, assisting caseworkers, and spending time with my neighbors, it became clear to me that almost everyone was waiting for someone. Many were waiting for decisions about family sponsorship cases. Others were waiting because their family had been separated by UNHCR or the US government based on case composition rules and some members had departed before others. Nuclear families would constitute a single case, while "extended" kin, including married children or any children over the age of twenty-one could be "linked"—they could depart at different times—possibly years apart and could receive different final determinations, potentially separating them permanently. Many family and social networks included some people with resettlement cases and some without.

My neighbors, who had arrived in Columbus from Kenya only days after I did and whom I had met at the airport when I accompanied Ikran to greet them, were anxiously waiting for their adult daughter with her husband and children. Nearby, a woman who lived with her daughter and sick husband was desperately hoping to be reunited with her two children from a first marriage, as well as her niece, the daughter of her deceased brother. Another neighbor and her two children were waiting for a younger daughter who was being cared for by her grandmother in Dadaab. To be waiting for someone seemed more common than not among people arriving in Columbus.

Kathryn was a white woman, born and raised in Columbus, who had worked for ORA since she had graduated from college a few years earlier. She formed close friendships with several of her colleagues as well as with ORA clients. She often spent time with Ikran, along with the family with whom Ikran lived—a woman and her six children, whose husband remained in Kenya. It was Kathryn who suggested I talk with Dahir, the young man who was waiting for his mother and younger siblings who were in Kakuma. Dahir's persistence and obvious frustration had affected Kathryn—in part because of the sheer frequency of his trips to ORA to voice his grievances and try to procure updates on his family's case. He had struck a chord with her. His complaints were directed toward problems that, for the most part, she was powerless to solve, which she found distressing but also illuminating. His continuous pleas highlighted the human costs of a bureaucratic and security juggernaut and the stress that people faced in their waiting without answers.

Dahir, his mother, and his siblings had begun their resettlement case from the Kakuma refugee camp in Kenya in 2007. The case remained pending for five years, until they were called for an interview in 2012. Because Dahir and his brother were twenty-two and twenty-three by that time—no longer minors—they were separated from their family's case. Their individual cases moved through the system, and Dahir arrived in Columbus in 2013, a week after his brother. But when I met Dahir in 2015, two years later, his mother and siblings had not arrived. In Kakuma, Dahir had worked for an international organization, acting as a liaison between it and his community and as a representative to donors. Perhaps in part because of his ability to take advantage of scarce opportunities in Kakuma and his connections to international NGOs there, he had high hopes for life in the US, which had been frustrated in his first years in the country.

It was difficult to find a time to meet with Dahir, given his work driving a truck between Columbus and Indianapolis six days a week. Sundays were for sleeping, laundry, and talking to family back in Kenya. But we finally found a day to meet for lunch when Dahir woke up, before starting his shift in the afternoon. Ginevra—a staple restaurant for ORA staff and the local Somali community—is casual, with tile floors, simple tables, and a long counter up front where to-go orders are dispensed. A drive-through window offers the ultimate American convenience, where patrons pick up lunch or large aluminum trays of rice, pasta, and meat for events and gatherings. Inside, a partition divides the men's seating area from the area for women, families, and mixed-gender diners, like restaurants in Eastleigh. On the day we met, jazz music was playing loudly. We ordered pasta and goat meat, but Dahir's lunch sat untouched as he talked animatedly. Having assisted a Canadian researcher in Kakuma, he was at ease and eager to talk, encouraging me to record him. When he explained that he had to find money each month for his mother, as well as his own daily expenses, I asked how much he sent back. Dahir answered:

> Quite a lot of money. We send back $1,000 a month, sincerely. I pay $500 per month; my brother pays $500 per month. My mom has diabetes, [high] blood pressure; she was treated for cancer. So all that, in Kakuma refugee camp, they don't get enough assistance for medical. And food and all that stuff. I have to take my siblings to school—pay for their school. That's why my dreams ended. My dream was to get further education—to do finance and accounting or po-

litical science as an activist. So those all—shattered. Because I had to work full time, seven days a week, sixty hours a week to make sure that they are living a sustainable life. Work overtime, work overtime, contribute, buy a car, went to DMV, did the exam, got my permit, did the road test. Same [for] my brother. We help each other. Some of the challenges that we had, like driving, we solved that one. The second challenge was a job; now we are working. The third challenge was getting a paycheck—we're living paycheck to paycheck; we can't save money. I probably cannot save money while my mom is dying, when she needs quick medical assistance. My siblings need something to eat. They need to go to school. They need to look at their future. As a breadwinner, both me and my brother, we were already resettled to the United States of America. So, my mom doesn't have help [at home], so the only help that she waits for from God is from me and my brother. We have to contribute money to make her life look more decent, more healthful, and that's why after two years we are still facing that challenge.

Dahir went on,

Someone who has a bright future in front of him—wants to be a young entrepreneur or businessman or an activist—can't go to college. I can't go to college because this small amount of money that I'm getting to sustain myself—pay my bills, my insurance, car, my fuel, my rent and all that—I have to work extra hours to cover the bills of my mom. Why is it that two of us, who came here to the United States of America, successfully, nothing was asked? Our process was quick, from the beginning! Finished medical [screening], six months later, [when] my medical [certification] was still good for one month [*snaps fingers to indicate the speed at which the process suddenly unfolded after years of waiting*]. My brother came, I came, and we expected that our mom and siblings would follow us not more than six months. It's now about three years.

Up at the counter, I see an ORA caseworker with a woman and three children. He is ordering their first meal in the United States since they have yet to go grocery shopping and get oriented in their new kitchen. The restaurant offers ORA a discount—$10 instead of $12 for rice and meat with salad.

"So this is the biggest challenge," says Dahir, who still has not looked at his food.

Our hands are tied. . . . Our lives are not complete without our family. And family to me—my mom is the only person that we look up to right now. My dad died of the same challenges. He had cancer. He never had medical assistance, no one had sent him money, no one took him to hospital, and that's why we are working six days a week to try to get enough money to make sure she is getting assistance and treatment. That's the thing she needs to have. And at least basic things like food, going to school [for the kids], clothing and all that. She doesn't need much. But that's the problem—the biggest problem is [that] my mind is in Kenya; my body is in America. You know what I'm saying? I always think of her. Right now, I'm a truck driver, but sometimes my job is a risk because sometimes I'm thinking too much of my mom. Sometimes you are on the road, they can call you and say, "Hey, Dahir, your mom is sick. She's been in the hospital for a week and no one was helping her." You know what I'm saying? She was taking care by herself! Okay, we met the financial expectation, but she cannot get the care that we used to give her. We used to take her to the hospital, back and forth, bring her home, whatever she's unable to do, help her to do. You know what I'm saying? So these are the challenges we're facing.

I still don't have any answers. I look for answers. I say, "Why? Why are my siblings who are under eighteen years locked up for security issues? Why is my mom's case on hold?" "On hold" means you have security problems! I mean, I mean, I mean—okay, I can have security problems because of the last name I have and as a youth. The government can say, "Hey this person *could* be involving himself in gang issues or terrorist issues," but such people—I don't think so! When I hear "security issues" of Homeland Security, my assumption is someone who has a bad background. But such kids, they don't have! When I ask such questions, I get no answers back. Neither [ORA] nor the government have given me any information. And that leaves us still—someone like me, twenty-five years old, came here when I was twenty-three years old, expecting much, expecting a future, expecting to meet my dreams, to get my degree, to pursue my education until master's or PhD—you see what I'm saying? To help people! Help the youth! Create opportunities for them! Advocate for their rights! And without my family, I don't think I can drive to my dreams. Because I'm already locked up! I'm working six days, only get Sunday off, and when I come [home on] Sunday, I'm already tired. Wash my clothes, look up some things . . . that's it. I drive eleven hours a day, take ten hours rest, give two hours to talk to my family. This is the challenge that we have been receiving from day one up to right now. Working here, making sure you pay your bills. Cope with your challenges. Right now, what we are lacking . . . if we had our family with us, there's somewhere I could work part-time. Even work for [ORA] as an interpreter or work as a case worker. Get eight hours a day, work three days, go to school! You know what I'm saying? Go to school!

Dahir's voice rang with exasperation. He is "already locked up," his "hands are tied"—the separation of his family caused many challenges for everyday life and fulfilling anything resembling what he had hoped for in a place that he imagined to be a land of opportunity. Whether because of separate "linked" cases like Dahir's, waiting for long-delayed family reunification cases, or separation from kin and community who had no case at all, many people who had arrived through the refugee resettlement program could relate to Dahir's stress and the pain of waiting through an opaque and uncertain process.

As Cawo Abdi's research (2015) demonstrates, newly arrived Somali Americans' hopes for life in the United States are often unmet for multiple reasons, the complications of family separations being one. Tied to Dahir's psychological and emotional well-being was the disruption of networks of care—a critical consequence of the ways in which families are constituted through US refugee policy. On one hand, he was able to provide his mother and siblings with greater financial assistance after coming to the US. However, his mother lost her primary caregivers when her adult children departed. Dahir also calculated that if his family were united, he would have greater capacity to pursue his goals.

The previous chapter demonstrated the ways in which family separation informs the lives of people left behind in places like Kenya when their family members move. Those who arrive in places like the United States struggle to manage a different set of conditions structured by the US economy without the networks of care on which they once relied, in addition to new responsibilities to support family they left behind. Writing about Somali women in Columbus and Minneapolis, Abdi notes that "extended female family members played a vital role in women's economic pursuits in Somalia, and their absence is a key challenge for Somali women in their employment pursuits in the diaspora"—specifically in the United States, where women "who work in low-paying sectors cannot afford private child care and still meet their family's needs" (2015, 192). Those who are ineligible for family reunification—adult children, siblings, aunts, cousins—are "exactly those relations most likely to provide practical and moral support to a new mother and to help care for a young baby," as Feldman-Savelsberg writes of Cameroonian mothers in Berlin and German immigration policies (2016, 190)—a point that applies to Somali and other women in the US. Data from the early 2010s shows well over 50 percent of Somali Americans living below the poverty line, more than double the rate of the poorest native-born Americans (Abdi 2015, 206–7). The disruption of networks of caregiving combined with the lack of support for childcare in the United States contribute to the challenges of building economic stability. Even single working men like Dahir and his brother, who would appear free from the financial burdens of family, are often supporting a family that was not able to come united, including siblings, parents, and others.

In the summer of 2015, nearly three years after the US Refugee Family Reunification Program reopened, not one person in Columbus had received a family member through the program. Some had been waiting since before the program had been suspended in 2008. Everyone—both applicants and ORA staff alike—began to wonder if anyone would ever arrive. For many, Trump's executive orders on immigration of 2017, colloquially named the "Muslim ban," prolonged that waiting even further; whole childhoods were passing in the absence of longing parents and children. People with parents, siblings, spouses, or children in precarious situations, like Dahir's mother and siblings, spent years going through weekly or monthly rituals of seeking answers about stalled cases, and then, after 2017, doing so with the dread of watching the obstacles mount.

In Dahir's account of life in the United States, threads of family obligation and government securitization intermingle. The strain of life in a refugee camp never lifted as his mind, as he put it, remained in Kenya with his mother, worrying about her health. When he said, "My mind is in Kenya; my body is in America," he drew on a common trope used in talking about *buufis,* the desire to go abroad. Horst quotes a student in the Dadaab camps describing buufis as "a disease that attacks people who are mentally in America and physically in Ifo" (one of the Dadaab camps) (2006b, 167). Others put it this way: "The person who has buufis is someone who is crazy; his mind is not settled. He is here, but his mind is elsewhere" (Jacobsen 2011, quoted in Carrier 2016, 115). Dahir reverses the trope of mind-body separation typically used to describe a longing to leave Africa. Stating that his body is in the United States while his mind is in Kenya suggests that buufis—longing for resettlement—can be multidirectional. He shows how desire to be somewhere else is tied not to a universal diasporic experience but here to the difficulty of a family separation expected to be resolved but that is tied up in opaque state security processes.

Like many, Dahir shouldered new burdens: learning to live in a new place, meeting his own and his family's expenses, managing the strain of a solitary low-wage job with demanding hours, and reckoning with the disappointment of his own dreams. The outcome of Dahir's family's case, which I learned of a year after leaving Columbus, punctuates the uncertainty of living under a regime of securitized humanitarianism, even after settling in the United States permanently.

Suspect Money Transfers outside Global Banking

On a summer day, I accompanied a Somali case worker, Asad, and a Congolese family for whom I was acting as a Swahili interpreter, to the Franklin County Office of Jobs and Family Services. The family had just arrived in the US, and the parents were applying for government benefits, which they would rely on while attending English-language training and looking for work. In the waiting room, I chatted with a young Somali man, Warsame, a college student who was working as an interpreter over the summer. He had come from Kenya several years prior, and we talked about Nairobi, Kenyan politics, and his life in the US. Describing his family, Warsame spoke candidly about money issues, saying, "Yeah, my dad is old school. He gets social security, and he sends 80 percent of it back home to his nephews and nieces. Even if he doesn't have enough. We tell him, 'Dad, you need that money!' But he just sends it. Then he asks us for money."

"Why do you think people have that practice?" I asked. "Why do people feel so strongly the obligation to help people back home?"

"Long time ago, we were nomads," Warsame began. "So, everyone in the family lived together. People didn't live separately. They lived all together in one place, so any money was shared by everyone. So, my dad would never see his brother's kids as separate."

"He sees them like his own children?" I asked.

"Yes, definitely. My dad even sends his tax refunds. Like me, if I get $2,000 [refunded] from taxes, I save that. But my dad? No, he wouldn't even think of saving it. There's no saving. My dad has been here for six years, but if you look at his bank account, you wouldn't believe it. There's nothing. But on the other hand, he doesn't help his own sons [in Ohio]. Like my younger brother, he's seventeen, sometimes he needs something, 'cause he's still young. But my dad thinks if you're here, you're okay; you don't need to be helped. And also it's the name. Your name is enhanced by helping. Or at least not ruined by not helping."

"So, you value maintaining the social relationships by supporting relatives over your own needs and wants," I concluded.

"Yes, definitely," Warsame replied. "Like my dad, he always tells us, 'When I die, keep helping them.'"

"So, do you send money back to Kenya? Or Somalia?"

"No, I don't send money. I tell people I'm a student and working; I can't send anything now. And you know, you could have been supporting someone for years and years and years, and then you stop for two months and it's like you're dead to them!"

Later, in the car, I asked Asad, "Does this create conflicts in families, if you can't fulfill someone's expectations of what you should be sending them?"

"Oh yes, definitely," he replied. "Yes, like for Eid.[2] For Eid, you want to give your children something nice; they have to have something to enjoy. But if you tell the relatives back home, 'I don't have money to send you. My kids need Eid,' they tell you, 'You're selfish! You're lying!' They don't believe that you don't have enough money."

Habiba, a staff member who came to the US as a teenager (chapter 4), put this in stark terms as well. When I asked her when she began supporting her biogenetic parents in Somalia, she replied,

> As soon as I came to the US. I got a job at Wendy's after about three months. I was making $70 per week. It was $4.25 per hour. I worked part-time. Saturday and Sunday, I worked the full day, and Friday after school. I thought I had to be responsible. My mom never called and asked for money. My dad didn't call and ask. When I came to America, my goal was to go to school, get a job, and maybe bring my family. But then there was the reality check—I can't bring anyone.[3] Most Somali people support other people. They can't save money— you will be here poor forever. There's always a mom who needs an operation, a cousin who is getting married, someone who's sick. With the little coming in each month, you're carrying other people. Because someone carried you, and now it's your turn.

Paralleling some of the grievances expressed by Warsame and others, sociologist Abdi warns that remittance sending should not be romanticized, because it often places serious financial burden on already strapped new immigrants, affecting the ability of their children to integrate and thrive (2015, 213–18). At the same time, the deeply felt social obligation to send money is one of the transnational ties that sustain people in Somalia and the African Somali diaspora (as well as other migrant-sending countries in the global South) and that contribute to the creation of connected diaspora communities.

Alongside conflicting views within the community about sending remittances is the suspicion with which remittances are often viewed from outside. The US government has understood sending money throughout the Somali diaspora and to Somalia in particular under the rubric of risky money transfers that can trigger investigations of material support for groups such as al-Shabaab (Reitman 2021; see also James 2011). In the immediate aftermath of

9/11, President Bush pronounced money the "lifeblood of terrorist operations" (Neumann 2017, 93), initiating a new counter-terror financing regime with the signing of Executive Order 13224. The order called for freezing assets of individuals, groups, and bankers (Dean, Thompson, and Keatinge 2013) and employing anti-money-laundering regulations to combat terrorism, though the effectiveness of these methods as anti-terror tools has come under scrutiny (Al-Jarani 2017). These new regulations placed a disproportionate burden on small companies, such as Somali *xawaala* businesses, that serve communities associated with locations deemed high-risk (Cooper & Walker 2016).

Xawaala (transfer) is a money transfer system used throughout the Middle East, South Asia, and the Horn of Africa. Beginning in the 1990s, the Somali xawaala system expanded globally, as Somalia's civil war created a larger and more far-reaching Somali diaspora. Since then, several transnational xawaala companies have emerged, providing an essential service since the collapse of many Somali institutions and the absence of a globally connected, formal banking industry inside the country, whose national economy has been described as "not-official/not-unofficial" (Little 2003, 4). Shortly after 9/11, the US government shut down al-Barakaat, the most widely used Somali xawaala company at the time, due to allegations that the company's service had been used to transfer money to al-Qaeda. The allegations were based on a "paucity of public information at the time" and were announced using prejudicial language that led to "deep mutual suspicion" between xawaala operators and regulators (Cockayne with Shetret 2012, 35). After al-Barakaat closed in 2001, a company called Dahabshiil (gold smelter) filled the gap it had left open.

Companies such as Dahabshiil work through an extended network of operators and the transfer of debts. Money paid by a customer on Morse Road in Columbus can be available to a relative in Mogadishu within twenty-four hours. The repayment to the sending agent is made later (Lindley 2010, 36). Still, Dahabshiil and other xawaala companies rely on banks in the places from which money is being sent. Under the Obama administration, the Federal Reserve sent cease-and-desist letters to banks where Somali xawaala companies held accounts (Lee 2019, 2361). In February 2015, a month before I arrived in Columbus, the last bank working with Dahabshiil, Merchants Bank of California, shut Dahabshiil's accounts, threatening remittances from the US to Somalia altogether (Oxfam 2015).

Later that spring, I went to the Dahabshiil office in the Banadir Mall on Cleveland Avenue in Columbus, hoping to send some money to a friend in Kenya and to learn what, if anything, had changed. Two men standing outside the office informed me that they were no longer in operation due to the recent changes. If I was sending money to Kenya, they said, I could use a new mobile app that connected directly to Kenya's mobile money transfer service, M-Pesa. This worked well. But there was no such option in Somalia, which had no access to similar systems nor to other international services such as Western Union or MoneyGram. Somalia was suddenly cut off from over a billion dollars that flowed into its economy annually—more than it received in humanitarian aid, development aid, and foreign direct investment combined (Oxfam 2015, 1; Reckard and White 2015). When the former prime minster of Somalia, Abdiweli Sheikh Ahmed, came to speak in Columbus in April 2015, he devoted his talk at the Ohio State University to the crisis of the new regulations that were cutting off remittances from the US to Somalia, impressing on the audience the life-saving importance of keeping xawaala operators working.

On social media and beyond, Somali diasporans protested the regulations that had pressured US banks to close Somali xawaala accounts. On Twitter, they used the hashtags #IFundFoodNotTerror and #SomaliLifeline to challenge the logic behind the regulations that pushed US banks to prohibit xawaala operators from holding accounts. Organizations like Oxfam used images of women in Somalia to create a gendered visual link between Somali remittances and the funding of women's businesses and essential goods like food for families—images that sought to disrupt the association between remittances and terrorism. By the summer of 2015, Dahabshiil operators were able to legally reopen, though many in the Somali community worried that they could close again at any time, given government suspicion of xawaala and the continuously shifting regulations that made it difficult for operators to stay in business. Sending money was a fraught act not only as a mode of managing real and perceived inequalities across the diaspora, as scholars such as Abdi (2015) and Lindley (2010) have shown, but also one that global North governments deem suspicious, constructing transnational Somali families and social networks as inherently linked to security risks.

Vetting

Writing about the emergence of a permanent war on terrorism in 9/11's aftermath, Nicholas De Genova comments, "The Cold War's specter of foreign infiltration never afforded migrants as such a prominence in the nationalist imagination at all comparable to that which presently congeals around Arab and other Muslims living in the United States, and which has figured 'immigration' in general as an utterly decisive site in the ostensible War on Terror" (2007, 423–24). In our conversations, long-time veterans of refugee resettlement work often emphasized that "everything changed" after 9/11. Refugee resettlement was part of broader transformations during this period in which "the US security state did nothing less than reinvent itself, imagining and pursuing a new planetary concept of American power organized around the anticipation and pursuit of terror" both on foreign and domestic planes (Masco 2014, 193–94).

The creation of the Department of Homeland Security (DHS) in 2002 involved the dissolution of Immigration and Naturalization Services (INS), which had been housed under the Department of Justice. INS was replaced by three new agencies under DHS: Customs and Border Protection (CBP), Immigration and Customs Enforcement (ICE), and Citizenship and Immigration Services (USCIS). In the wake of this major institutional transformation, security protocols for every refugee undergoing screening to enter the United States also changed—more so for those coming from countries of concern to the United States, like Somalia. In comparison to the pre-9/11 period, a much larger set of data sources was employed to check names and birth dates of people considered for resettlement to the US (Martin 2005, 71–72). The Department of Homeland Security, the Department of State, the FBI, the National Counterterrorism Center, and the Department of Defense are all involved in screening people referred to the US Refugee Admissions Program. Layers of biographical and biometric checks using fingerprints are conducted against multiple US government agency databases (Center for American Progress 2015).

Although special clearances called Security Advisory Opinions had been used by the US government in the past, they became required for "a far wider range of individuals, sometimes based on nationality and sometimes on other criteria," in the refugee program (Martin 2005, 72). All Somali men between 16 and 50 have been subject to Security Advisory Opinions (SAOs), and others may also be flagged for various reasons (Refugee Council USA 2017). Along with the Consular Lookout and Support System name check used for all applicants, those requiring an SAO have their name run through additional government databases (Martin 2005, 72). In refugee camps, birthdates are often recorded as January first because of lack of birth records or for the purpose of streamlining administrative procedures. And Somalis often have names that are commonly shared across many Muslim countries. A name match in a database can cause a case's rejection, even if it is nearly impossible that the person listed in the database and the person referred to the US Refugee Admissions Program are the same, because that possibility cannot be conclusively ruled out. Dahir was baffled by the holdup of his mother and siblings' case because a sick woman and her children did not fit the typical profile of a person of concern to the US government, especially since he and his brother—the more likely targets of increased scrutiny based on gender and age—had passed through without a problem.

Although after 9/11 the US resettlement program underwent widespread changes related to security protocols, it remained largely under the radar of public discussions about immigration. Long oriented around Cold War geopolitics, refugee resettlement had received bipartisan support as a humanitarian program in the decades before the new millennium (Espiritu 2006; Loescher, Betts, and Milner 2008; Tang 2015). As historian Roger Daniels writes, the passage of the 1980 Refugee Act, which systematized refugee admissions to the US, was "spectacularly uncontroversial." The bill, co-sponsored by Democrat Edward Kennedy and Republican Strom Thurmond, passed in the Senate by a vote of 85–0 (2004, 204). After the November 2015 terror attacks in Paris, which coincided with large numbers of people fleeing to Europe from Syria's brutal civil war and Central Americans at the US-Mexico border receiving increased national media coverage, refugee resettlement became a target of scrutiny.

Much of the political rhetoric about refugees during this period focused on "vetting." In a speech on the presidential campaign trail in the summer of 2016, Donald Trump (2016a) stated that his opponent Hillary Clinton's plans involved "admitting hundreds of thousands of refugees from the Middle East with no system to vet them, or to prevent the radicalization of their children." Trump (2016b) advocated "extreme vetting" as a solution and "ideological certification to make sure that those we are admitting to our country share our values and love our people." His rhetoric and that of other nationalist populist leaders in Europe and elsewhere centered refugees and refugee admissions policies in growing public debates about control over national borders and about national identity, which included coded and explicit statements excluding racialized minorities from the national body.

Although people who had worked in the refugee field authored op-eds and posted on social media about the "extreme vetting" already involved in refugee resettlement, the allure of widespread political rhetoric about the dangers of people coming from places Trump called "shithole countries" proved compelling to many in the United States (Dawsey 2018). In a book published in 2004, Daniels wrote that "the notion that the United States was obligated to take in refugees of all kinds and have a relatively generous policy toward them had become part of a general consensus" (204). But between 2017 and 2018, the percentage of Americans who said the US did not have a responsibility to accept refugees increased from 41 percent to 43 percent among all polled and from 62 percent to 68 percent among people who identified as Republicans (Hartig 2018). In 2016, many Americans had rallied around Trump's call for eliminating immigration by people who practice the Islamic faith—an idea that would be put into action in the 2017 executive orders on immigration that barred people from several Muslim-majority countries, including Somalia. Political rhetoric that centered the US refugee program marked a dramatic shift. Alongside the rising securitization of refugee admissions, public opinion about accepting refugees soured. The effects of increasing securitization of immigration and humanitarian programs like refugee resettlement came to life in the lived experiences of people like Dahir.

Becoming a Suspect

As Mohamed and I were sitting in a restaurant in Eastleigh a couple of months before he would depart for Toronto, he leaned over a glass of mango juice, eyes wide, to tell a story. He had run into an old classmate at a cybercafé earlier in the week. The young woman was Somali Canadian but had gone to Kenya for high school—a common way for parents to guide teenagers to develop Somali language skills and cultural and religious values—known as *dhaqancelin* (to return to culture); the "returnees" were known as *dhaqan celis* (see also Abdi 2015; Carrier 2016; Tiilikainen 2011). Mohamed and the young woman had been in school together for a year before he graduated, and had known each other fairly well. They had said hi to each other at the cybercafé, and the young woman began to tell Mohamed about her recent trip to Mogadishu to see relatives.

"You know," Mohamed added, "even if you are in another country, you don't cut your ties to your relatives back home."

"Of course," I nodded.

The young woman had traveled to Somalia with a female relative, whom he described as "a big suspect," reportedly suspected of financing al-Shabaab. The evidence upon which that allegation was based was unknown to me. "When she returned to Kenya, the Canadian embassy had been tracking her," Mohamed told me. "She received a message from them telling her to come to the embassy. When she came, they *cut* her passport," he said, clipping his fingers forcefully in the air, miming the destruction of the precious document.

He continued,

> She's a suspect now. She has to apply as if she's never been to Canada before. She says now they are listening to her phone calls. But how do you see Sophi, a girl of nineteen years, financing al-Shabaab? I asked her, "Is there anything true about that?" "No!" she said. "Nothing." But that embassy must be very strong, they must know something. But the lady she traveled with is *known*. As I was standing there, I was thinking, "Is there a satellite watching me? If I'm seen with this girl, will I be denied my visa?" I was just shaking. I was standing back from her, though I was trying to act calm. As if her blood could be a grenade. Yesterday I was walking by the mosque. I saw her and just crossed to the other side.

Canadian and US governments have used guilt by association in antiterror tactics both before and since 9/11 (Cole 2001; Cole and Dempsey 2006; Roach 2003; Scahill 2006): "it is not probable cause but the guilt by association with certain ideas, people, or organizations that guides the logic behind who becomes a suspect" (Rana 2011, 150). Guilt by association was a principle used during the McCarthy era, reignited with the 1996 antiterrorism act, and expanded by the post-9/11 USA PATRIOT Act (Cole and Dempsey 2006), which relies on ethnic and racial profiling (Cole 2001). Canada's Anti-terrorism Act, also passed in 2001, similarly employs the concept.

While aspects of the story remained unknowable to me, its importance as an ethnographic fact emerges in the life the story took on in Mohamed's imagination. His fear of satellite-based surveillance speaks to the "fear and paranoia that come with subjection to surveillance and suspicion" (Al-Bulushi 2021, 2). It also reflects the reality of the "watchful vigilance against risky bodies . . . through the universe of satellites currently orbiting the earth, of which 400 out of 950 are owned by the US" (Besteman 2020, 114). Mohamed's articulation of the "known" woman and his fear of his former classmate places guilt by association at the forefront of his understanding of himself as Somali and Muslim in the context of a global war on terror and his own migration dreams. As he saw how his classmate became implicated by her association with a "known suspect," he feared that he, too, could become a suspect based upon the same logic. Guilt by association becomes a kind of contagion. Mohamed's classmate's new status as a suspect and the fear of possible deportation from Canada produced Mohamed's fear of her physical presence, causing him to cross the road to avoid her when he saw her the next day. In saying "her blood could be a grenade," he evoked the physical proximity of her body to his own—their "association"—as endangering his safety. What did he imagine the metaphorical grenade would explode?

In Eastleigh, people articulated fear of others through the metaphor of body parts as weapons. Often, they evoked such images to describe their sense that their own bodies were feared—seen as dangerous Muslims in a Kenyan imaginary—particularly in the aftermath of the al-Shabaab attack on the Westgate shopping mall. When someone felt they were regarded with suspicion by non-Somalis in a public space—a matatu, for example—they might say, "They acted as if my head was a bomb," commenting on the fear that they perceived they inspired in others. But in this case, another person's body was frightening to Mohamed. In his turn of phrase, her blood—central in Somali conceptions of kinship, evoking their shared identity—posed a risk. But crucially, the young woman was frightening only if refracted through the surveillance of powerful governments in the global North, which had the power to determine Mohamed's fate. Here, he articulated the anxieties that pervade being a member of a surveilled community—"Is there a satellite watching me?"—and that being seen with a person suspected by the Canadian government could cause his own family sponsorship case to be denied.

Because of the security situation in Somalia and after a small number of diasporans traveled to Somalia following the US-backed Ethiopian invasion of 2006 to fight against foreign military occupation, any travel to Somalia has been deemed suspicious by the US government.[4] Yet many Somalis, like people from other immigrant communities, desire resettlement and naturalization in global North countries not so that they can sever ties with their homeland but so that they can travel back and forth to Somalia and neighboring countries, benefiting from mobility enabled by a US or other powerful passport. Earning US dollars allows people to participate in civic and business life in Somalia and support relatives there. This "additive" conception of citizenship can conflict with normative US ideas about citizenship that seek to eliminate "the potential disruptiveness of diversity" (Coutin 2003, 512–15) and to "domesticate the foreign" (522). The metaphor of "naturalization" itself biologizes citizenship and reinforces the idea of an exclusive link between one citizen and one nation. Yet for many, US residence and citizenship are often employed to strengthen rather than diminish ties with a homeland (Coutin 2003, 511). In this sense, despite the nuclear-family model of resettlement-case composition truncating possibilities for sponsoring large networks of kin, transnational families are maintained in long-distance forms. Travel between North America and Somalia and the mobility of capital between the US and Somalia through money transfer systems outside formal banking create lifeworlds cast as suspicious by national security agencies.

Back at the restaurant on Morse Road in Columbus, Dahir wondered aloud if his mother's case had been put on hold because of a mistaken identity. He wondered if one of his siblings shared a name with a high-profile terrorist—a 9/11 bomber or one of the attackers in the 1998 embassy bombings in Kenya. He wondered if the government had suspended the case because he hadn't fully paid off his government loan for the airline ticket that brought him to the US, or if the money he sent back to his family made the US government perceive them as less worthy of resettlement since they received assistance from outside. As Al-Bulushi writes of Muslim activists in Kenya trying to grasp the violence of transnational policing they are subject to, "The rumors and conspiracy theories that emerge in these contexts become a means through which to engage with uncertainty . . . and to process the simultaneous display and disavowal of imperial power" (2021, 7). Through his own speculations, Dahir evoked a looming black hole of information and the ways in which "encounters with the bureaucracy of immigration and resettlement fragment what for the refugees are meaningful wholes (such as families)" (Besteman 2014, 427).

Dahir's lack of knowledge about his family's case counterposed with the state's work to extract knowledge about his family exists in a broader matrix of counter-terror tactics aimed at the Somali American community. Dahir's embodied and affective daily life—driving a truck in the American Midwest while his mind is in Kenya where his mother seeks cancer treatment—is structured by his ongoing relationship with state security through his mother's case. In his indignation and his continual attempts to obtain information, Dahir also levelled a moral critique against these regimes, which fragment the moral whole of an idealized family and family unity.

"A Matter of Discretion"

A year after our lunch on Morse Road, while listening to the recording of our interview play from my laptop, I sent Dahir a message, hoping to hear good news about his mother's case. Dahir's WhatsApp profile showed him wearing a suit jacket, sitting alone on a bench. His profile status read, "I love hoyo mcn"—short for *hooyo macaan*—a common phrase meaning "sweet mother." Dahir wrote back right away, informing me that his mother's case had been rejected. When I asked what reason had been given, he forwarded me the USCIS letter. The letter, addressed to his mother, began by explaining the laws under which she had applied for resettlement. It then stated, "For the reason or reasons indicated below, we have determined that you are not eligible for resettlement to the United States." The remainder of the letter enumerated seven possible reasons for rejection, some of which had multiple sub-reasons listed beneath and all of which had an empty check box next to them, except for the last. According to the letter, Dahir's mother had *not* been rejected on account of (1) failing to establish that she is a person of special humanitarian concern, (2) failing to establish that she meets the definition of a refugee, (3) persecuting others, (4) having been already resettled in a third country, (5) being inadmissible based on specified US criteria, or (6) finding her claim for resettlement not credible.

Rather, it was the seventh and final reason, next to which the box had been marked with an "X." It read, "Other Reasons: After a review of all of the information concerning your case, including your testimony, supporting documentation, background checks, country condition and other available information, your application for refugee resettlement in the United States under Section 207 of the Immigration and Nationality Act has been denied as a matter of discretion for security-related reasons."

Through US management of immigration under the Department of Homeland Security and governance of transnational money transfers through the Department of the Treasury, Somali Americans and many others experience themselves as suspects even after years, sometimes decades of navigating the patchwork of institutions and regulations that constitute refugee resettlement from Africa. Caring for their kin abroad—through sponsorship programs, helping with resettlement cases, and sending remittances—troubles US national security ideals. Transnational kinship provokes anxieties about national borders, for which "the family" stands as a miniature.

Conclusion

IN THE INTRODUCTION OF this book, I recounted the story of Jacqueline, a single woman who lived with Claire, Innocent, and their children but was denied a place on their resettlement case. That was not the first time that the composition of Claire and Innocent's case had been called into question. Among their young children was thirteen-year-old Aline, the biogenetic daughter of Claire's brother, who had lived with Claire and Innocent since she was around eight, before the family had fled eastern Congo. Aline had initially been included on their resettlement case. But when her biogenetic parents suddenly arrived in Nairobi after having lost contact for years, a US-based NGO partnering with UNHCR decided she should be removed from it and rejoin her biogenetic parents and siblings. This was an outcome that had not been requested by either set of parents and that opposed Aline's own stated wishes. Because Aline would eventually be left behind when Innocent and Claire departed for the United States, she returned to her biogenetic parents to begin getting used to living with them. The NGO's decision removed her from the family with whom she had lived since earlier in her childhood and returned her to a family she had not seen for nearly six years. She began a difficult adjustment to a new life without the parents and siblings she had known and without the hope of resettlement in her future (Balakian 2023).

While UNHCR advocates for a flexible and "culturally sensitive" approach to family (2011, 178), how the composition of resettlement cases is ultimately decided also depends on government regulations and priorities, as well as the nuances of decision-making among UN and NGO staff members. From the standpoint of the US government as well as organizations like the one that decided Aline's case, it is normal for children to live with their biogenetic parents, and it is often seen as abnormal or dysfunctional for a child to live in the care of other relatives (see Briggs 2020; Stack 1974). UNHCR and partnering NGOs often decide issues surrounding family composition with government regulations in mind and have a risk-management approach to child protection in which biogenetic parents are seen as best. Today, many global North countries prioritize or enforce the biogenetic nuclear family through DNA testing (Hautaniemi 2007; Heinemann and Lemke 2014; Helén 2014). UNHCR and NGOs therefore also emphasize nuclear family composition because these organizations must refer cases that comply with government policies. The US has historically accepted the largest number of people through resettlement globally, and thus a majority of resettlement cases from Kenya have long prioritized compliance with US policies. Maintaining a child on a family's case when her biogenetic parents were nearby was seen as concerning. Sending a child to the United States with parents who were not her biogenetic mother and father also invited the possibility that Aline or her biogenetic parents could later claim the right for them to join her in the US, a practice that would facilitate undesirable "chain migration" and misuse of the system.

Defining family in refugee resettlement involves priorities and calculations on the part of people with decision-making power that often conflict with priorities and wishes of the families involved. Bureaucratic categories often hamper the creative work of kinship and care, particularly among those with limited power to press decision-makers at UNHCR, NGOs and governments to enact their own visions of what is right for their families, communities, and futures. Given the bureaucratic need to define and categorize, alongside the role of the war on terror and the logic of humanitarianism in delineating "the family" in particular (if at times contradictory) ways, questions about the meanings and boundaries of kinship take on urgent significance.

Anthropologists have long debated the meaning of kinship—one of anthropology's original objects of study beginning in the nineteenth century. In the 1960s and '70s, the "genealogical grid"—a tool to map relations of genealogical descent, imagined as universally applicable for charting kinship in societies across the world—began to be seen as a culturally particular construct (Schneider 1972). Did mapping genealogical relations really show how kinship existed out in the world? Or, as some now argued, was this tool a reflection of a culturally specific notion of kinship that existed in North America and

Britain? Biology, or genealogical relations, was not kinship, David Schneider and others argued (see Franklin and McKinnon 2001). Rather, kinship in the United States—or at least some normative version of it—rested upon particular *beliefs* about the biological facts of reproduction, or genealogical relations, which mid-century Anglophone anthropologists imposed onto other societies (Schneider 1980).

From the 1980s, anthropologists—including those in wealthy, post-industrialized societies—continued to study the evolving ways in which relations defined as familial were lived and experienced. This included "the complex traffic between different cultural registers, including that of science," and the power of science "in defining and naturalizing the modalities of human relations" (Franklin and McKinnon 2001, 15). Kinship involves long-standing practices of widely shared child-rearing responsibilities (Gottlieb 2004, 2009), deep traditions of child fosterage and even the denial of biological parenthood (Alber 2003), changing notions of relatedness embedded in evolving reproductive technologies (Carsten 2004), transnational adoption and kinship among adoptees (Kim 2010), spiritual kinship (Thomas 2021), queer and chosen families of other kinds (Weston 1991), and families created in the context of managing insecurity (Gale 2007; Piot with Batema 2019; Utas 2005), among other possibilities. Kinship practices vary widely, and the people most central to one's sense of identity and belonging and most involved in labors of care often fall outside the nuclear family and other relations forged through marriage or reproduction.

Marshall Sahlins defined kinship as "mutuality of being" and kin as "people who are intrinsic to one another's existence." This definition, he argued, covers "the variety of ethnographically documented ways that kinship is locally constituted" (2013, 2). Any biogenetic relationship can be made "postnatally or performatively by culturally appropriate action" (2). In different contexts, substances other than genetic material, such as breast milk or food generate familial belonging as those substances are habitually provided and consumed (Carsten 1995; Sahlins 2013). Rituals and lived practices of many kinds make kinship as much as kinship is constituted through sexual reproduction.

The ways in which people constitute or configure relatedness for the purposes of managing bureaucratic and political processes, or social needs, do not exist outside kinship. Marriages that strengthen alliances of families or polities; giving birth in order to secure status or an heir; inviting those not related by blood or marriage into the fold of familial traditions to meet the needs of care and social well-being—the purposes for making kin are many. Kinship forged or reconfigured to fit the definition of family constructed by powerful states is often considered fraudulent, perhaps at the most basic level because, as historian Lorraine Daston argues, evidence is considered "incompatible with intention" (1994, 244). A family created in order to access resettlement is no family at all, so the logic goes. But the stories of many people in this book hoping to resettle in North America, Europe, Australia, and elsewhere show that the contours of kinship are far more varied and complex than the notion of "fraud" captures. People become kin in many ways and for many reasons. Making kinship responds to immigration policies but also to the intersections of culturally particular norms of identity and belonging and to the social pressures that emerge from death and displacement. Family also takes on new meaning for people seeking to resettle precisely because it is the category prioritized by the institutions that control immigration. We might ask what other social units or categories could structure and organize the resettlement of displaced people? We should also ask how people who have been displaced can determine their own futures in new ways.

"The family is an object of political struggle around the world" (Giddens 2000, 70), and state and non-state institutions define "the family" in ways that support their ideological and pragmatic aims. Legislating issues surrounding marriage and reproduction and what constitutes a family or household is central to contemporary politics. In the United States, legalizing same-sex marriage in 2015 and overturning *Roe v. Wade* in 2022, which had federally legalized abortion since 1973, are just two recent examples. In the US and beyond, debates about welfare and social programs, economic policy, education, and healthcare rest on particular visions of what a family should look like and how it should function. Engineering society through policies and programs pertaining to family and family life is visible in eugenics and campaigns of forced sterilization; pro-natalist policies that encourage marriage and birth; or anti-natalist policies to curb population growth or curb it in certain communities. The family is often perceived as a force for social stability and moral order, demonstrated by the attention it is explicitly and implicitly given in political debates and agendas.

As this book has shown, DNA testing and related policies facilitate the resettlement of families that are culturally normative in places like the US (biogenetic nuclear families) and exclude relations deemed illegitimate, threatening, or deviant—polygynous families or those composed of people whose relations are deemed nonessential by a dominant US standard. At the same time, DNA testing stems "chain migration," supposed risks to national security, and what governments perceive as the misuse of humanitarian charity. Yet considering the intrinsic flexibility of kinship and its meanings across place and time contributes to a different story about genetic science as border security and the notion of "family composition fraud" than the one told by powerful institutions that manage mobility today. People assign many different meanings to their social worlds in the aftermath of civil wars. People are embedded in multiple networks of kin and care. The bureaucratic requirement that we be members of just one family—like Aline, who was separated from one set of parents on account of finding the other—troubles the practical work of kinship, particularly for people on the move, who give and rely on care that often extends beyond a single biogenetic nuclear family household.

The multiplicity of "family" for people on the move is shown in granular detail in a 2022 memoir chronicling a nine-year-old's journey from El Salvador to California to reunite with his parents. The parents of the author Javier Zamora left their home country during its civil war and tumultuous aftermath, leaving him in the care of his maternal grandparents and aunt. His book, titled *Solito*, is the story of a child migrating "alone." But in another sense, it is the story of the relations that sustain him in his parents' absence, first in his hometown and then on a journey across multiple countries. Coyotes give Zamora and three strangers papers allowing them to present themselves as a Mexican family (mother, father, and two children), making them less suspicious to authorities. But the "paper" family becomes real from the standpoint of Zamora in profound ways. At the end of the book, in Arizona, they prepare to part ways:

> I didn't realize we were going to opposite sides of the country. . . . I don't want to be separated from my second family . . .
> "You want to clean your feet?"
> Chino pulls my shoelaces loose. It distracts me. I swipe his hand and take my shoes off and dump dirt on the carpet, wipe the twigs and grass from my socks. There's dirt in between my toes. They smell but no one says anything.
> "Wash them." He opens the water bottle. . . . He pours the water on my toes, and I wipe them clean with my hands. The water seeps into the carpet. Chino stretches his pants so I can wipe my feet dry on them.

The memoir, which Zamora dedicates to his "second family," meditates on the ways in which two people who begin as strangers take care of Zamora through a perilous and punishing journey. Chino cleaning Zamora's feet before saying goodbye invokes this continuous embodied work of caring for another.[1]

This story—like those of Nadifa Mohamed's young character and "the lie her heart wanted to tell"; Habiba's uncle's family that became her own; Mohamed's chronicling of his life with Ahmed, the paternal relative who became his brother; Aline's separation from Claire and Innocent's case; Abdirahman's ruminations on DNA testing and his removal from his aunt's resettlement case to Sweden; Fardowsa's separation from a world of care and her attempt to rebuild one through her children, and others recounted in this book—tell us how the experiences of care, the making of kinship, and loss and separation are structured by violent conflict, as well as by humanitarian responses and migration policies.

Unsettled

In one sense, the separation of families and communities in the process of refugee resettlement and, paradoxically, family reunification are manifestations of the security logics, humanitarian triage, and nuclear family norms that undergird these transnational processes. More generally, they are an outgrowth of the desire among wealthier nations to restrict pathways to authorized immigration, which demand narrow definitions of who qualifies. At the same time, the story of the US Refugee Family Reunification Program and the introduction of DNA testing can be put into conversation with "a long history in the Americas of interrupting relations of care, kinship, and intimacy," giving rise to "new regimes of racialized rightlessness" (Briggs 2020, 12). In *Taking Children*, on the history of the US government's removal of children from Black, Native American, and Latinx communities, Laura Briggs argues that "child taking" is "a counterinsurgency tactic [that] has been used to respond to demands for rights, refuge, and respect by communities of color and impoverished communities" (12–13). Taking children and separating enslaved Black American families were used as tools of subjugation and terror. In the twentieth century, Black and Native American communities demanding rights were targeted by the US child welfare system and some of their children were placed in foster care. Native American families were also separated through the Indian boarding school system, which began in the 1870s and lasted until the 1970s (Briggs 2020; see also Strong 2001). Using the nuclear, heterosexual family as a standard and pathologizing care given by other adults or single mothers have often justified child taking (Briggs 2020, 62).

Separating families and criminalizing nonnormative forms of kinship and sexuality has also been part of US histories of immigration and deportation. Post–World War I deportation regimes used the category "likely to become a public charge" in order "to mask a much broader agenda of moral policing" and produced family separations in its wake (Pope-Obeda 2021, 120). Criminalizing poverty and relying on racist stereotypes, deportation operated "as a mechanism to police morality, allowing an administrative agency of the state to decide and enforce the boundaries of normative sexuality and family structure" (115)—with immigrant women who had children out of wedlock targeted for deportation.

The separation of children, including babies and toddlers, from their parents and guardians at the US-Mexico border, with no systems in place to reunify them, represents a dramatic newer manifestation of family separations. The zero tolerance policy under the Trump administration—spearheaded by administration advisor Stephen Miller and instituted in 2017—intentionally used taking children to deter people from crossing the US-Mexico border to legally seek asylum. This policy was deemed wildly impractical and immoral by many working for US Homeland Security at the time. But buck passing and bullying within the administration allowed the policy to be pushed through, and thousands of children were removed and detained in special facilities. Their parents, who were detained separately, often in different states, were denied information about their children's locations and about when and if they would be reunited. Many were deported *without* their children. Years later, hundreds of children had been lost in the system and had yet to be reunited. The separation of children was not an unintended consequence; it was the goal in a broader deterrence strategy. As Attorney General Jeff Sessions reportedly stated, "We need to take away children" (Dickerson 2022).

Starting in the early 2000s, DNA testing and greater surveillance of family composition in refugee family reunification—a program primarily relied upon by people from African countries—was instituted by the US and other global North governments as an anti-fraud and counter-terror instrument. The separation of family members outside the biogenetic nuclear family has been one consequence of DNA testing and related case composition regulations. This policy has roots in a specific transnational, post-9/11 history. DNA testing was a response to people using a humanitarian program in ways that exceeded the limits of humanitarian charity. It should also be read alongside longer histories of US policies that have separated families, particularly immigration policies. As of the mid-2010s, 16.7 million people in the US lived in mixed-immigration-status households, at risk of separation by deportation (Castañeda 2019, 9). In the government's fiscal year 2023, US officials deported 142,580 people from about 180 countries (Sacchetti 2023). In a context in which family separation through deportation from the US is largely an accepted feature of American life, it is not surprising that people left behind in African camps and cities when the people on whom they rely resettle would be invisible.

Official norms and procedures across institutions involved in refugee re-settlement largely take for granted the scarcity of resettlement opportunities as a natural state of affairs. Stories in this book tell of the everyday ways that people resist or refuse the notion that resettlement—often the only safe and legal way to migrate to countries that offer a path to citizenship—is a privilege for the 1 percent, rather than a right and a lifeway rooted in long histories of mobility and migration. Strategies employed by many people living as refugees in Kenya—strategies often cast as "fraudulent," or corrupt, illicit, or immoral—constitute "the refusals of lives to submit to new orders" (Rosas 2012, 130), a global regime that pushes people to the margins of the "national order of things" (Malkki 1995b) and outside citizenship.

The modern liberal state, as Hagar Kotef (2015) argues, sees movement in ambiguous ways: a form of freedom but also a threat to order that must be controlled. Prior to the state's "monopolization of the legitimate means of movement"—its exclusive claim to authorize and criminalize movement across borders—human migration was managed, experienced and imagined differently (Torpey 1998). In pre-colonial African societies, Achille Mbembe (2018) writes, sovereignty was not expressed through "control of a territory, physically marked with borders." Instead, "you dominated by integrating foreigners. All kinds of foreigners." European explorers, missionaries, settlers, and colonial administrators were not required to apply for visas to enter territories in the Americas, Africa, and Asia that they colonized and where they had established entities to extract resources and labor between the fifteenth and twentieth centuries. Only later did the passport and visa systems emerge worldwide, which made it difficult or impossible for most people in formerly colonized countries to move in the reverse direction.

Today, the sheer luck of where we were born structures our rights to cross borders. The passports of the world are of vastly unequal value: A US passport allows a person to enter 188 countries with no prior government authorization. A Somali or a Congolese passport, by contrast, grants a person entry into only 33 or 39 countries, respectively. As Besteman writes, the fortification of contemporary national borders, and borders between the global North and global South is a system of "extraordinary inequality, expense, damage, and immorality" that "cannot last." Those moving to escape unlivable circumstances at home and to seek better possibilities elsewhere "will not stop moving" (2020, 128). "Life exceeds borders. . . . Borders veer to porousness. They portend crossings" (Rosas 2023, 147). Moving, after all, has always been part of the human story. That story is not one of disconnected individuals. It is a story of people moving in response to the needs, abilities, and circumstances of social groups—families, households, communities (Arar and FitzGerald 2023, 74–105)—and the desire to protect and care not only for oneself but also for others.

Early in my fieldwork, I was introduced to a woman who told me that her child had been taken to the US by her former husband "by fraud" and that she hoped that DNA testing proving her maternity would help her reunite with her daughter. If people living as refugees struggle with differences between their social worlds and the dominant categories of the resettlement system, people also quickly learn new rules and adopt the language of governments and NGOs to articulate their claims. In this sense, this book is not only about differing ways of reckoning relatedness but also about the multiple ways in which "the family" is deployed by migrating people and their advocates to claim a right to move, as well as by governments and international organizations in their desire to control mobility.

The family and the intrinsic flexibility of social ties—the ability for someone to become kin and be cared for in many ways—provides possibilities for people living as refugees to reject powerful obstructions to crossing certain borders. Just as enforcing boundaries of the family informs the fortification of national borders, the flexibility of the family and the work of care also enables those on the move to unsettle borders, even as spaces for doing so narrow. People positioned as refugees by the current global order have asserted their own social obligations against policy definitions, where kinship fulfills needs in a world of increasing global interconnection and inequality.

Moving

On a Monday in November 2014, I headed to the IOM Transit Center to deliver a bushel of diapers. On a few occasions, I had conducted the cultural orientation for people leaving Kenya through the UK refugee program. (No matter that I wasn't from the UK, they said; it was all scripted.) An American friend in Kenya had connected me to IOM, and I took the opportunity to observe and participate in that moment of the resettlement process. I no longer remember why I had a grocery bag full of diapers that had to be brought to the Transit Center—the place where IOM facilitated cultural orientations and where people stayed before being transported to Jomo Kenyatta International Airport. The diapers may have been a donation I had been asked to take over by a Kenyan staff member who lived in my neighborhood. I took them that Monday so that I had a reason to enter the compound and say my goodbyes to Mohamed before he left for the airport.

Finally, he was going to join his uncle Ali in Canada and his uncle's wife and their three children. Traveling with him was Issa, his uncle's wife's brother. Ahmed, with whom Mohamed had grown up, was not leaving with them. He had been called about the scheduling of his cultural orientation that morning, but they didn't know when he would join them or why his case was taking longer than theirs. Without their parents physically present, Mohamed and Ahmed had, in some sense, raised each other—each had been the other's constant companion through moves across countries and cities and camps, through deaths and departures of friends and family members, through finishing high school and entering adulthood. Now, they would be separated for this next period of their journeys.

Three cars had accompanied Mohamed and Issa to the Transit Center that morning. Ahmed and their friends all came as far as the gates and took photos together. I met them inside. Mohamed was distracted by his phone and then asked to use mine. "Traveling to Toronto Canada family and friends wish me safe journey," he had posted on Facebook. Now the post had seventy-eight Likes and sixty-two Comments. I was busy watching the activity at the Transit Center, while he was busy watching the activity on his post. People milled about outside in the courtyard. They lined up to have their temperature taken. Special regulations had been put in place because of the ongoing Ebola outbreak, though the outbreak was thousands of miles across the continent. The assembled families were departing for Louisville, Baton Rouge, Salt Lake City, Buffalo, and other US cities. Most of the travelers wore casual clothing—Somali women in informal *dirac*, loose-fitting cotton dresses, and headscarves that they would wear at home or running errands. Issa wore jeans and black sneakers, a shirt, and a scarf around his neck—a practical move for the cold airplane and cold Toronto, where he would arrive the next day. But

Mohamed had had a perfectly tailored suit made for the occasion. "I don't want anyone saying I looked rough when I came to Canada," he said, considering the moment a historic one in his life but also imagining the hierarchies and stereotypes that would follow him. A little girl standing nearby told Mohamed that she had already lived in America and now they were returning. When Mohamed asked her questions about her life there, her brother overheard. "She's lying!" he said. "We've never been to America!" We all laughed. No one wanted to look like a newcomer.

Behind the building, away from the commotion of weighing bags, taking temperatures, kids in motion, I took a short video on my phone of Mohamed and Issa, asking them, "What do you expect in your first years in Canada?" Mohamed discussed "living with the people of Canada happily" and "respecting the rule of law of the country." His formality and self-consciousness on the recording reminded me of his precarity in this process, even, perhaps especially, as he prepared to board a plane. I put my phone away. The conversation moved to different thoughts. Mohamed said that he had left his house at eight o'clock yesterday evening to go somewhere that he could call his family back in Somalia. He had just left his building when he saw members of the General Service Unit—the paramilitary branch of the police.

"If you pass them, they'd just grab you," he said.

"Yeah, but you should never turn around when you see police," Issa commented.

"They never saw me," Mohamed replied.

Issa recounted being slapped in the face at Pangani Police Station during Operation Usalama Watch.

I forgot to ask Mohamed if he was ever able to call his family.

He looked around. "I'm just realizing I'm in a place I can't get out of," he said, observing the gates of the compound.

The majority of his life had now been spent outside Somalia, in a place where he could not appeal to rights attached to citizenship. In the year leading up to his departure, he discussed returning home to visit his elderly father and his brothers, but the journey involved far too many risks and complications. In the end, he left Kenya without having seen his parents or brothers after he left Somalia as a ten-year-old child. Since that time, he had lived with his uncle Abdiqani, Ahmed's father; with the trucker and his wife whom Abdiqani employed; with another young uncle who had moved to Kenya from Sweden to marry; with his sister, Zamzam, and her husband in Dadaab; and finally with just Ahmed and then Ahmed and Issa, where they were tightly bonded. They developed connections of many kinds with the many classmates, friends, and neighbors with whom they had shared their lives. They had also been supported and guided by their family members abroad. Their networks of kin were multiple. The people with whom they shared a "mutuality of being" were many and would still grow. And their need for those connections were particular in the absence of their mothers and fathers, their siblings, and the communities where they had been born.

At four o'clock, everyone was called to weigh their carry-on luggage. The big bags had already been transported to the airport. In a lull, Mohamed called me aside. An acquaintance, Shamso, had been calling him all morning, asking for help with fare, about three thousand Kenyan shillings (about US$30) to go to Mombasa so that she could get a document she needed. "I told her, 'I don't have anything left. Except some money for travel,'" Mohamed said.

In the morning, she had come to his apartment. He had waited for her there, delaying his departure for the Transit Center as she struggled to find his place. Mohamed introduced her to Ahmed, who gave her some of Mohamed's things that he wasn't taking with him. "But she was demanding more," Mohamed said.

"Don't worry," I told him.

"Please, Sophi, if you can, assist her with something."

I was struck that he was still thinking about Shamso moments before his departure.

Suddenly, the bus was there, its engine running. As Mohamed boarded, he turned on the stairs. I snapped a photo. In it, he smiles widely, a backpack slung over his suited shoulder. As the bus rumbled out of the gate and onto the road, I followed in my little Toyota Starlet. My route home was the same as the bus's route on Thika Highway. As I passed them on the highway, I waved, and Mohamed and Ahmed waved back, along with some of the little kids on the bus. I pulled into the Oil Libya petrol station and watched them go by. Turning on Muthaiga Roundabout, the bus headed in the other direction—back toward town, toward the airport—and then they were out of sight.

In Canada, they first lived in the finished basement of their uncle's home in a Toronto suburb. "The sun is here," Mohamed wrote me, "but it's inactive." If he stood out on the street of the quiet cul-de-sac, he would see only a single jogger go by in a sweatsuit or the occasional person hopping into their car. Only the groan of the occasional garage door would pierce the quiet day, as minivans and SUVs left—the only sign of the people inside them. It was cold, gray, and silent.[2]

Mohamed and Issa worried that Ahmed wouldn't ever arrive, but after about a year he finally did. Issa went to work in Alberta in the oil fields. Later he got married. Mohamed and Ahmed eventually saved up enough money to leave their uncle's suburban home and move into the city. They are working. Sending money to their families in Somalia. Sometimes dreaming of Somalia and of people in Kenya. Slowly, imperceptibly, they begin to know new people, begin to get used to a new life. They chat with people around the world, people they know from their lives in Nairobi. Some are still there, in Eastleigh. Some are in other places. They still talk about resettlement, about *buufis*, about family reunification cases, and family sponsorship processes. A relative has left Somalia for Kenya. An old neighbor and her mother get to the UK. A desperate friend goes to Libya to try to cross the Mediterranean. People are in motion, but not without incredible effort. Mohamed sometimes remembers people like Shamso and wonders what happened to her. He thinks of many people and their webs of obligation and belonging—where they are trying to go and to whom.

Notes

Introduction

1. All names of interlocutors are pseudonyms unless otherwise indicated in the text.

2. Analysis that closely followed the 2008 shutdown of the US Refugee Family Re-unification Program includes a report by Jill Esbenshade (2010) and a law review article by Emily Holland (2011).

3. Arar and FitzGerald argue that scholars often treat the 1951 Convention as the beginning of the refugee regime. However, religious, legal, and ideological traditions from outside Europe and prior to the twentieth century fundamentally contributed to the legal refugee regime we have today (2023, 46–73).

4. In 2022, Kenya passed a new Refugee Act, which, among other things, would enable refugees from the six other countries in the East African Community (EAC) to relinquish refugee status and use their status as EAC citizens to live and work in Kenya. This would theoretically increase their rights in the country (Refugees International 2022). Notably, Somalia is not an EAC country. The Kenyan act's impact will take time to assess.

5. Scholars such as Liisa Malkki and Jason De León have used composites drawn from years of research, a practice I follow briefly here. De León, for example, created a composite vignette to "bring the reader phenomenologically closer to the everyday terror" of his interlocutors' journeys as undocumented migrants crossing from Mexico to the United States (2015, 44). For ethical reasons, he could not accompany interlocutors through the desert, so he produced a narrative based on hundreds of interviews and conversations to bring stories of the desert to life. Malkki created "narrative panels," which combined elements that were continually repeated by the people she interviewed, to convey the powerful sense of collective voice, the "repetition and thematic unity" in Burundian refugees' accounts of violent histories (1995a, 56–58).

6. In the Kinyamulenge and Kinyarwanda languages, an individual from the Banyamulenge community would be referred to as *Munyamulenge*. Because of how the

ethnonym has come into the English language and for accessibility for readers not familiar with the grammar of this and many related languages, I use *Banyamulenge* for both the name of the community and an individual from it throughout the book.

7. UNHCR is the primary organization responsible for referring refugees for resettlement to host governments, but a few NGOs conduct the same work.

8. In Kenya and many other global South contexts, asylum seeker status refers to the status of a person who has approached UN or government authorities to request refugee status and awaits the determination of their case. Refugee status refers to the status of a person who has passed through the refugee status determination process and whose asylum case has been positively determined. In the US, a person who comes through the US Refugee Admissions Program applies for Lawful Permanent Resident status after a year and can apply for citizenship after five years.

9. Hagar Kotef (2010) uses this same term in a different way: to describe the ways in which delivery of humanitarian aid can make violence possible, specifically writing on Israeli delivery of humanitarian aid during the 2008 war on Gaza.

10. Fassin defines "moral sentiments" as "the emotions that direct our attention to the suffering of others and make us want to remedy them." These moral sentiments are deployed in what he calls "humanitarian government"—"actions conducted in order to manage, regulate, and support the existence of human beings" (2012, 1). For Fassin, these moral sentiments are paradoxically directed toward people who are viewed as unequal (poorer, more vulnerable) to those taking action but also simultaneously viewed with solidarity, as "fellows" (3).

Chapter 1: The Figure of the Fraudulent Refugee

1. In 2015, this system changed so that people received a reply from UNHCR by text to their phone.

2. The diversity of immigrants that have come to the US since the passage of the Immigration Act of 1965 was not the intended outcome of those who sponsored it, who expected the changed quota system would favor immigrants from southern and eastern Europe (Daniels 2004, 135).

3. The Department of Homeland Security was established in 2002 under President George W. Bush after 9/11 to oversee a "comprehensive national strategy to safeguard the country against terrorism and respond to any future attacks" (US Department of Homeland Security n.d.). Immigration and Naturalization Services, which had overseen immigration affairs prior to 9/11, became US Customs and Border Protection (CBP), US Immigration and Customs Enforcement (ICE), and US Citizenship and Immigration Services (USCIS), all under Homeland Security. USCIS oversees the US Refugee Admissions Program.

4. A pseudonym.

5. Ilana Feldman makes a related point about humanitarian communication to Palestinians (2018, S162–63).

Chapter 2: Selling Cases and Eating Money

1. See Mahmood Mamdani's *Good Muslim, Bad Muslim: America, the Cold War, and the Roots of Terror* (2004) for a discussion about the burden of proof necessary to

demonstrate allegiance to "the West" held by Muslims in the United States after 9/11 and the ways in which that burden of proof was structured around the moralizing labels of "good Muslim" and "bad Muslim."

2. Instead of creating pseudonyms for the many names of people and places Yvette included in her letter of appeal, I have simply indicated where a proper name was in the original text.

3. A different way of indicating "Banyamulenge"

4. A person of the Bembe ethnic group.

5. Banyamulenge people sometimes referred to Congolese of other ethnic communities simply as "Congolese."

6. The Swahili *nimetupwa* can mean "I've been thrown out," "dumped," or "left to fend for myself."

7. Anthropologists have pointed out the indeterminacy of the ways in which identity papers actually work to confer rights and protection (Kelly 2006) and their ambiguous effects as simultaneously enabling states to control populations and to imbue the same populations with rights that give them recourse against the state (Gordillo 2006). While many Nairobi residents who possessed refugee identity documents (both from UNHCR and the Kenyan government) often decried their powerlessness in the face of changing state policies and extortive Kenyan police or their inability to authorize crossing international borders or even moving within Kenya unencumbered— people such as Yvette revealed that they held practical and symbolical significance.

8. In a different case, Peter Redfield (2011) argues that Médecins Sans Frontières and other humanitarian organizations strategically make political or ethical compromises in order to maintain access to sites where they work.

9. One manifestation of the racialization of the categories Hutu and Tutsi was fixation on stereotypical phenotypic differences, such as nose shape (Des Forges 1999, 215). The racializing of these categories has a long history, institutionalized through practices of European colonial governance (Mamdani 2001, 76–102)

10. *Gacaca* courts were the local Rwandan system for trying alleged genocide perpetrators, distinct from the International Criminal Tribunal that tried high-ranking Rwandan officials.

Chapter 3: Mending Broken Bones

1. Indian immigrants lived for centuries along the Swahili coast of eastern Africa as part of Indian Ocean commercial networks. After the construction of the Uganda railway in the 1890s Indian immigration shifted from Zanzibar to Kenya (Brennan 2012, 49).

2. Garissa is an ethnically Somali city, like many of the Kenyan cities and towns near Somalia's border.

3. The Somali word *xerada* (the camp) can also be used for a place where domesticated animals are kept.

4. At the time, Somalis had prima facie refugee status in Kenya, meaning they were granted refugee status automatically on the basis of conditions in their country.

5. One of Kenya's major ethnic groups, from the region of Central Kenya where Nairobi is located.

Chapter 4: Testing DNA and Transforming Kin

1. The war in Somalia's northwest (a region known as British Somaliland from the 1880s until Somali independence in 1960) was a separatist movement brutally countered by Barre's Somali government by bombing major cities and violently targeting civilians. The war ultimately resulted in the region becoming the autonomous but unrecognized Republic of Somaliland.

2. For a discussion of the introduction of DNA testing in the US refugee program from a legal perspective, see Holland 2011.

3. As of 2014, twenty-one countries used DNA testing in their immigration systems for family reunification, including the UK, Canada, Australia, and many countries in continental Europe (Helén 2014, 349, 357).

4. In a document titled "Fraud in the Refugee Family Reunification (Priority Three) Program," the State Department's Bureau of Population, Refugees, and Migration (2009) reported: "We were . . . only able to confirm all claimed biological relationships in fewer than 20% of cases (family units). In the remaining cases, at least one negative result (fraudulent relationship) was identified, or the individuals refused to be tested."

5. Najib evoked a widespread idea that gendered expectations in North America and Europe clashed with Somali values. This concept spread through personal anecdotes and through representations of Somali life in diaspora, such as Mahamed Abdullahi Sangub's 1998 play *Qabyo* (Abdi 2015, 171).

Chapter 5: Resettled Families in an Age of Global Security

1. A pseudonym.

2. The Eid holiday that concludes the month of Ramadan usually includes a large feast and gifts and special outings for kids.

3. As described in chapter 4, Habiba could not sponsor her biogenetic parents to come to the United States because she came as the daughter of her *abti*, her mother's brother.

4. Despite public perceptions, even the US National Counterterrorism Center has noted, "Most of [al-Shabaab's] fighters are predominantly interested in the nationalistic battle against the FGS [Federal Government of Somalia] and not supportive of global jihad" (National Counterterrorism Center n.d.).

Conclusion

1. Given the Catholic tradition about which Zamora writes early in the book, the foot washing also calls to mind Jesus washing his disciples' feet at the Last Supper, symbolizing another kind of "mutuality of being" (Sahlins 2013, 2).

2. My husband and I visited Mohamed at his new home in Canada a few months after he arrived during a short trip back to North America.

Works Cited

Abdi, Cawo M. 2015. *Elusive Jannah: The Somali Diaspora and a Borderless Muslim Identity*. Minneapolis: University of Minnesota Press.

Abel, Sarah. 2021. *Permanent Markers: Race, Ancestry, and the Body after the Genome*. Chapel Hill: University of North Carolina Press.

Abu El-Haj, Nadia. 2012. *The Genealogical Science: The Search for Jewish Origins and the Politics of Epistemology*. Chicago: University of Chicago Press.

Abu Lughod, Lila. 2002. "Do Muslim Women Really Need Saving? Anthropological Reflections on Cultural Relativism and Its Others." *American Anthropologist* 104 (3): 783–790.

Agamben, Giogio. 1998. *Homo Sacer: Sovereign Power and Bare Life*. Translated by Daniel Heller-Roazen. Stanford: Stanford University Press.

Alber, Erdmute. 2003. "Denying Biological Parenthood: Fosterage in Northern Benin." *Ethnos* 68 (4): 487–506.

Al-Bulushi, Samar. 2019. "#SomeoneTellCNN: Cosmopolitan Militarism in the East African Warscape." *Cultural Dynamics* 31(4): 323–349.

———. 2021. "Citizen-Suspect: Navigating Surveillance and Policing in Urban Kenya." *American Anthropologist*. 123 (4): 819–832.

Al-Jarani, Yusef. 2017. "A War Developing Countries Cannot (Afford to) Win." *Yale Law & Policy Review*. 35 (2): 585–602.

Amos, Deborah. 2016. "For Refugees and Advocates, an Anxious Wait for Clarity on Trump's Policy." November 15. *Morning Edition*, National Public Radio. https://www.npr.org/sections/parallels/2016/11/15/502010346/for-refugees-and-advocates-an-anxious-wait-for-clarity-on-trumps-policy.

Arar, Rawan, and David FitzGerald. 2023. *The Refugee System: A Sociological Approach*. Cambridge: Polity Press.

Arendt, Hannah. (1951) 1973. *The Origins of Totalitarianism*. New York: Harcourt, Brace, Jovanovich.

Balakian, Sophia. 2016. "'Money Is Your Government': Refugees, Mobility, and Unstable Documents in Kenya's Operation *Usalama* Watch. *African Studies Review* 59 (2): 87–111.

———. 2020. "Navigating Patchwork Governance: Somalis in Kenya, National Security, and Refugee Resettlement." *African Studies Review* 63 (1): 43–64.

———. 2023. "Of Aunts and Mothers: Refugee Resettlement, the Nuclear Family, and Caring for 'Other' Children in Kenya." *Ethnic and Racial Studies.* 46 (2): 213–232.

Bamford, Sandra, and James Leach. 2009. *Kinship and Beyond: The Genealogical Model Reconsidered.* New York: Berghahn.

Barata, Llilda P., Helene Starks, Maureen Kelley, Patricia Kuszler, and Wylie Burke. 2015. "What DNA Can and Cannot Say: Perspectives of Immigrant Families about the Use of Genetic Testing in Immigration." *Stanford Law & Policy Review* 26: 597–638.

Bayart, Jean-François. 1993. *The State in Africa: The Politics of the Belly.* London: Longman.

Beneduce, Roberto. 2015. "The Moral Economy of Lying: Subjectcraft, Narrative Capital, and Uncertainty in the Politics of Asylum." *Medical Anthropology* 34 (6): 551–571.

Besteman, Catherine. 1999. *Unraveling Somalia: Race, Violence, and the Legacy of Slavery.* Philadelphia: University of Pennsylvania Press.

———. 2014. "Refuge Fragments, Fragmentary Refuge." *Ethnography* 15 (4): 426–445.

———. 2016. *Making Refuge: Somali Bantu Refugees and Lewiston, Maine.* Durham: Duke University Press.

———. 2019. "Militarized Global Apartheid." *Current Anthropology.* 60 (S19): S26–S38.

———. 2020. *Militarized Global Apartheid.* Durham: Duke University Press.

Brennan, James. 2012. *Taifa: Making Nation and Race in Urban Tanzania.* Athens: Ohio University Press.

Briggs, Laura. 2020. *Taking Children: A History of American Terror.* Berkeley: University of California Press.

Buhain, Venice. 2015. "FBI's Seattle Somali Community Outreach Programs Targeted for Spying, Report Says." *The Seattle Globalist.* January 30, 2015. http://www.seattle globalist.com/2015/01/30/seattle-fbi-community-outreach-fbi-spy-plans/33068.

Bureau of Labor Statistics. 2015a. "Unemployment Rates for Large Metropolitan Areas Annual Average Rankings Year: 2015." https://www.bls.gov/lau/malrgrank15.htm.

———. 2015b. "Unemployment Rates for States, 2015 Annual Averages." https://www.bls.gov/lau/lastrk15.htm.

Bureau of Population, Refugees, and Migration. 2009. "Fraud in the Refugee Family Reunification (Priority Three) Program." February 3, 2009. https://2009-2017.state.gov/j/prm/releases/factsheets/2009/181066.htm.

Cabot, Heath. 2013. "The Social Aesthetics of Eligibility: NGO Aid and Indeterminacy in the Greek Asylum Process." *American Ethnologist* 40 (3): 452–66.

———. 2014. *On the Doorstep of Europe: Asylum and Citizenship in Greece.* Philadelphia: University of Pennsylvania Press.

———. 2019. "The Business of Anthropology and the European Refugee Regime." *American Ethnologist* 46 (3): 261–275.

Carrier, Neil C. M. 2016. *Little Mogadishu: Eastleigh, Nairobi's Global Somali Hub.* New York: Oxford University Press.

Carsten, Janet. 1995. "The Substance of Kinship and the Heat of the Hearth: Feeding, Personhood and Relatedness among Malays in Pulau Langkawi." *American Ethnologist* 22 (2): 223–241.

———. 2004. *After Kinship.* Cambridge: Cambridge University Press.

Castañeda, Heide. 2019. *Borders of Belonging: Struggle and Solidarity in Mixed-Status Immigrant Families.* Stanford: Stanford University Press.

Center for American Progress. 2015. "Infographic: The Screening Process for Entry to the United States for Syrian Refugees." November 18, 2015. https://www.american progress.org/issues/immigration/news/2015/11/18/125812/infographic-the-screen ing-process-for-entry-to-the-united-states-for-syrian-refugees/.

Clark-Kazak, Christina R. 2011. *Recounting Migration: Political Narratives of Congolese Young People in Uganda.* Montreal: McGill-Queen's University Press.

Cockayne, James 2012. "Capitalizing on Trust: Harnessing Somali Remittances for Counterterrorism, Human Rights and State Building." With Liat Shetret. Global Center on Cooperative Security.

Coe, Cati. 2014. *The Scattered Family: Parenting, African Migrants, and Global Inequality.* Chicago: University of Chicago Press.

Cohen, Cathy. 2004. "Deviance as Resistance: A New Research Agenda for the Study of Black Politics." *Du Bois Review* 1 (1): 27–45.

Cole, David. 2001. "Secrecy, Guilt by Association, and the Terrorist Profile." *Journal of Law and Religion.* 15 (1/2): 267–288.

Cole, David, and James X. Dempsey. 2006. *Terrorism and the Constitution: Sacrificing Civil Liberties in the Name of National Security.* 3rd ed. New York: The New Press.

Cole, Jennifer. 2004. "Fresh Contact in Tamatave, Madagascar: Sex, Money, and Intergenerational Transformation." *American Ethnologist* 31 (4): 573–588.

Collier, Jane, Michelle Z. Rosaldo, and Sylvia Yanagisako. 1997. "Is There a Family?: New Anthropological Views." In *The Gender/Sexuality Reader: Culture, History, Political Economy.* Edited by Micaela Di Leonardo and Roger N. Lancaster, 71–81. New York: Routledge.

Columbus City Schools. 2012. "Comprehensive Financial Annual Report." https://www. ccsoh.us/site/handlers/filedownload.ashx?moduleinstanceid=14140&dataid=198 50&FileName=2012%20Final%20Columbus%20Report%20for%20Audit%20CAFR.pdf.

Connor, Phillip, and Jens Manuel Krogstad. 2016. "5 Facts about the Global Somali Diaspora." Pew Research Center, June 1, 2016. https://www.pewresearch.org/short-reads /2016/06/01/5-facts-about-the-global-somali-diaspora/.

Cooper, Karen, and Clive Walker. 2016. "Security from Terrorism Financing: Models of Delivery Applied to Informal Value Transfer Systems." *The British Journal of Criminology* 56 (6): 1125–1145.

Copeland, Libby. 2020. *The Lost Family: How DNA is Upending Who We Are.* New York: Abrams.

Coutin, Susan Bibler. 2000. *Legalizing Moves: Salvadoran Immigrants' Struggle for U.S. Residency.* Ann Arbor: University of Michigan Press.

———. 2003. "Cultural Logics of Belonging and Movement: Transnationalism, Naturalization, and U.S. Immigration Politics." *American Ethnologist* 30 (4): 508–526.

Dachenbach, Laura. 2015. "Journeys of the Diaspora." *614 Columbus*, March 3, 2015. http://614columbus.com/2015/03/journeys-of-the-diaspora/.

Daniel, E. Valentine, and John Chr. Knudsen. 1995. *Mistrusting Refugees*. Berkeley: University of California Press.

Daniels, Roger. 2004. *Guarding the Golden Door: American Immigration Policy and Immigrants since 1882*. New York: Hill and Wang.

Daston, Lorraine. 1994. "Marvelous Facts and Miraculous Evidence in Early Modern Europe." In *Questions of Evidence: Proof, Practice, and Persuasion across the Disciplines*. Edited by James Chandler, Arnold I. Davidson, and Harry D. Harootunian. 243–74. Chicago: University of Chicago Press.

Davis-Sowers, Regina. 2006. "Salvaging Children's Lives: Understanding the Experiences of Black Aunts Who Serve as Kinship Care Providers within Black Families." PhD dissertation, Georgia State University.

———. 2012. "'It Just Kind of Like Falls in Your Hands': Factors that Influence Black Aunts' Decision to Parent Their Nieces and Nephews." *Journal of Black Studies* 43 (3): 231–250.

Dawsey, Josh. 2018. "Trump Derides Protection for Immigrants from 'Shithole' Countries." *The Washington Post,* January 12, 2018. https://www.washingtonpost.com/politics/trump-attacks-protections-for-immigrants-from-shithole-countries-in-oval-office-meeting/2018/01/11/bfc0725c-f711-11e7-91af-31ac729add94_story.html.

De Genova, Nicholas. 2002. "Migrant 'Illegality' and Deportability in Everyday Life." *Annual Review of Anthropology* 31: 419–447.

———. 2007. "The Production of Culprits: From Deportability to Detainability in the Aftermath of 'Homeland Security.'" *Citizenship Studies* 11 (5): 421–448.

De León, Jason. 2015. *The Land of Open Graves: Living and Dying on the Migrant Trail*. Oakland: University of California Press.

Dean, Aimen, Edwina Thompson and Tom Keatinge. 2013. "Draining the Ocean to Catch One Type of Fish: Evaluating the Effectiveness of the Global Counter-Terrorism Financing Regime." *Perspectives on Terrorism* 7 (4): 62–78.

Des Forges, Alison. 1999. *Leave None to Tell the Story: Genocide in Rwanda*. New York: Human Rights Watch.

Dickerson, Caitlin. 2022. "'We Need to Take Away Children': The Secret History of the U.S. Government's Family-Separation Policy." *The Atlantic*, August 7, 2022.

Drotbohm, Heike. 2020. "Care and Reunification in a Cape Verdean Family: Changing Articulations of Family and Legal Ties." *Ethnography* 21 (1): 48–70.

Easton-Calabria, Evan, and Annelisa Lindsay. 2013. "Toward Durable Solutions for Protracted Congolese Refugees in Rwanda." *Oxford Monitor of Forced Migration* 3 (2): 58–66.

Ellison, James. 2009. "Governmentality and the Family: Neoliberal Choices and Emergent Kin Relations in Southern Ethiopia." *American Anthropologist* 111 (1) :81–92.

Esbenshade, Jill. 2010. "An Assessment of DNA Testing for African Refugees." Washington, DC: Immigration Policy Center. https://www.americanimmigrationcouncil.org/research/assessment-dna-testing-african-refugees

Espiritu, Yến Lê. 2006. "Toward a Critical Refugee Study: The Vietnamese Refugee Subject in US Scholarship." *Journal of Vietnamese Studies* 1 (1–2): 410–33.

Etienne, Mona. 1979. "The Case for Social Maternity: Adoption of Children by Urban Baule Women." *Dialectical Anthropology* 4 (3): 237–242.

Evans-Pritchard, E. E. 1940. *The Nuer: A Description of the Modes of Livelihood and Political Institutions of a Nilotic People.* Oxford: Oxford University Press at the Clarendon Press.

———. 1951. *Kinship and Marriage among the Nuer.* Oxford: Clarendon Press.

Farah, Nuruddin. (1986) 2000. *Maps.* New York: Penguin Books.

Fassin, Didier. 2011. "*Noli Me Tangere:* The Moral Untouchability of Humanitarianism." In *Forces of Compassion: Humanitarianism Between Ethics and Politics.* Edited by Erica Bornstein and Peter Redfield, 35–52. Santa Fe: School for Advanced Research Press.

———. 2012. *Humanitarian Reason: A Moral History of the Present.* Berkeley: University of California Press.

Fassin, Didier, and Estelle d'Halluin. 2005. "The Truth from the Body: Medical Certificates as Ultimate Evidence for Asylum Seekers." *American Anthropologist* 107 (4): 597–608.

Federal Bureau of Investigation. 2009. "Memo: Implementation of Specialized Community Outreach Team (SCOT)." January 7, 2009. https://www.brennancenter.org/sites/default/files/analysis/FN%20126%20(FN%20126%20(Federal%20Bureau%20of%20Investigation,%20Memo%20to%20All%20Field%20Offices--Implimentation%20of%20Specialized%20Community%20Outreach%20Team).pdf

Feldman, Ilana 2007. "Difficult Distinctions: Refugee Law, Humanitarian Practice, and Political Identification in Gaza." *Cultural Anthropology* 22 (1): 129–69.

———. 2018. "Care and Suspicion: Corruption as Definition in Humanitarian Relations." *Current Anthropology* 59 (S18): 160–170.

Feldman, Ilana, and Miriam Ticktin. 2010. "Introduction: Government and Humanity." In *In the Name of Humanity: The Government of Threat and Care.* Edited by Ilana Feldman and Miriam Ticktin, 1–26. Durham, NC: Duke University Press.

Feldman-Savelsberg, Pamela. 2016. *Mothers on the Move: Reproducing Belonging between Africa and Europe.* Chicago: University of Chicago Press.

Ferguson, James. 2006. *Global Shadows: Africa in the Neoliberal World Order.* Durham, NC: Duke University Press.

Franklin, Sarah, and Susan McKinnon. 2001. "Relative Values: Reconfiguring Kinship Studies." In *Relative Values: Reconfiguring Kinship Studies.* Edited by Sarah Franklin and Susan McKinnon, 1–25. Durham, NC: Duke University Press.

Gale, Lacey Andrews. 2007. "Bulgur Marriages and 'Big' Women: Navigating Relatedness in Guinean Refugee Camps. *Anthropological Quarterly* 80 (2): 355–78.

Garnier, Adèle, Kristin Bergtora Sandvik, and Liliana Lyra Jubilut. 2018. "Refugee Resettlement as Humanitarian Governance: Power Dynamics." In *Refugee Resettlement: Power, Politics, and Humanitarian Governance.* Edited by Adèle Garnier, Liliana Lyra Jubilut, and Kristin Bergtora Sandvik, 1–27. New York: Berghahn Books.

Geschiere, Peter. 2013. *Witchcraft, Intimacy and Trust: Africa in Comparison.* Chicago: University of Chicago Press.

Giblin, James L. 2005. *A History of the Excluded: Making Family a Refuge from State in Twentieth-Century Tanzania*. With Blandina Kaduma Giblin. Athens: Ohio University Press.

Giddens, Anthony. 2000. *Runaway World: How Globalization Is Reshaping Our Lives*. New York: Routledge.

Glinton, Sonari. 2016. "A Diversified Economy Cushions Columbus, Ohio, from Downturns." *All Things Considered,* National Public Radio, September 19, 2016. https://www.npr.org/2016/09/19/494561019/a-diversified-economy-cushions-co lumbus-ohio-from-downturns

Gordillo, Gastón. 2006. "The Crucible of Citizenship: ID-Paper Fetishism in the Argentinean Chaco." *American Ethnologist* 33 (2): 162–176.

Gottlieb, Alma. 2004. *The Afterlife Is Where We Come from: The Culture of Infancy in West Africa*. Chicago: University of Chicago Press.

———. 2009. "Who Minds the Baby? Beng Perspectives on Mothers, Neighbors, and Strangers as Caretakers." In *Substitute Parents: Biological and Social Perspectives on Alloparenting across Human Societies*. Edited by Gillian Bentley and Ruth Mace, 119–38. Oxford: Berghahn Books.

Government of Canada. 2023. "Groups of Five: About the Process." https://www.cana da.ca/en/immigration-refugees-citizenship/services/refugees/help-outside-cana da/private-sponsorship-program/groups-five.html.

Guardian. 2015. "Fact Checking Donald Trump's Recent Claims: From Mexico to San Francisco." July 7, 2015. https://www.theguardian.com/us-news/reality-check/2015 /jul/07/fact-checking-donald-trump.

Hannaford, Dinah. 2017. *Marriage without Borders: Transnational Spouses in Neoliberal Senegal*. Philadelphia: University of Pennsylvania Press.

Haraway, Donna J. 1997. *Modest_Witness@Second_Millenium.FemaleMan_Meets_ OncoMouse: Feminism and Technoscience*. New York: Routledge.

Hardt, Michael, and Antonio Negri. 2000. *Empire*. Cambridge, MA: Harvard University Press.

Hargreaves, Katrina. 2006. "Constructing Families and Kinship through Donor Insemination." *Sociology of Health and Illness* 28 (3): 261–83.

Hartig, Hannah. 2018. "Republicans Turn More Negative toward Refugees as Number Admitted to U.S. Plummets." *Pew Research Center*, May 24, 2018. https://www. pewresearch.org/short-reads/2018/05/24/republicans-turn-more-negative-toward -refugees-as-number-admitted-to-u-s-plummets/

Hautaniemi, Petri. 2007. "Diasporic Authenticity: Connecting Genes and Building Families through DNA-testing in Somali Family Reunification in Finland." In *From Mogadishu to Dixon: The Somali Diaspora in a Global Context*. Edited by Abdi M. Kusow and Stephanie R. Bjork, 119–132. Trenton, NJ: Red Sea Press.

Hayden, Sally. 2019. "Asylum for Sale." *100 Reporters*, April 6, 2019. https://100r.org/ 2019/04/unhcr-corruption-refugee-resettlement/

Heinemann, Torsten, and Thomas Lemke. 2014. "Biological Citizenship Reconsidered: The Use of DNA Analysis by Immigration Authorities in Germany." *Science, Technology, & Human Values* 39 (4): 488–510.

Helén, Ilpo. 2014. "Biological Citizenship across the Borders: Politics of DNA Profiling for Family Reunification." *Distinktion (Aarhus)* 15 (3): 343–360.

Helmreich, Stefan. 2001. "Kinship in Hypertext: Transubstantiating Fatherhood and Information Flow in Artificial Life." In *Relative Values: Reconfiguring Kinship Studies*. Edited by Sarah Franklin and Susan McKinnon, 116–143. Durham, NC: Duke University Press.

Hodžić, Saida. 2017. "Introduction." In *Maintaining Refuge: Anthropological Reflections in Uncertain Times*. Edited by David Haines, Jayne Howell, and Fethi Keles, 157–158. Committee on Refugees and Immigrants; Society for Urban, National, and Transnational/Global Anthropology; American Anthropological Association. https://mason.gmu.edu/~dhaines1/CORI_2017_Final.pdf

Holland, Emily. 2011. "Moving the Virtual Border to the Cellular Level: Mandatory DNA Testing and the U.S. Refugee Family Reunification Program." *California Law Review* 99 (6): 1635–1682.

Horst, Cindy. 2006a. "*Buufis* amongst Somalis in Dadaab: The Transnational and Historical Logics behind Resettlement Dreams." *Journal of Refugee Studies* 19 (2): 143–157.

———. 2006b. *Transnational Nomads: How Somalis Cope with Refugee Life in the Dadaab Camps of Kenya*. New York: Berghahn Books.

Howell, Signe. 2003. "Kinning: The Creation of Life Trajectories in Transnational Adoptive Families." *Journal of the Royal Anthropological Institute* 9 (3): 465–484.

Hunt, Nancy Rose. 2008. "An Acoustic Register, Tenacious Images, and Congolese Scenes of Rape and Repetition." *Cultural Anthropology* 23 (2): 220–253.

Human Rights Watch. 2015. "Kenya: Counterterrorism Operation Undermines Rights." January 29, 2015. https://www.hrw.org/news/2015/01/29/kenya-counterterrorism-operations-undermine-rights

Hyndman, Jennifer. 1997. "BorderCrossings." *Antipode* 29 (2): 149–176.

Ibrahim, Ahmed. 2018. "The Shari'a Courts of Mogadishu: Beyond 'African Islam' and 'Islamic Law.'" PhD dissertation, Graduate Center, City University of New York.

Ivey, Paula K. 2000. "Cooperative Reproduction in Ituri Forest Hunter-Gatherers: Who Cares for Efe Infants?" *Current Anthropology* 41 (5): 856–66.

Jacobsen, Anna. 2011. "Making Moral Worlds: Individual and Social Processes of Meaning-Making in a Somali Diaspora." PhD dissertation, Washington University, St. Louis.

James, Erica Caple. 2010. *Democratic Insecurities: Violence, Trauma, and Intervention in Haiti*. Berkeley: University of California Press.

———. 2011. "Governing Gifts: Law, Risk, and the 'War on Terror.'" *UCLA Journal of Islamic and Near Eastern Law* 10 (1): 65–84.

Jansen, Bram J. 2008. "Between Vulnerability and Assertiveness: Negotiating Resettlement in Kakuma Refugee Camp, Kenya." *African Affairs* 107 (429): 569–587.

Kapteijns, Lidwien. 2013. *Clan Cleansing in Somalia: The Ruinous Legacy of 1991*. Philadelphia: University of Pennsylvania Press.

Kelly, Tobias. 2006. "Documented Lives: Fear and the Uncertainties of Law during the Second Palestinian Intifada." *Journal of the Royal Anthropological Institute* 12 (1): 89–107.

Kim, Eleana. 2010. *Adopted Territory: Transnational Korean Adoptees and the Politics of Belonging*. Durham, NC: Duke University Press.

Kimball, Spencer. 2015. "Somali Americans Allege Discrimination." *Deutsche Welle*.

December 9, 2015. http://www.dw.com/en/somali-americans-allege-discrimination
-in-us-counterterrorism-policies/a-18710323

Knudsen, John Chr. 1995. "When Trust is on Trial: Negotiating Refugee Narratives."
In *Mistrusting Refugees*. Edited by E. Valentine Daniel and John Chr. Knudsen, 13–
35. Berkeley: University of California Press.

Kohler-Hausmann, Julilly. 2007. "'The Crime of Survival': Fraud Prosecutions, Community Surveillance, and the Original 'Welfare Queen.'" *Journal of Social History*
41 (2): 329–354.

Koko, Sadiki. 2014. "The *Movement due 23 Mars* and the dynamics of a failed insurgency in the Democratic Republic of Congo." *South African Journal of International Affairs* 21 (2): 261–278.

Kotef, Hagar. 2010. "Objects of Security: Gendered Violence and Securitized Humanitarianism in Occupied Gaza. *Comparative Studies of South Asia, Africa, and the
Middle East* 30 (2): 179–91.

———. 2015. *Movement and the Ordering of Freedom: On Liberal Governances of Mobility*. Durham, NC: Duke University Press.

Lee, Stephen. 2019. "Family Separation as Slow Death." *Columbia Law Review* 119 (8):
2319–2384.

Lewis, I. M. 1994. *Blood and Bone: The Call of Kinship in Somali Society*. Lawrenceville,
NJ: Red Sea Press.

Lindley, Anna. 2010. *The Early Morning Phone Call: Somali Refugees' Remittances*.
Oxford: Berghahn Books.

Little, Peter. 2003. *Somalia: Economy without State*. Bloomington: Indiana University
Press.

Lochery, Emma. 2012. "Rendering Difference Visible: The Kenyan State and Its Somali
Citizens." *African Affairs* 111 (445): 615–639.

Loescher, Gil, Alexander Betts, and James Milner. 2008. *The United Nations High
Commissioner for Refugees (UNHCR): The Politics and Practice of Refugee Protection into the Twenty-first Century*. London: Routledge.

Lonsdale, John. 1992. "The Moral Economy of Mau Mau: Wealth, Poverty, and Civic
Virtue in Kikuyu Political Thought." In *Unhappy Valley: Conflict in Kenya and
Africa*. Edited by Bruce Berman and John Lonsdale, 315–504. London: James
Currey.

Lowe, Lucy. 2019. "Refusing Cesarean Sections to Protect Fertile Futures: Somali Refugees, Motherhood, and Precarious Migration." *American Ethnologist* 46 (2):
190- 201.

Malkki, Liisa H. 1995a. *Purity and Exile: Violence, Memory, and National Cosmology
among Hutu Refugees in Tanzania*. Chicago: University of Chicago Press.

———. 1995b. "Refugees and Exile: From 'Refugee Studies' to the National Order of
Things." *Annual Review of Anthropology* 24: 945-523.

———. 1996. "Speechless Emissaries: Refugees, Humanitarianism, and Dehistoriciza-
tion." *Cultural Anthropology* 11 (3): 377–404.

———. 2010. "Children, Humanity, and the Infantilization of Peace." In *In the Name of
Humanity: The Government of Threat and Care*. Edited by Ilana Feldman and
Miriam Ticktin, 58–86. Durham, NC: Duke University Press.

Mamdani, Mahmood. 2001. *When Victims Become Killers: Colonialism, Nativism, and the Genocide in Rwanda*. Princeton, NJ: Princeton University Press.

———. 2004. *Good Muslim, Bad Muslim: America, the Cold War, and the Roots of Terror*. New York: Pantheon Books.

Martin, David A. 2005. *The United States Refugee Admissions Program: Reforms for a New Era of Refugee Resettlement*. Migration Policy Institute.

Masco, Joseph. 2014. *The Theater of Operations: National Security Affect from the Cold War to the War on Terror*. Durham, NC: Duke University Press.

Mbembe, Achille. 2018. "The Idea of a Borderless World." *Africa is a Country*. https://africasacountry.com/2018/11/the-idea-of-a-borderless-world

Mburu, Nene. 2005. *Bandits on the Border: The Last Frontier in the Search for Somali Unity*. Trenton, NJ: Red Sea Press.

McConnell, Tristan. 2014. "Rwanda's Disappearing Dissidents." *The World*, November 23, 2014. https://www.pri.org/stories/2014-11-23/rwanda-s-disappearing-dissidents

McIntosh, Janet. 2016. *Unsettled: Denial and Belonging among White Kenyans*. Oakland: University of California Press.

Meiu, George Paul. 2017. *Ethno-erotic Economies: Sexuality, Money, and Belonging in Kenya*. Chicago: University of Chicago Press.

Minority Rights Group International. 2015. "State of the World's Minorities and Indigenous People 2015—Kenya." July 2, 2015. https://www.refworld.org/docid/55a4fa506.html.

Mohamed, Nadifa. 2014. *The Orchard of Lost Souls*. First American Edition. New York: Farrar, Straus and Giroux.

Moodie, Ellen. 2010. *El Salvador in the Aftermath of Peace: Crime, Uncertainty, and the Transition to Democracy*. Philadelphia: University of Pennsylvania Press.

———. 2022. "Expert Witnessing in the Asylum Economy." *Annals of Anthropological Practice* 46 (1): 72–75.

Mutongi, Kenda. 2017. *Matatu: A History of Popular Transportation in Nairobi*. Chicago: University of Chicago Press.

National Counterterrorism Center. n.d. "Terrorist Groups: Al-Shabaab." Counterterrorism Guide. Office of the Director of National Intelligence. Accessed March 7, 2024. https://www.dni.gov/nctc/groups/al_shabaab.html.

Neumann, Peter R. 2017. "Don't Follow the Money: The Problem with the War on Terrorist Financing." *Foreign Affairs* 96 (4): 93–102.

Notermans, Catrien. 2004. "Fosterage and the Politics of Marriage in East Cameroon." In *Cross-Cultural Approaches to Adoption*. Edited by Fiona Bowie, 48–63. London: Routledge.

Oka, Rahul Chandrashekhar. 2014. "Coping with the Refugee Wait: The Role of Consumption, Normalcy, and Dignity in Refugee Lives at Kakuma Refugee Camp, Kenya." *American Anthropologist* 116 (1): 23–37.

Oliver, Kelly. 2017. *Carceral Humanitarianism: Logics of Refugee Detention*. Minneapolis: University of Minnesota Press.

Ole Lenku, Joseph. 2014. "Press Statement by Cabinet Secretary for Interior and Coordination of National Government on Refugees and National Security Issues on 26th March 2014." https://www.hrw.org/sites/default/files/related_material/PRESS

%20STATEMENT%20BY%20CABINET%20SECRETARY%20FOR%20INTER
IOR%20%20COORDINATION%20OF%20NATI%20%20%20.pdf.

Ong, Aihwa. 1999. *Flexible Citizenship: The Cultural Logics of Transnationality.* Durham, NC: Duke University Press.

Oxfam. 2015. "Hanging by a Thread: The Ongoing Threat to Somalia's Remittance Lifeline." Adeso, Global Center on Cooperative Security, and Oxfam, February 19, 2015. https://oxfamilibrary.openrepository.com/bitstream/handle/10546/344616/bn-hanging-by-thread-somalia-remittances-190215-en.pdf;jsessionid=7F9E0963FB9 66DFDE3EF83C6BD980270?sequence=14.

Oxford English Dictionary. 2023. "Fraud." https://www.oed.com/search/dictionary/?scope=Entries&q=fraud.

Pavanello, Sara, Samir Elhawary, and Sara Pantuliano. 2010. "Hidden and Exposed: Urban Refugees in Nairobi, Kenya." London: Humanitarian Policy Group.

Petryna, Adriana. 2013. *Life Exposed: Biological Citizens after Chernobyl.* Princeton: Princeton University Press.

Peutz, Nathalie. 2006. "Embarking on an Anthropology of Removal." *Current Anthropology.* 47 (2): 217–241.

Pierre, Jemima. 2020. "The Racial Vernaculars of Development: A View from West Africa." *American Anthropologist* 122 (1): 86–98.

Piot, Charles. 2010. *Nostalgia for the Future: West Africa after the Cold War.* Chicago: University of Chicago Press.

Piot, Charles. 2019. *The Fixer: Visa Lottery Chronicles.* With Kodjo Nicolas Batema. Durham, NC: Duke University Press.

Pope-Obeda, Emily. 2021. "'Let Them Deport Me, I Will Come Back to Him Again': Romance, Affective Relations, and the US Deportation Regime, 1919–1935." In *Emotional Landscapes: Love, Gender, and Migration.* Edited by Marcelo J. Borges, Sonia Cancian, and Linda Reeder, 112–130. Urbana: University of Illinois Press.

Povinelli, Elizabeth A. 2005. "A Flight from Freedom." In *Postcolonial Studies and Beyond.* Edited by Ania Loomba, Suvir Kaul, Matti Bunzl, Antoinette Burton, and Jed Esty, 145–165. Durham, NC: Duke University Press.

Prunier, Gérard. 2009. *Africa's World War: Congo, the Rwandan Genocide, and the Making of a Continental Catastrophe.* Oxford: Oxford University Press.

Rapp, Rayna, Deborah Heath, and Karen-Sue Taussig. 2001. "Genealogical Dis-ease: Where Hereditary Abnormality, Biomedical Explanation, and Family Responsibility Meet." In *Relative Values: Reconfiguring Kinship Studies.* Edited by Sarah Franklin and Susan McKinnon, 384–409. Durham, NC: Duke University Press.

Ramsay, Georgina. 2018. *Impossible Refuge: The Control and Constraint of Refugee Futures.* New York: Routledge.

Rana, Junaid Akram. 2011. *Terrifying Muslims: Race and Labor in the South Asian Diaspora.* Durham, NC: Duke University Press.

Reckard, E. Scott, and Ronald D. White. 2015. "Money Transfers Cut Off to Somalia." *Los Angeles Times.* February 5, 2015. http://www.latimes.com/business/la-fi-merchants-bank-somalia-20150206-story.html

Redfield, Peter. 2011. "The Impossible Problem of Neutrality." In *Forces of Compassion: Humanitarianism between Ethics and Politics.* Edited by Erica Bornstein and Peter Redfield, 53–70. Santa Fe: School for Advanced Research Press.

Redfield, Peter, and Erica Bornstein. 2011. "An Introduction to the Anthropology of Humanitarianism." In *Forces of Compassion: Humanitarianism between Ethics and Politics*, edited by Erica Bornstein and Peter Redfield, 3–30. Santa Fe: School for Advanced Research Press.

Refugee Consortium of Kenya. 2014. *Is My Claim Meritorious? Congolese Experience of the Refugee Status Determination Process in Kenya*. Nairobi: Refugee Consortium of Kenya and the Danish Refugee Council.

Refugee Council USA. 2017. "Security Advisory Opinion Fact Sheet." January 13, 2017. https://rcusa.org/resources/security-advisory-opinion-fact-sheet/.

Refugees International. 2022. "What Does Kenya's New Refugee Act Mean for Economic Inclusion?" May 4, 2022. https://www.refugeesinternational.org/reports/2022/4/29/what-does-kenyas-new-refugee-act-mean-for-economic-inclusion.

Refugee Processing Center. 2020. "Refugee Admissions by Region: Fiscal Year 1975 through September 30, 2020." Graph. https://www.wrapsnet.org/documents/Refugee%20Admissions%20by%20Region%20since%201975%20as%20of%2010-5-20.pdf.

Reitman, Janet. 2021. "I Helped Destroy People." *The New York Times Magazine*. September 1, 2021. https://www.nytimes.com/2021/09/01/magazine/fbi-terrorism-terry-albury.html

Roach, Kent. 2003. *September 11: Consequences for Canada*. Montreal: McGill-Queen's University Press.

Rosas, Gilberto. 2012. *Barrio Libre: Criminalizing States and Delinquent Refusals of the New Frontier*. Durham, NC: Duke University Press.

———. 2023. *Unsettling: The El Paso Massacre, Resurgent White Nationalism, and the US-Mexico Border*. Baltimore: Johns Hopkins University Press.

Rud, Jeremy. 2023. "Asylum Text Analytics as an Algorithmic Silver Bullet: The Impossible Quest for Automated Fraud Detection." June 20, 2023. *Talking Politics*. https://talkingpoliticsonline.blogspot.com/2023/06/asylum-text-analytics-as-algorithmic.html.

Rushdie, Salman. 1991. *Midnight's Children*. New York: Penguin Books.

Sacchetti, Maria. 2023. "Deportations of Migrants Rise to More Than 142,000 under Biden." *Washington Post*, December 29, 2023. https://www.washingtonpost.com/immigration/2023/12/29/immigrants-ice-border-deportations-2023/.

Sackett, Blair. 2023. "A Uniform Front?: Power and Front-Line Worker Variation in Kakuma Refugee Camp, Kenya." *Ethnography* 24 (1): 106–131.

Sahlins, Marshall. 2013. *What Kinship Is—and Is Not*. Chicago: University of Chicago Press.

Sandvik, Kristin Bergtora. 2011. "Blurring Boundaries: Refugee Resettlement in Kampala—between the Formal, the Informal, and the Illegal." *Political and Legal Anthropology Review* 34 (1): 11–32.

———. 2018. "A Legal History: The Emergence of the African Resettlement Candidate in International Refugee Management." In *Refugee Resettlement: Power, Politics, and Humanitarian Governance*. Edited by Adèle Garnier, Liliana Lyra Jubilut, and Kristin Bergtora Sandvik, 46–69. New York: Berghahn Books.

Scahill, Timothy. 2006. "The Domestic Security Enhancement Act of 2003: A Glimpse into a Post-PATRIOT Act Approach to Combating Domestic Terrorism." *CR: The New Centennial Review* 6 (1): 69–94.

Schatzberg, Michael G. 2001. *Political Legitimacy in Middle Africa: Father, Family, Food.* Bloomington: Indiana University Press.

Scherz, China. 2011. "Protecting Children, Preserving Families: Moral Conflict and Actuarial Science in a Problem of Contemporary Governance." *Political and Legal Anthropology Review.* 34 (1): 33–50.

Schneider, David M. 1972. "What is Kinship All About? In *Kinship Studies in the Morgan Centennial Year.* Edited by Priscilla Reining, 32–63. Washington, DC: Anthropological Society of Washington.

———. (1968) 1980. *American Kinship: A Cultural Account.* 2nd edition. Chicago: University of Chicago Press.

———. 1984. *Critique of the Study of Kinship.* Ann Arbor: University of Michigan Press.

Shapiro, Dani. 2019. *Inheritance: A Memoir of Genealogy, Paternity, and Love.* New York: Alfred A. Knopf.

Shaw, Jonathan Edwards. 2018. "Youth and Therapeutic Insurgency in Eastern Congo: An Ethnographic History of Ruga-Ruga, Simba, and Mai-Mai Movements, 1870-Present." PhD dissertation, University of Michigan.

Sheik, Salah Abdi. 2007. *Blood on the Runway: The Wagalla Massacre of 1984.* Kenya: Northern Publishing House.

Sheikh, Hanna. 2019. "Counter-Extremism as Surveillance on the Somali Diaspora." *Anthropology News* 60 (5): e143-e146.

Smith, Constance. 2019. *Nairobi in the Making: Landscapes of Time and Urban Belonging.* Suffolk: James Currey.

Smith, Lindsay Adams. 2016. "Identifying Democracy: Citizenship, DNA, and Identity in Postdictatorship Argentina." *Science, Technology, and Human Values* 41 (6): 1037–1062.

Speed, Shannon. 2006. "At the Crossroads of Human Rights and Anthropology: Toward a Critically Engaged Activist Research." *American Anthropologist* 108 (1): 66–76.

Stacey, Judith. 1996. *In the Name of the Family: Rethinking Family Values in the Postmodern Age.* Boston: Beacon Press.

———. 1998. *Brave New Families: Stories of Domestic Upheaval in Late Twentieth Century America.* Berkeley: University of California Press.

Stack, Carol B. 1974. *All Our Kin: Strategies for Survival in a Black Community.* New York: Harper & Row.

Stearns, Jason. 2011. *Dancing in the Glory of Monsters: The Collapse of the Congo and the Great War of Africa.* New York: PublicAffairs.

Strong, Pauline Turner. 2001. "To Forget Their Tongue, Their Name, and Their Whole Relation: Captivity, Extra-Tribal Adoption, and the Indian Child Welfare Act." In *Relative Values: Reconfiguring Kinship Studies.* Edited by Sarah Franklin and Susan McKinnon, 468–493. Durham: Duke University Press.

Sugarman, Julie, and Courtney Geary. 2018. "English Learners in Ohio: Demographics, Outcomes, and State Accountability Policies." Migration Policy Institute. https://www.migrationpolicy.org/sites/default/files/publications/EL-factsheet2018-Ohio_Final.pdf.

Suhrke, Astri and Adèle Garnier. 2018. "The Moral Economy of the Resettlement Regime." In *Refugee Resettlement: Power, Politics, and Humanitarian Governance.*

Edited by Adèle Garnier, Liliana Lyra Jubilut, and Kristin Bergtora Sandvik, 244–252. New York: Berghahn Books.

TallBear, Kimberly. 2013. *Native American DNA: Tribal Belonging and the False Promise of Genetic Science*. Minneapolis: University of Minnesota Press.

Talle, Aud. 2004. "Adoption Practices among the Pastoral Maasai of East Africa: Enacting Fertility." In *Cross-Cultural Approaches to Adoption*. Edited by Fiona Bowie, 64–78. London: Routledge.

Tamarkin, Noah. 2020. *Genetic Afterlives: Black Jewish Indigeneity in South Africa*. Durham, NC: Duke University Press.

Tang, Eric. 2015. *Unsettled: Cambodian Refugees in the New York City Hyperghetto*. Philadelphia: Temple University Press.

Thomas, Todne. 2021. *Kincraft: The Making of Black Evangelical Sociality*. Durham, NC: Duke University Press.

Thompson, Charis. 2001. "Strategic Naturalizing: Kinship in an Infertility Clinic." In *Relative Values: Reconfiguring Kinship Studies*. Edited by Sarah Franklin and Susan McKinnon, 175–202. Durham: Duke University Press.

Thompson, Vincent B. 1995. "The Phenomenon of Shifting Frontiers: The Kenya-Somali Case in the Horn of Africa, 1880s-1970s." *Journal of Asian and African Studies* 30 (1–2): 1–40.

Thomson, Marnie Jane. 2012. "Black Boxes of Bureaucracy: Transparency and Opacity in the Resettlement Process of Congolese Refugees." *Political and Legal Anthropology Review* 35 (2): 186–205.

———. 2018. "'Giving Cases Weight': Congolese Refugees' Tactics for Resettlement Selection." In *Refugee Resettlement: Power, Politics, and Humanitarian Governance*. Edited by Adèle Garnier, Liliana Lyra Jubilut, and Kristin Bergtora Sandvik, 203–222. New York: Berghahn Books.

Thomson, Susan. 2013. *Whispering Truth to Power: Everyday Resistance to Reconciliation in Postgenocide Rwanda*. Madison: University of Wisconsin Press.

Ticktin, Miriam. 2011. *Casualties of Care: Immigration and the Politics of Humanitarianism in France*. Berkeley: University of California Press.

———. 2020. "On Refugees and Innocence." *Public Seminar*. January 16, 2020. https://publicseminar.org/2020/01/on-refugees-and-innocence/#:~:text=In%20this%20sense%2C%20by%20valorizing,its%20accompanying%20forms%20of%20violence.

Tiilikainen, Marja. 2011. "Failed Diaspora: Experiences of Dhaqan Celis and Mentally Ill Returnees in Somaliland." *Nordic Journal of African Studies* 20 (1): 71–89.

Torpey, John. 1998. "Coming and Going: On the State Monopolization of the Legitimate 'Means of Movement.'" *Sociological Theory* 16 (3): 239–259.

Trump, Donald. 2016a. "Donald Trump's National Security Speech." June 13, 2016. *Politico*. https://www.politico.com/story/2016/06/transcript-donald-trump-national-security-speech-224273

———. 2016b. "Donald Trump's Full Immigration Speech." August 31, 2016. *Los Angeles Times*. https://www.latimes.com/politics/la-na-pol-donald-trump-immigration-speech-transcript-20160831-snap-htmlstory.html

Turton, E. R. 1972. "Somali Resistance to Colonial Rule and the Development of Somali Political Activity in Kenya, 1893–1960." *Journal of African History* 13 (1): 119–143.

United Nations. 1948. *The Universal Declaration of Human Rights.* https://www.un.org /en/universal-declaration-human-rights/

UNHCR. 1951. "Convention Relating to the Status of Refugees." http://www.unhcr.org /en-us/3b66c2aa10

———. 1997. *UNHCR Resettlement Handbook.* Geneva: UNHCR.

———. 2011. *UNHCR Resettlement Handbook.* Geneva: UNHCR.

———. 2015. "Resettlement Fact Sheet 2015." https://cnnc.uncg.edu/wp-content/up loads/2017/03/UNHCR_Resettlement_Fact_Sheet_2015.pdf

———. 2016. *Ukweli Hauna Mwanandani.* Arnold Temple Visuals. Vimeo. https:// player.vimeo.com/video/162950859

———. 2022. "Global Report 2021: East and Horn of Africa and Great Lakes." https://re porting.unhcr.org/globalreport2021/ehagl#:~:text=By%20the%20end%20of%2020 21,shortages%2C%20insecurity%20and%20localized%20violence.

———. 2023. "Mid-year Trends 2023." https://www.unhcr.org/us/media/mid-year -trends-2023.

UN Security Council. 2014a. "Final Report of the Group of Experts on the Democratic Republic of the Congo." January 23, 2014. https://www.securitycouncilreport.org/ atf/cf/%7B65BFCF9B-6D27-4E9C-8CD3-CF6E4FF96FF9%7D/s_2014_42.pdf.

———. 2014b. "Midterm Report of the Group of Experts on the Democratic Republic of the Congo." June 25, 2014. https://www.securitycouncilreport.org/atf/cf/%7B65BF CF9B-6D27-4E9C-8CD3-CF6E4FF96FF9%7D/S_2014_428.pdf.

US Department of Homeland Security. n.d. "Creation of the Department of Homeland Security." Accessed July 12, 2022. https://www.dhs.gov/creation-department-home land-security.

US Department of State. n.d.(a). "Refugee Admissions." Accessed December 1, 2016. https://www.state.gov/j/prm/ra/.

US Department of State. n.d.(b). "The Immigration and Nationality Act of 1952 (The McCarran-Walter Act)." Accessed March 7, 2024. https://history.state.gov/mile stones/1945-1952/immigration-act.

Utas, Mats. 2005. "Victimcy, Girlfriending, Soldiering: Tactic Agency in a Young Woman's Social Navigation of the Liberian War Zone." *Anthropological Quarterly* 78 (2): 403–430.

Voutira, Eftihia, and Barbara Harrell-Bond. 1995. "In Search of the Locus of Trust: The Social World of the Refugee Camp." In *Mistrusting Refugees.* Edited by E. Valentine Daniel and John Chr. Knudsen, 207–24. Berkeley: University of California Press.

Weiss, Meira. 2001. "The Children of Yemen: Bodies, Medicalization, and Nation-Building." *Medical Anthropology Quarterly.* 15 (2): 206–221.

Weitzberg, Keren. 2017. *We Do Not Have Borders: Greater Somalia and the Predica-ments of Belonging in Kenya.* Athens: Ohio University Press.

Weston, Kath. 1991. *Families We Choose: Lesbians, Gays, Kinship.* New York: Columbia University Press.

———. 2001. "Kinship, Controversy, and the Sharing of Substance: the Race/Class Pol-itics of Blood Transfusion." In *Relative Values: Reconfiguring Kinship Studies.* Edited by Sarah Franklin and Susan McKinnon, 147–74. Durham: Duke University Press.

White, Luise. 1990. *The Comforts of Home: Prostitution in Colonial Nairobi*. Chicago: University of Chicago Press.

———. 2000. *Speaking with Vampires: Rumor and History in Colonial Africa*. Berkeley: University of California Press.

Whittaker, Hannah. 2008. "Pursuing Pastoralists: The Stigma of *Shifta* during the 'Shifta War' in Kenya, 1963-68." *Eras* 10.

———. 2015. "A New Model Village? Nairobi Development and the Somali question in Kenya, c. 1915–1917." *Northeast African Studies* 15 (2): 117–140.

Zamora, Javier. 2022. *Solito*. New York: Hogarth.

Zong, Jie, and Jeanne Batalova. 2015. "Refugees and Asylees in the United States." *Migration Policy Institute*. Accessed March 7, 2024. https://www.migrationpolicy.org/article/refugees-and-asylees-united-states-2013.

The Grip of Sexual Violence in Conflict:
Feminist Interventions in International Law
Karen Engle
2020

When Misfortune Becomes Injustice: Evolving Human
Rights Struggles for Health and Social Equality
Alicia Ely Yamin
2020

The Politics of Love in Myanmar: LGBT Mobilization
and Human Rights as a Way of Life
Lynette J. Chua
2018

Branding Humanity: Competing Narratives of
Rights, Violence, and Global Citizenship
Amal Hassan Fadlalla
2018

Remote Freedoms: Politics, Personhood and Human
Rights in Aboriginal Central Australia
Sarah E. Holcombe
2018

Letters to the Contrary: A Curated History of
the UNESCO Human Rights Survey
Edited and Introduced by Mark Goodale
2018

Just Violence: Torture and Human Rights in the Eyes of the Police
Rachel Wahl
2017

For a complete listing of available titles in this series, visit
the Stanford University Press website, www.sup.org.

The authorized representative in the EU for product safety and compliance is:
Mare Nostrum Group B.V.
Mauritskade 21D
1091 GC Amsterdam
The Netherlands
Email address: gpsr@mare-nostrum.co.uk

KVK chamber of commerce number: 96249943

The authorized representative in the EU for product safety and compliance is:
Mare Nostrum Group
B.V Doelen 72
4831 GR Breda
The Netherlands

www.ingramcontent.com/pod-product-compliance
Lightning Source LLC
Chambersburg PA
CBHW031056280326
41928CB00049B/744